Masculinity and the
British Organization
Man since 1945

Masculinity and the British Organization Man since 1945

MICHAEL ROPER

OXFORD UNIVERSITY PRESS

1994

Oxford University Press, Walton Street, Oxford OX2 6DP
Oxford New York Toronto
Delhi Bombay Calcutta Madras Karachi
Kuala Lumpur Singapore Hong Kong Tokyo
Nairobi Dar es Salaam Cape Town
Melbourne Auckland Madrid
and associated companies in
Berlin Ibadan

Oxford is a trade mark of Oxford University Press

Published in the United States
by Oxford University Press Inc., New York

British Library Cataloguing in Publication Data
Data available

Library of Congress Cataloging in Publication Data
Roper, Michael, 1959–
Masculinity and the British organization man since 1945 /
Michael Roper.
Includes bibliographical references.
1. Executives—Great Britain.   2. Women executives—Great Britain.
3. Sex discrimination in employment—Great Britain.
4. Sex role in the work environment—Great Britain.
5. Masculinity (Psychology)
I. Title.
HD38.25.G7R66   1993   331.4'133'094—dc20   93–15075
ISBN 0–19–825693–0

Set by Hope Services (Abingdon) Ltd.
Printed in Great Britain by
Biddles Ltd.
Guildford & King's Lynn

Preface

This book began its life as a Ph.D. thesis on the post-war generation of British managers. It has slowly evolved since then, reworked in between various research and teaching jobs. Despite this it is still partly a product of me as I was when I carried out my interviews in 1987–8: an Australian graduate historian in my late twenties, the son of public sector professionals, uncertain about the kind of career I wanted, and asking questions about my own masculinity. I was completely fascinated by the managers that I met during the field-work. Initially my interest was aroused by the confidence that they radiated, by their articulacy, and by their ability to fashion a story of upward mobility with the autonomous 'I' at its centre. Occasionally, however, this appearance of solid confidence gave way, and I saw glimpses of the intimacies that are exchanged between men in business, or heard confessions of extreme vulnerability. In my very first interview, a senior manager in a large manufacturing firm presented a beautifully clear and elegant explanation of the complex body of competition law that he dealt with. When I commented on his enthusiasm for the work, he remarked, 'No. I'm just always frightened,' and went on to reflect on what a poor example he had set his son of how an organization man and father should behave.

This book explores tensions like this between the rational discourse of management, and the emotions of organization men. The book's narrative is shaped by the similarities and differences between me and the managers I myself interviewed in age, nationality, class, and masculinity. A brief biography of each interviewee is provided in the appendices. You may find it helpful to consult this as you read, so that the voices in the text are set in the context of the speaker's life history. In order to ensure anonymity the names of interviewees and their companies have been disguised.

Many people have helped the project reach fruition, from those who vetted the original proposal and read early drafts of my graduate work, to those who passed opinions on the book's photographs and title. I would like to thank my interviewees first of all, for their generosity and willingness to talk with me. Paul Thompson supervised the thesis, while Leonore Davidoff provided invaluable comments on various drafts of it. I am deeply indebted to them for their assistance, both practical and intellectual. A number of people encouraged me along the path from thesis to book. Heartfelt thanks to John Tosh for his friendship, comments, and unfailing support. Also to my sister and friend, Lyndal Roper, who, by comment and example, showed me how one goes about making a book. Others helped me to put shape to various drafts, among them Guy Boanas, Cynthia Cockburn, Ian Craib, Tim Edwards, David Goodman, Jeff Hearn, Ludmilla Jordanova, Anne McElroy, David Morgan, Jim Obelkivich, Ray Pahl, and Ken Plummer. Much of the thinking-through of the book's themes went on in a study group on the history of masculinity which met in London between 1988 and 1991. I would like to thank everyone in that group, but particularly Kelly Boyd, Norma Clarke, Graham Dawson, Joy Dixon, Peter Lewis, Keith McClelland, and Jonathan Rutherford. Romano Dyerson was very supportive during the couple of years when, embarked on new research, I could not put pen to page. David Mayers and Peter Evans have assisted me greatly with the creative aspects of the book. My thinking was also stimulated by the Social History MA students that I taught at Essex in my first year there. More than anyone else, in our talks together, in her confidence in me, and in her comments on my work, Yasmin Lakhi has helped me to complete the book.

I am extremely grateful to the Leverhulme Trust, which supported my research for three months in between jobs. The London Business School, and Professor John Kay in particular, were also generous in allowing me time on the book.

Earlier versions of parts of this work have appeared in M. Roper and J. Tosh (eds.), *Manful Assertions: Masculinities in Britain since 1800* (London: Routledge, 1991), and *Life Stories/Récits de vie*, 4 (International Sociological Association; 1988). I am grateful to the publishers for permission to reproduce this material. I should also like to thank the following for illustrations: Alcatel Business Systems, Associated Press, BTR Group, Gestetner, Guardian News Services Ltd, The London Business School, Midland Bank plc, Philips Electronics UK Ltd, and TSB Bank plc. Ravi Mirchandani at Penguin Books provided useful information on sales of their historical titles, and Katie Vandyck took some excellent photographs for me. Finally, many thanks to David Musson at Oxford University Press for his insightful comments and editorial suggestions.

MICHAEL ROPER

Essex University
September 1992

Contents

Appendices

List of Illustrations

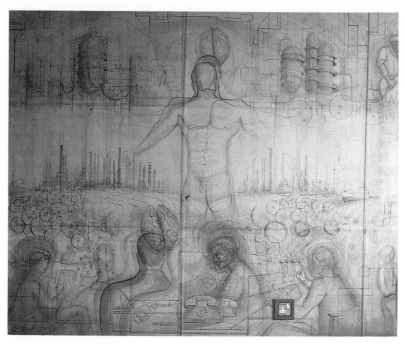

1 'Industrial man'

This mural, completed in 1966 was commissioned by an oil company for the newly established London Business School. Based on Da Vinci's *The Proportions of the Human Figure*, its message is that industry is a human endeavour. Yet the image is highly gender specific. The body's penis and the phallic smokestacks which are clustered around it neatly demonstrate the links between male sexuality and the 'mens work' of production.

Theodore Hancock, 1966

Introduction

The term 'organization man' was coined by business commentators in the 1950s to describe the growing armies of career managers in public corporations.[1] Its ambiguity captures the central problem of this book. While the word 'man' implies a common humanity including women and men, the image evoked by writers like C. W. Mills of 'the salaried bureaucrat, with brief case and slide rule' is at the same time undeniably masculine.[2] 'Organization man' suggests impartiality. It conjures up the image of a classless, genderless, disembodied administrator who—in contrast to the owner–manager of old—can exercise complete neutrality in decision-making.[3] The bureaucrat's power is vested in the ability to act, as Max Weber put it, 'without regard to persons'.[4] Yet, despite its meritocratic ring, the expression has a deeply gendered significance. The image is of a certain *kind* of man: single-minded in his pursuit of career success but a responsible bread-winner and loyal servant of the company. It reflects a clear division of labour between men and women: the organization man's extreme devotion to company and career was, after all, facilitated by the servicing work of secretaries and wives. To be a successful organization man means conforming to certain emotional constraints, learning to exercise intellect but suppress passion. As C. W. Mills described it in an imaginary tutorial for aspiring managers: 'Be calm, judicious, rational; groom your personality and control your appearance; make business a profession.'[5]

This book is based on the life stories of thirty senior managers—twenty-five men and five women—who began their careers in the post-war period at the high point of the 'organization society'.[6] It explores the masculine identity of 'organization man', and the kind of emotional life which the post-war generation lived amidst a

1

business environment that seemed to demand personal detachment. Historians and sociologists of business have often contrasted the modern bureaucrat's analytical skills with the era of family capitalism, when company strategies were guided by the owner's intuition. In contrast, this book argues that management continues to operate in non-rational ways, even in the age of the bureaucracy. Business might be described as an 'emotional economy' in which organization men negotiate the satisfactions and discontents of masculinity. The pleasure of technical innovation or of seeing a new product through to market, the explosive mixture of rivalry and generosity that surrounds management succession, the hard bargaining of industrial relations—at every level, managerial functions involve the dramatization of emotions among men.

A study of this emotional economy among men illuminates gender inequalities and how they are perpetuated in management. Women are entering management in increasing numbers at junior and middle levels, but continue to be under-represented in senior posts. Less than 1 per cent of the top 180 British companies have a woman on their main board.[7] Researchers have described this in terms of a 'glass ceiling' which prevents women from reaching senior management. At the same time we know very little about the men whose interests are served by that ceiling. The links *between* the systematic exclusion of women and the gender identities of the men who dominate British corporations have yet to be traced. A factor which has influenced this neglect is the organization man's ability to present himself as a professional first and foremost, his masculine identity hidden by the cloak of objectivity.

The image of the manager as rational thinker is evident in a wide range of writings. Organization studies have often followed Max Weber in defining bureaucratic authority as non-subjective.[8] Frederick Taylor's 'scientific' manager earned the right to control the production worker by virtue of his superior powers of reason.[9] Managerial economics, drawing on the neo-classical model, assumes that managers are rational men who respond in the most efficient possible way to market forces.[10] Business historians have charted the growth of modern management in terms of a transition from informal to systematic structures. As family capitalism gave way to the corporate economy, the owner–manager to the career manager, so management was transformed from an art to a profession regulated by formal systems of training, entry, and promotion.[11] Liberal–

feminist critiques of management during the 1970s and 1980s showed that, despite this supposed movement towards a meritocracy in management, the rules continued to favour men. Attempts to achieve equality concentrated on improving practices in key areas like recruitment, training, and promotion. Yet this approach sustained the notion of organizations as resource-allocating systems, and of leadership as no more than the logical channelling of those resources. 'Gate-keeping' practices could be formalized so that sexist beliefs would not distort the selection process. Lack of professional practice was the problem, rather than the beliefs of the professional men who governed those practices. Even the pro-feminist men's movements of the 1970s played a part in perpetuating the myth of management as a purely analytical process, and of the manager as dispassionate. They regarded the post-war organization man as a symbol of middle-class men's inability to express their emotions.[12] Such men had caused hurt to themselves, their partners, and their children by repressing their caring, nurturing, 'feminine' sides.

These diverse commentaries depict the modern manager in a similar way, defining his masculinity and his fitness for management in terms of his cognitive abilities. Yet, as Arlie Hochschild points out in her book *The Managed Heart*, while the air of personal warmth which the woman flight attendant or secretary presents to clients is engineered to some extent 'from above' by the corporation and is sold in exchange for a wage, the interesting thing about senior managers is the degree to which their emotions are invested in what they do.[13] They both create and internalize what Hochschild calls 'corporate feeling rules'. For corporate decision-makers,

> the ties between self and work are many and diffuse. Here years of training and experience, mixed with a daily carrot-and-stick discipline, conspire to push corporate feeling rules further and further away from self-awareness. Eventually these rules about how to see things and how to feel about them come to seem 'natural', a part of one's personality. The longer the employment and the more rewarding the work in terms of interest, power and pay, the truer this becomes.[14]

The organization men in this study did a lot of 'deep acting' on behalf of the company. They routinely demonstrated their expertise and fascination with technology as clues to the quality of their company's products. When quelling industrial disputes they strove to project a persona of absolute confidence and authority. So close were the ties between self and company that the managers they chose as successors were men in their own image. One of the things which made management enjoyable for my interviewees was the considerable opportunity it afforded for self-expression. A focus on the post-war generation and how it sustained the masculine identity of organization man through work forces us to consider management as 'emotional labour' in a way that the literature on women in management, business history, and organization studies has usually failed to do.

Thus the questions that need to be asked about organization men do not concern their emotional inexpressivity, but rather what kinds of emotions they express in their work, and how these have become part of the ordinary conduct of business. Three aspects of these questions are addressed in the book. Its principal topic is men and masculinity. Previous works—like Hochschild's—have addressed the ways in which women's subordination in employment is related to the emotional labours they perform, particularly the enhancing of others' self-worth. Yet we lack an equivalent understanding of the emotional economy that operates among men at work. The post-war organization man depended upon women to safeguard his gentler emotions. Yet this 'mothering' by women did not mean that men's work life was devoid of affections. Robert Bly, the self-proclaimed guru of America's men's movement, has commented on the need for middle-class men to recover a 'fierce' spirit, celebrating the bonds between men in events such as ritual initiations to manhood. Corporations, he claims, emasculate men, doing 'so much work to produce the sanitized, hairless, shallow man'.[15] Bly here fundamentally misunderstands the dynamics of corporate life. Business thrives on precisely the kind of close relations between men that Bly now wishes to revive. Organization men were attracted to management partly because of the opportunities it provided for the expression of homosocial affections.

The second thing to note about this study is its focus. It does not claim to describe an emotional make-up which is 'typical' of male managers in general. As Appendix I makes clear, the research is confined to one nation, one generation, and one economic sector: the post-war entrants to management in British manufacturing industry. Born between 1922 and 1937, they reached senior management and late career in the 1980s. Limiting the study in this way enables a more historically informed and more differentiated perspective on masculinity.[16] When management writers have introduced a gender perspective that treats men *qua* men, the result too often confirms the myth of men as the more emotionally detached sex.[17] The life stories of managers in this study provide a counterpart to the collective post-war image of the rational bureaucrat. The organization man's image of manhood is the product of life experiences specific to one generation: being a young soldier in war or national service; learning about the industry in 'hands-on' fashion through prolonged training; living through the peaks and troughs of the economic cycle from the post-war boom to the decline of manufacturing in the early 1980s. Most important, the members of this generation stand at the crossroads of family and managerial capitalism. When they began their careers in the 1950s, the majority of Britain's largest firms were family owned. Organization men helped introduce a more professional approach to management, but were not, for the most part, formally trained as managers. Their image of themselves as men is profoundly influenced by their historical position between these two epochs. By examining the self-perceptions of organization men in the light of this historical past, looking at how their work experiences shaped their gender identities, this book seeks to avoid treating masculinity in a categorical way.

In focusing on the organization man this study also contributes to our understanding of the post-war gender order in Britain, with its extreme separation of spheres between women and men. Existing work in this area has highlighted the factors bearing on the post-war cult of motherhood, including government campaigns to increase the birth rate, policies on welfare provision, the work of psychologists like D. W. Winnicott and John Bowlby, and the expansion of consumer advertising.[18] While we now know a little about the implications for middle-class women of the home-maker/bread-winner divide, its significance for middle-class men is less clear. How did men experience the role of bread-winner, which paradoxically defined their domestic identity primarily in terms of their work activities? Despite the work of sociologists in the 1950s on men and careers, we lack a body of literature which, like the feminist work on women, interprets the experiences and perceptions of men from a gender perspective. We know a lot about the class origins and work habits of the organization man, but precious little about his relations with women or his self-image as a man.

The third aspect which distinguishes this work is its use of the life-history method. In this open-ended approach to interviewing, informants are encouraged to structure their own narratives as much as possible, the researcher's interest lying as much in the mythical and symbolic aspects of the account as its factual content. It is a method that, because it encouraged organization men to reflect on the personal dimensions of their public activities, leads me to question the image of the dispassionate bureaucrat. Despite the post-war culture of separate spheres, the organization man's conception of management was greatly influenced by his experiences in the domestic sphere. Relations between younger and older men, for example, might involve an intensity of affection and a language of intimacy that is usually associated with sexual relationships. A preoccupation with cultural aspects of the separation of spheres has prevented us from seeing how sexual and familial metaphors shaped the post-war generation's understanding of work.[19] Managerial work offered organization men a wide range of expressive modes, from typically masculine postures of cold-hearted calculation, to being 'mothered' by a secretary, or 'mothering' young managers by developing them in career terms. This ability to establish the emotional economy on behalf of others in the organization distinguished the men's psychic investments in work from those of the women who serviced their material and emotional needs. Through their freedom to fashion work roles, men obtained polymorphous pleasures from the corporate life. The organization man is known for the instrumental nature of his actions; understanding his power involves being aware of the colourful emotional life which he created amidst the monochrome structures of the bureaucracy.

Perhaps the principal advantage of the life-history method is that it so clearly illuminates the complexity of links between the psychic and social dimensions of gender. Men's exclusion of women from the top jobs in management cannot be understood by reference to material factors alone, a point which is sometimes missed by social scientists.[20] At the same time, however, most attempts to analyse gender segregation from a psychological perspective adopt a far too categorical conception of masculinity. In the object-relations approach revived by Nancy Chodorow in the late 1970s, men's need to dominate women is seen to result from the difficulty which they experience in dis-identifying with the mother, and securing a separate, masculine identity.[21] This theory has been used in a wide variety of fields, ranging from studies of gender segregation in science, the military, and business,[22] to the 'men's-studies' literature which seeks to understand men's supposed emotional inarticulacy.[23] The social oppression of women is—to varying degrees—seen as a defensive response, provoked by men's desire to protect a fragile masculine identity.[24]

Psychoanalytic concepts are essential if we are better to comprehend the points of intersection between men's behaviour in organizations and their fantasies. Object relations sheds light on many common dilemmas in masculinity, particularly the tendency for men to feel insecure about their gender identity. The problem with most of the studies which deploy such concepts is that they collapse the social and psychic dimensions of masculinity. They adapt concepts derived from the analysis of individual case histories, but use them only to explain collective phenomena such as gender segregation. Subjectivity itself holds little interest. Psychoanalysis is used instead to furnish a schematic explanation for social inequalities. All men— regardless of age, social class, ethnicity, or race—are seen to suffer from difficulty in establishing intimacy, a tendency that stems from the male child's need to reject his original closeness with the mother. Hence the psychologists Liam Hudson and Bernadine Jacot comment that, 'in the field of emotional relations the "male" male is bound to be at a disadvantage'.[25] Such approaches also perpetuate a kind of psychic determinism, regarding work institutions as little more than stages for re-enacting a set piece Oedipal transition. The majority of men in this study were brought up in 'typical' families, with a mother as primary carer. Nevertheless they did not work out the dilemmas of masculinity in identical ways. While they did often experience their gender identity as tenuous, and strove to shore it up through career achievement, their ways of dealing with psychic dilemmas took quite different forms. One man sought to dominate our interview through his iron handshake, prolonged stares, and gruff demeanour, while others treated the interview as a kind of confessional, explaining how oppressed they had felt by the pressure to act tough. Each was revealing insecurities about his gender, but in strikingly different ways.

The main difference between this study and the recent reworkings of object relations is that, where the latter begin with the proposition that men are afraid of personal intimacy, I explore how management exploits the affective bonds between men. The remainder of this introduction illustrates the ways in which one company man projected an image of dispassion—the bureaucratic ideal type—while living a vivid emotional life through work. The life story of Sir Peter Aldridge is in some ways a microcosm of the rise of professional management. Aldridge was born into a working-class family in 1917, his mother a laundry worker, his father a railway porter. After a succession of manual jobs, in 1938 he became one of the first British graduates in economics. Just before the war he joined a family-owned multinational textile company, Chemtex. Although he was initially 'made to feel inferior' by the public-school-educated managers who dominated its board, Aldridge achieved considerable career success. He became finance director of Chemtex in the early 1960s, and chairman in the mid-1970s. At one level Aldridge's story is a straightforward narrative of the opening-up of management to talent. Aldridge himself presented his story as a triumph of merit over privilege.

Aldridge prided himself on having introduced a more professional approach to management at Chemtex. Where the gentleman managers at Chemtex had operated a promotion system based on social connections, Aldridge had introduced an assessment system in his capacity as chairman. He promoted himself in our interview as the archetypal rational man. He had been 'to some extent the thinker', creating logical management systems where once 'there was no formal planning team, no formal strategy planning'. On becoming chairman he had sought to provide 'the institutionalization that the old organization had lacked'. Aldridge also approached our interview as a kind of strategic exercise. He was particularly anxious that it should have a clear structure. Over tea beforehand he explained that he wished to split the session into two. In the first half he would talk about management succession at Chemtex and his role in formalizing the process. In the latter half he would outline the main stages in his career path. True to his word, the section on succession covered three themes: management recruitment, training, and motivation. Each theme was divided into subtopics, starting with a description of the way things were handled before he took over as chairman, followed by a summary of the management systems he had installed, and then an update on the strategies followed by his successor. At the end of each topic he would recap the main points ('So what have we said? . . . We've said . . .'), as if I were a student and he was delivering a lecture. The process of remembering did not seem to kindle excitement. The structure he put on this part of his story had the effect of preventing intimacy between us, as if he were reliving the past boundaries between his private and public lives. This was not done in a defensive way. Rather, Aldridge seemed to judge that the discourse of bureaucratic rationality was appropriate for an ex-manager being interviewed by a student of business history. Where I experienced difficulty in drawing him out during the initial stages of our interview, he feared that 'it all spilled out a bit'.

The first half of Aldridge's life story thus confirmed the ideal type of the rational organization man. The second half, where he explained his own work history, was rather more puzzling. It, too, was logically ordered, following a linear form which began with his parents' background and ended with his retirement. The more I pored over the transcript and listened to the tape, however, the more I began to see contradictions between the measured tones of Aldridge the organization man, and the emotional needs that drove his ambition. Success in class terms was ultimately less important to him than the desire to be remembered as a tough leader. Yet he doubted that he had ever achieved this standing in the eyes of other men. Sometimes he fashioned a tale where promotion had been won by being tougher than others, while at other moments he clearly felt more a victim than an aggressor.

His quest to prove his masculinity to me is evident in the heroic mode through which he described his career. Not only was he a strategy-maker, he had toughened himself through physical labour. After leaving school he had worked 'in a really rather rough part of south London, in a factory', combining this with a disciplined regime of evening study: 'My Saturday evenings were my leisure. And only that evening.' Although the work itself was purely sedentary, his descriptions of his early career are peppered with military metaphors. A first post at Chemtex in 1938, formulating a plan to boost exports, had prepared him for intelligence work during the war. 'I'd already tasted blood,' he explained. After the war he had been sent to Europe to set up joint ventures between Chemtex and European textile firms. He had thus been 'engaged in very rough, unpleasant situations', at a time when life in England was 'rather cosy and easy'. This experience, he explained, had showed him how to manipulate others through aggression: 'You just had to show who was boss and bang the table and be rather rough and unpleasant.' Management to Aldridge is not simply a matter of intellect. It is mixed up with normative ideas about the kinds of masculine qualities that make a good manager. A successful manager commands authority by cultivating aggression.

Aldridge played up his success in acting tough, but hinted that he had also been a victim of the competitive culture at Chemtex. His reason for seeking promotion was profoundly defensive: he wished to escape being bullied by other men. This feeling of insecurity was not something which he could confide to his colleagues; it was only to be shared with wives. As he explained in one of two indirect mentions of a wife: 'I remember, in 1958, when they put me on the board, going home and saying, you know. "They've put me on the board, thank God I now can't be pushed around." That was my first feeling: "Thank God I now can't be pushed around."' Aldridge's obvious abilities in the new management skills of strategy and finance were not enough. Success had also required that sensitive qualities—shyness, for example—were 'knocked out of me'. In order to avoid being bossed around, he had needed to learn to dominate others. His driving ambition was to be in a position where he could not be oppressed by other men.

In the first half of our interview, Aldridge spoke as a representative of Chemtex. He depicted management as a process of logical decision-making, conducted without regard to personal interests. In the second half he represented it as a highly emotive activity. Aldridge made no attempt to square the institutional and biographical narratives. His personal experience of management was of a struggle to maintain a sufficiently masculine identity, but this had no place in the public discourse of bureaucratic rationality. Aldridge had deeply conflicting feelings about the culture at Chemtex, in which qualities of aggression were indispensable, as did most of the men I interviewed. They occasionally portrayed themselves as masters of the art of being 'rough and unpleasant'. Yet the cult of toughness seemed to manipulate them as much as they it. What are we to make of this split between the public and private discourses of organization men? Aldridge's measured tones, the air of clear-minded authority, provided a means of concealing the passionate battle for power between organization men. This battle has been described in terms of its class dimensions, gentlemen amateurs against professional managers, in the context of the transition from family to corporate capitalism. The ideal types of the gentleman inheritor and the organization man are also deeply gendered, conveying different images of the masculine qualities desirable in a leader.

Aldridge's story illustrates the main themes of this book. It shows us that the relationship between masculinity and management cultures is not at all straightforward. Aldridge's identity as a man and a manager was influenced by the economic changes which occurred during his working life. The value which he placed on logical thinking as a prerequisite for management reflected his historical position in the vanguard of the managerial revolution. Aldridge's story also illustrates the paradox that, despite men's systematic domination of management, they do not experience themselves as powerful. Feelings of inadequacy pressed more urgently on them than those of manly virility. Like his fellow managers, Aldridge relied upon his wife to manage these feelings of vulnerability. In this way, organization men inverted the social relations of gender. Women, not men, were the powerful sex. Object relations, with its focus on mother–child relationships, illuminates this tendency for men to live the more 'feminine' aspects of themselves through women. What it does not illuminate so well is the emotional economy that flourished among men, with its peculiar 'love–hate' relationships, as one manager described them. Moreover, the approaches based on object relations tend to understate differences in the social backgrounds and psychic complexes of men. For example, while Aldridge alluded to his wife as the more emotionally attuned partner in their marriage, he completely reversed these gender roles when describing his parents. He considered that he had derived more 'masculine' qualities from his mother, while he idealized his father's gentleness:

> My mother was a very strong character. And certainly encouraged
> . . . What else? She . . . instilled certain very strong principles about hon-
> esty . . . What else from her? Hard work, obviously, that's it. Father, my
> father? He was a saintly figure. Hadn't got the self confidence to take on
> even a foreman's job when it was offered . . . A saintly figure.

We need to become more aware of complexities like these in the psychic identities of men. In addition, we need to be able to distinguish more clearly between different levels of discourse about masculinity in management. The dominant public discourse in the post-war period was of the manager as rational man. This, however, concealed the fears and desires which lay behind the seemingly methodical actions of organization men. Rather than plotting a process of increasing objectivity, this book details the range of emotional investments which organization men made in their work. My contention is that the psychic dynamics of relations between men in management provide important clues about their resistance to sex equality.

The book as a whole is divided into three parts. Part One sets out the theoretical and historical context of the study. Chapter 1 explores the range of business domains in which masculinity is visible: in collective representations like that of the rational manager, in managerial divisions of labour, and in the subjective identities of organization men. Chapter 2 outlines the industrial context in which the post-war generation spent their careers, and compares their stories with the historical narrative of the rise of professional management. It shows how a focus on masculinity alters the modernist picture of linear progress towards the rational bureaucracy.

Part Two deals with the relations between organization men. Here the focus is not explicitly on exclusionary practices, but on the ways in which men advantaged each other. Chapter 3 illustrates this through a study of relations between younger and older managers. Previous works have pointed out the institutional function of mentors in bringing through a younger generation to power. However, little attention has been paid to the extraordinary emotional intensity of the relationship. Intimacy between older and younger men continues to flourish in the modern corporation, despite the formalization of recruitment and promotion. Chapter 4 turns from the emotional bonds among men, to competition between them. In the company men's life stories, career progress was won through confrontations with other managers and shop-floor workers. The professional ideal is not much in evidence here either. Masculinity was measured through a hierarchy which owed little to professional status, but which inverted the class order so that those at the bottom—ex-engineers who had proved themselves on the shop-floor—became its best exemplars of the masculine ideal. Chapter 5 looks in more detail at the relationship between masculinity and production. Organization men were as passionate about products as they were about their past mentors. Product fetishism also went against the grain of corporate capitalism. It demonstrated the organization man's attempts to perpetuate the traditions of family capitalism, with its characteristic conception of products as standard-bearers for the founding family. The post-war generation cultivated this love of products in the face of growing demands for restraint from cost-cutting financiers.

While these early chapters focus on the public sphere of production, they show that relationships within management often replicated those in the 'private' sphere of family. Attachments between older and younger men were modelled on those between father and son, or man and wife. The organization man's fascination for process machinery and products was also expressed in familial and sexual ways, men imagining products either as fragile creations in need of fatherly protection, or as objects of desire whose beauty was inspirational. Similarly, the cult of toughness championed by organization men was founded upon an opposition between the 'soft' domain of home and the 'hard' work of manufacturing. Familial and sexual dramas were continually played out by organization men, dramas created around the cultural separation of work and home.

The two chapters in Part Three further illuminate these dramas by analysing the men's depictions of women. They look at the links between exclusion and the bread-winning–home-making divide. The post-war celebration of femininity as motherhood operated across the domestic and business domains. My interviewees portrayed women as carers above all else, regardless of whether they were secretaries, wives, or colleagues. Women's labours at work supported the truly productive business between men. A competent woman manager easily threatened the men's vision of themselves as family, company, and national bread-winners. Masculinity for the organization men was built on career achievement; they themselves, however, never felt this edifice to be secure.

NOTES

1. C. W. Mills, *White Collar: The American Middle Classes* (New York, 1956); W. H. Whyte, *The Organization Man* (Harmondsworth, 1963). For parallel British studies of organization men, see J. M. Pahl and R. E. Pahl, *Managers and their Wives: A Study of Career and Family Relationships in the Middle Class* (London, 1971), esp. ch. 2; C. Sofer, *Men in Mid-Career: A Study of British Managers and Technical Specialists* (Cambridge, 1970).
2. Mills, *White Collar*, p. x.
3. As J. Acker states it, 'In organizational logic, both jobs and hierarchies are abstract categories that have no occupants, no human bodies, no gender' ('Hierarchies, Jobs, Bodies: A Theory of Gendered Organizations', *Gender and Society*, 4/2 (June 1990), 139–58).
4. M. Weber, 'Bureaucracy', in H. Gerth and C. W. Mills (eds.), *From Max Weber: Essays in Sociology* (London, 1948), 215.
5. Mills, *White Collar*, 81.
6. See Appendix I for further information on the sample. P. Thompson and D. McHugh provide a good summary of the post-war ideal of the rationally planned 'organisation society' (*Work Organisations: A Critical Introduction* (London, 1990), 13–16).

INTRODUCTION

7. Hansard Society, *Report of the Hansard Society Commission on Women at the Top* (London, 1990), 60, table 4.2. The figures do not include non-executive directors.
8. For a good critique of the rationalist strain in organization studies, see R. Pringle, 'Bureaucracy, Rationality and Sexuality: The Case of Secretaries', in J. Hearn, D. L. Sheppard, P. Tancred-Sheriff, and G. Burrell (eds.), *The Sexuality of Organization* (London, 1989), esp. 158–63.
9. R. M. Kanter, *Men and Women of the Corporation* (New York, 1977), 20–3.
10. The work of M. Porter (esp. *The Competitive Advantage of Nations* (London, 1990)) provides a good example of the rationalist strain in writings about business strategy. A useful commentary on the strategy literature can be found in D. Knights and G. Morgan, 'Corporate Strategy, Organizations, and Subjectivity: A Critique', *Organization Studies*, 12/12 (1991), 251–73.
11. For examples, see A. D. Chandler, *The Visible Hand: The Managerial Revolution in American Business* (Cambridge, Mass., 1977); H. Perkin, *The Rise of Professional Society: England since 1880* (London, 1989); or R. Locke, *Management and Higher Education since 1940: The Influence of America and Japan on West Germany, Great Britain and Japan* (Cambridge, 1989). Ch. 2, sect. i, below treats these business histories in more detail.
12. For example, F. Bartolome comments that male managers are 'limited by a role definition obliging them to be super-masculine, super-tough, super-efficient, and super strong' ('Executive as Human Beings', in J. H. Pleck and J. Sawyer (eds.), *Men and Masculinity* (Englewood Cliffs, NJ, 1974), 101. See also A. Tolson, *The Limits of Masculinity* (London, 1977), 86–91; R. L. Ochberg, 'The Male Career Code and the Ideology of Role', in H. Brod (ed.), *The Making of Masculinities: The New Mens' Studies* (Boston, 1987), 173–95.
13. A. R. Hochschild, *The Managed Heart: Commercialization of Human Feeling* (Berkeley, Calif., 1983), 7–8.
14. Ibid. 155.
15. R. Bly, *Iron John: A Book about Men* (Longmead, Shaftesbury, Dorset, 1991), 6.
16. For a more detailed discussion of this theme, see M. Roper and J. Tosh, 'Historians and the Politics of Masculinity', in Roper and Tosh (eds.), *Manful Assertions: Masculinities in Britain since 1800* (London, 1991), 1–25.
17. M. Alvesson and Y. D. Billing, 'Gender and Organization: Towards a Differentiated Understanding', *Organization Studies*, 13/2 (1992), 73–102. Alvesson and Billing raise important criticisms of the women in management literature, particularly its tendency to treat masculinity 'as a unitary and unequivocal category' (p. 74).
18. P. Summerfield, *Women Workers in the Second World War: Production and Patriarchy in Conflict* (London, 1984), 190–1. See also D. Riley, *War in the Nursery: Theories of the Child and Mother* (London, 1983); J. Lewis, *Women in Britain since 1945: Women, Family, Work and the State in the Post-War Years* (Oxford, 1992).
19. A study that neatly illustrates the domestic discourses operating in business is R. Pringle, *Secretaries Talk: Sexuality, Power and Work* (Sydney, 1988).
20. As C. L. Williams aptly comments in her study of women and men in the US Marines, 'men's opposition to sexual integration cannot be explained entirely by the economic interests at stake in reserving all the best . . . jobs for them-

14

selves' (*Gender Differences at Work: Women and Men in Nontraditional Occupations* (Berkeley, Calif., 1989), 64).

21. N. Chodorow, *The Reproduction of Mothering: Psychoanalysis and the Sociology of Gender* (Berkeley, Calif., 1978).

22. See Williams, *Gender Differences at Work*; Hochschild, *Managed Heart*, 164–5n; and comments on E. F. Keller, *A Feeling For the Organism: The Life and Work of Barbara McClintock* (San Francisco, 1983), in J. Wajcman, *Feminism Confronts Technology* (Cambridge, 1991), 2, 7.

23. See A. Metcalf and M. Humphries (eds.), *The Sexuality of Men* (London, 1985); many of the contributors draw on Chodorow's work; in the introduction Metcalf explains that 'this book is concerned with exploring the consequences of modern man's lack of emotional knowledge and language' (p. 4). A more recent example is L. Hudson and B. Jacot, *The Way Men Think: Intellect, Intimacy and the Erotic Imagination* (London, 1991); Hudson and Jacot discern a preference among men for inanimate, technical pursuits, which they attribute to the 'male wound' suffered by boys as a consequence of having to renounce the emotional comforts provided by mothers (p. 45).

24. For good discussions of the problematic use of object relations in studies on masculinity, see L. Segal, *Slow Motion: Changing Men, Changing Masculinities* (London, 1990), 73–82; J. Sommerville, 'The Sexuality of Men and the Sociology of Gender', *Sociological Review*, 37/2 (May 1989), 277–308.

25. Hudson and Jacot, *The Way Men Think*, 45.

Part One

Masculinity and the
Rise of the
Organization Man

1

The Psychic Realm of Business

As that descent took its course the illusions and the dreams of 1945 would fade one by one—the imperial and Commonwealth role, the world-power role, British industrial genius, and, at the last, New Jerusalem itself, a dream turned to a dank reality of a segregated, subliterate, unskilled, unhealthy and institutionalised proletariat hanging on the nipple of state maternalism.[1]

Corelli Barnett, 1987

'Business' and 'masculinity' may seem at first sight to be only distantly related terms. Whilst business is an activity carried out in logically structured organizations for financial gain, 'masculinity' describes the gender attributes associated with men. Yet masculinity is visible in a variety of business domains: in the images of potency and emasculation used by journalists, economists, or even historians to depict economic activity; in the 'macho' ethos found in male-dominated industries such as manufacturing; and in the thrusting language used by individual managers when describing their work. Managers live out particular gender identities in the work they do, influencing the conduct of business in the process and how it is represented as a social category. In an influential essay, 'Gender: A Useful Category of Historical Analysis', the historian Joan Scott proposes a definition of gender that encompasses these different aspects.[2] She emphasizes its role in signifying power relations, and suggests that it has a number of linked elements. One concerns the manipulation of cultural symbols, and the norms which confer meaning on these symbols. Another concerns social institutions such as the economy, work organizations, marriage, and family. Finally, gender has a subjective aspect, relating to the identities of 'woman' and 'man' and how these are constructed through social institutions and 'historically specific cultural relations'.[3]

Taking the 'organization man' as its subject, this chapter highlights the interplay between these various aspects of gender. It sets out the principal domains of business in which masculinity operates: in collective discourses about management and the economy, in the historically shaped beliefs which structure relations between women and men in business institutions, and finally in the desires and fears which organization men revealed in the telling of their life histories. These domains relate to each other in complex ways. As we saw in the introduction, there are profound divergences between the collective and individual representations of masculinity in business. Whilst public representations commonly depict the manager as a rational actor, the non-rational aspects of masculinity are clearly apparent in the personal accounts of male managers. Organization studies have played a significant role in rendering this more subjective realm invisible. From Max Weber onwards, industrial researchers made men the object of study, but without recognizing their gender.[4] They depicted modern enterprises as characterized by rules, hierarchies, and objective knowledge, and as lying beyond the subjectivities of gender.

There are equally important reasons for studying the construction of masculinity in the institutions surrounding business. Family, public school, armed services, and marriage together shaped the organization man's identity as a man and manager. Yet the literature on women in management—with a few notable exceptions—has usually confined itself to the workplace. Formal and informal 'exclusionary mechanisms' are seen to underpin men's domination of senior management: discriminatory recruitment and promotion practices, the ideology of continuous service, lack of nursery provision, sexual harrasment, and the prevalence of 'men only' social activities.

A narrow focus on the mechanisms through which women are disadvantaged misses part of the story. It is also important to understand the kinds of psychic satisfactions which men derive from their social power as managers, and what those privileges are which they are so loath to relinquish. As Cynthia Cockburn has commented of men's resistance to equality in organizations, 'we have to look at what men as a sex gain from the *status quo*'.[5] Such a project demands that we understand the emotional dynamics of relations between men as well as how they exclude women. For example, authority relations among men in management operate in highly irrational ways. Managers often depict battles for supremacy between old and young in terms of competing images of masculinity. The post-war entrants considered that their technical expertise made them superior men to those they replaced, the 'gentleman amateurs' who had managed on the basis of mere intuition. Industrial restructuring during the 1980s called forth a new generation of hero. Now, business-school educated, highly mobile managers accuse the post-war entrants of being yesterday's men. In the quest for power, each generation promotes itself as more masculine than its predecessor. The history of business in Britain could be traced in terms of successive versions of masculinity, from the paternalism of the family capitalist, through the scientific rationality of the post-war organization man, to the 1980s revival of aggressive entrepreneurship in a mature corporate economy. It is important to recognize these variations in regimes, for business is often described as a 'masculine' pursuit, as if masculinity itself was a universal, unchanging quality.[6]

A further problem with studies based solely on the organizational setting is that the connections to other institutions, particularly the family are frequently left unexplored. Organization men began their careers during the 1950s, at a time when the 'separation of spheres' between home-makers and bread-winners was a middle-class norm. William H. Whyte movingly conveyed this in his contemporary description of American organization men as 'the ones of our middle-class who have left home, spiritually as well as physically, to take the vows of organization life'.[7] The managerial domain was firmly his; divisions of labour and notions of masculinity and femininity seemed fixed. Yet even among this generation the separation was actually rather complex, for the organization man's total commitment to career was only sustained by the unpaid work of wives and the underpaid work of secretaries, both of which could be managerial in content. Moreover, the reign of the organization man was short lived. The past two decades have seen increasing numbers of women in middle management, and 'dual-career' families becoming more common.[8] Slight in statistical terms, these stirrings of change in the gender order nevertheless threaten the organization man's identity as bread-winner.

Most accounts of business thus concentrate—consciously in the case of the women in management literature, and unconsciously in the case of 'classical' organization studies—on the cultural symbols or the institutional aspects of gender. By contrast, this study begins with the last of Scott's definitions: subjectivity. Below I draw on interviews and autobiographies in order to analyse the fantasies and repressions of organization men, and how these were played out in their work. The language that they used to describe their pasts, and the myths and fantasies that they conveyed in their reminiscences, provide important clues to subjectivity.[9] Memories act 'not only as special clues to the past, but equally as windows on the making and remaking of individual and collective consciousness', as Raphael Samuel and Paul Thompson remind us.[10]

Taking this view of oral narratives requires that we rethink the role of the researcher, and examine life-history narratives as *joint* productions rather than as mere windows on to the past. The particular emotional complexion of the company man's stories reflects certain fantasies about me as the interviewer, and vice versa.[11] A sociologist might approach a topic like this by considering the structural features of gender such as sexual divisions of labour. Instead, my starting-point is the meanings which organization men themselves attached to their work. This approach, as Rosemary Pringle explains, 'involves a consideration of the unconscious processes, the repressions and the fantasies that structure "consciousness", of the precariousness of "identity", and of the ways in which "experience" is interpreted through existing discourses'.[12] Life history helps make visible the connections between this psychic realm of business and the institutional structures that sustain men's dominance of management.

The remainder of this chapter sets the life histories of organization men in their cultural, institutional, and psychic contexts.[13] Section i examines the 1980s debates about economic decline in Britain to show how collective discourses about masculinity operate in the cultural milieu of business. Section ii explores the institutional contexts of work and home which shaped the organization man's identity as a man. The post-war generation of managers witnessed profound economic changes during their careers. Manufacturing was still dominated by family firms at the end of the war, but by the 1970s, corporate capitalism and the ethos of professional management held sway. This shift brought with it all kinds of tensions within management: between old and young, between those who had 'hands-on' experience and those who were business-school trained, and between functions such as production and finance.[14] As I shall argue below, competing images of masculinity formed the subtext of these tensions. The masculine identity of 'organization man' reflected not only the economic context, but also the divisions of labour between men and women. The men's depictions of women as colleagues, secretaries, and partners reveal much about their motivations for the exclusion of women from senior management. Gender inequalities are often conceived of in terms of a distinction between the occupational structure and the gender stereotypes attached to particular jobs. Models such as this separate categories which are symbiotic in people's minds. Moreover while the sex-typing of jobs is partially a product of historical time, a phenomenon outside the mind, sex stereotypes are continually reproduced at a psychic level. Section iii expands on this point. It argues that, while the organization man's masculinity was shaped by the institutional setting, it was equally fashioned in the interview itself. Interviews bring to light not only the facts of career history, but also its fantastic elements. My method in this project has been to track the organization man's comments back to the present, beginning with my role in the production of their stories. Only by comprehending all the planes on which gender operates—in the 'theatres of the mind'[15] as well as the discourses and structures of management—can we arrive at a satisfactory account of its workings.

i. Collective Discourses: Masculinity and Industrial Decline

In January 1980 the journal *Management Today* opened its editorial with the words: 'Today, there is no confidence about the future, in general or in detail.' It called upon Britain's businessmen to rally around and halt the economic slide, 'fighting aggressively' for market opportunities, improving the design of products to make them more competitive, and reining in the trade unions.[16] The journal detected a malaise among the country's industrial managers, who seemed powerless to prevent the traditional heartland of manufacturing from descending into recession. By 1982 things seemed to have grown worse. In that year Britain recorded its first ever trade deficit in manufactures, reflecting a continued erosion of the country's share in world exports from 33 per cent in 1900, to just 8 per cent.[17] Perhaps, *Management Today* mused tentatively, having lost its way in the heavy industrial sectors of machine tools and steel, Britain might seek a world lead in the—decidedly less heroic—sectors of 'brain-power and software'.[18]

Foreboding about the future led to vexed questioning of the past. Just how had British industry become so uncompetitive? Who was principally to blame for the decline? It was at this moment, amidst the crumbling foundations of British manufacturing, that a new historical industry emerged. In 1981 Martin Wiener's *English Culture and the Decline of the Industrial Spirit* appeared. It has become something of a classic text, selling 17,000 copies in the United Kingdom in the seven years after it went paperback in 1985, and stimulating debates between the business and academic communities which have lasted into the 1990s.[19] Wiener's style in the book was urgent and proselytizing. He took on cultural heroes of the British Left and Right, from the radical utopian William Morris to the imperialist Rudyard Kipling, and charged them all with the sin of anti-industrialism.[20] Even Britain's most prominent industrialists of the twentieth century, inheritors and self-made men alike, were found to lack the essence which generated economic progress: industrial spirit.[21] The book's reviewer for *Management Today* was the military historian Corelli Barnett, who offered generous praise to Wiener by claiming his own work of 1972, *The Collapse of British Power*, as its sire.[22] It was no accident that it should have been Barnett who offered his services to the journal as a kind of historian-cum-management consultant.[23] His own volume of 1987, *The Audit of War*, mounted a savage attack on the British education system.[24] Now amplifying Wiener, Barnett criticized academics for failing to provide suitable training for business. Since the nineteenth century, the élite universities of Oxford and Cambridge had only perverted the will to profit: 'Here amid the silent eloquence of grey Gothic walls and green sward, the sons of engineers, merchants, and manufacturers were emasculated into gentlemen.'[25] Ensconced within these very walls, Barnett promoted himself as the businessman's ally, the Cambridge Fellow who had dared to tutor men of the real world on the cause of Britain's industrial troubles.

Such literature caught the public imagination, partly by depicting Britain's economic problems as a 'social infection'.[26] More than this, however, the sickness was sexual in kind. Barnett believed that Britain's educationalists had 'emasculated' manufacturing, turning potential producers into public-school fops. Martin Wiener constructed a kind of spermatic economy in which 'industrial spirit' contained the seed of production. Decline stemmed from a shrivelling of the desire for profit, a waning of acquisitive, masculine drives. What made these 'decline histories' so compelling was that they presented organic images of the economy, picturing it as a damaged male body. In so doing they mobilized the fears of politicians, businessmen, and academics. Europe's 'sick man' was losing his potency, while the Establishment frittered away its energies in the feminine pastime of 'romantic imagination'.[27]

In order to illuminate the masculine imagery that underlies these 'decline histories', we need to analyse the narrative strategies they deploy. Weiner and his supporters portrayed the entrepreneurs of the nineteenth century as men who were initially fired by a desire for wealth, but who, once they had secured prosperity, gave up their industrial pursuits for a quiet life in the country. Gentility affected the sons of entrepreneurs in a negative way, their quasi-aristocratic education making them disdainful of technical expertise and leaching away the urge for wealth creation. Instead of supporting professional training for industry, inheritors prided themselves on their amateur status. Wiener's account gains its persuasive force by way of morally laden dichotomies between wealth creation and consumption, entrepreneurs and gentlemen, masculine and feminine. This tendency is especially evident when he describes the education of inheritors. Inverting the notion that public schools are forcing houses for 'making a man of him', Wiener views them as agents of emasculation.[28] They are 'nurseries' which 'nurture' imitation of the 'leisured, landed gentlemen' and a negative attitude towards production.[29] Wiener implies that inheritor managers lacked potency. They avoided risk and hard work in favour of soft domestic pleasures. Following a similar line of thought, Corelli Barnett depicts the ideal gentleman as 'the parfait knight, pure of face and blank of loins'.[30]

By extension, the nation as a whole suffers from a surfeit of non-masculine values. Businessmen, who should show 'dedication to work, the drive for profit, and the readiness to strike out on new paths', prefer instead the comforts of 'mother' nature—quiet rural homes away from the smoke and grit of production.[31] Profit-making, which should involve the harnessing of untutored aggression to industrial endeavour, had been 'muffled' by effeminate inheritors. 'Domestication of the wilder traits of earlier British behaviour' was to blame for the nation's poor economic performance over the past century, Wiener concluded.[32]

The 'decline thesis' thus proposed that Britain's economic fortunes could be explained in terms of a struggle between effeminate gentlemen and manful producers in which the former had retained their hegemony.[33] This bizarre history really only begins to add up when we situate it in the context from which its proponents wrote. Fundamental changes were taking place in British industrial culture during the 1970s and 1980s. 'Big science' and Harold Wilson's 'white-hot technological revolution' had not yielded the kinds of advantages hoped for.[34] The source of wealth creation was slowly shifting from manufacturing to services such as banking, insurance, retailing, and professional services. By 1980 the service sector accounted for half the share of Britain's GDP, a rise of almost 15 per cent over the figure in 1950.[35] Within manufacturing, 'paper entrepreneurialism', where the company acts as a kind of investor to its subsidiaries, seeking quick financial returns rather than creating new products, was at its zenith.[36] These changes went hand in hand with the elevation of new business heroes. Wiener's businessmen were thus not actually manufacturers, but men who sought profit. They had no inherent interest in technical merit or amateur knowledge, but were driven by the spirit of acquisition. In order to be re-empowered as an industrial nation, Britain needed 'aggressive and acquisitive capitalists'.[37]

These attempts to fashion masculinity around wealth creation can be traced back to the business commentators and economic historians of the 1960s and 1970s. Paradoxically, Wiener in his adversarial way discounted economic explanations of Britain's industrial performance. And yet his work parodied their prescriptions. For example, in his 1973 study of diversification in British firms, D. F. Channon tried to explain why post-war British managers had proved so tardy in adopting a multi-divisional structure.[38] Lack of will was the answer. Money-making was considered 'immoral' by the older generation of managers, in contrast to 'the new leaders . . . men of force who did not hesitate to use their . . . power of office in order to re-direct the enterprise'.[39] Channon's heroes of the early 1970s were men like Arnold Weinstock of GEC, Frank Kearton of Courtaulds, or Jim Slater of Slater Walker. Competitive spirit signifies virility in Channon's view. The new men lead the trend towards 'more aggression' in management, while 'lack of desire' characterizes their predecessors. In Channon's account the sources of industrial renewal lie deep within the psyche, in 'the will to be profitable or efficient'.[40]

In Graham Turner's comprehensive commentary of the late 1960s,

Business in Britain, it is once again the profit-conscious businessman who possesses virility.[41] This emerges particularly clearly in his depiction of Arnold Weinstock, who effected the merger of English Electric, AEI, and GEC to form the sprawling conglomerate of today. Weinstock symbolizes the displacement of masculinity from production and its transference to the pursuit of profit. Instead of the legendary cars which adorned the desks of ex-engineers in the 1960s, Turner tells us that Weinstock's desk featured a sheet of paper on which was listed the profit-and-loss statistics for American electrical firms, and the comparative figures for GEC. This was his 'spur' to action.[42] Weinstock himself equated masculinity with financial acumen, using the adjective 'manly' to describe the 'cold' but 'intelligent' businessmen he admired.[43] In his portrait of Weinstock, Turner articulates a contemporary perception that the character of managerial conquest was changing. Aggression is still the key quality needed in business, but not the physical bravado displayed by ex-engineers. It is the calculative rationality of the money-maker that drives industry forward.[44]

The decline histories of the 1980s clearly articulated this conception of profit as the principal signifier of managerial potency. Claiming to diagnose the ills of the past, they confidently held out the prescription for national revival. The key to economic health was the restoration of a business environment in which 'rugged individualists' could be given free rein.[45] By midway through the 1980s the language of thrusting masculinity had even taken root in national debates about economic policy. It was to be found in the Conservative government's manifesto for the 'enterprise culture'. According to the Chancellor at the time, Nigel Lawson, Britain's future economic success would not only depend on strategies such as privatization, reducing the burden of taxation or controlling inflation, but on 'changing psychology to change the business culture'.[46] Lawson and the Minister for Trade and Industry, Lord Young, argued that the nation's ability to compete had been weakened by an overprotective state. Aggressive entrepreneurialism would provide the antidote to this post-war culture of dependency. The British people must be weaned from what Conservatives sometimes called the 'nanny state'.[47] The Conservative diagnosis of the 'British disease' was thus identical to that provided by the historian Corelli Barnett in 1987: Britain was suffocating under a hegemony of feminine values, its 'unhealthy and institutionalised proletariat hanging on the nipple

27

of state maternalism'.[48] Supporters of the new regime such as Lord Young saw the organization man as part of the problem, his initiative having been stifled by life in the bureaucracy.[49] De-regulation, the fostering of competition, would strip away his homely comforts, and force him to play his appropriate role as bread-winner for the nation. In the enterprise culture, men would be separated from boys by competition in the market.[50] Describing the implications of this new order for business, in his keynote speech of 1987 the Director-General of the British Institute of Management revelled in metaphors of athletic, combative, and sexually potent manhood. He talked of the 'supple and fast-moving vigour . . . needed to beat off competitors and seize opportunities in the market-place'. Opportunities would abound for Wiener's heroes, businessmen 'with cutting edge'. In the new competitive age, manful struggle was the only solution. 'No business in Britain can expect shelter from the blast,' the Director-General warned, because 'somewhere in the world a competitor is honing his ability to win'.[51]

Images of virility and impotence abounded in the 1980s debates about Britain's economy, evoking the contrast between money-making entrepreneurs and the wealth-sapping public sector. The 'enterprise culture' aimed to cultivate an aura of manly heroism around money-making, so enhancing its legitimacy as a pursuit. Yet this conception of business was no more valid than its predecessors which emphasized intuition or professional knowledge as the marks of a true man and manager. We need only look at the transience of financial wizards, at their meteoric rise to prominence and their equally rapid disappearance, to realize this. Amidst the growing calls for 'long-termism', decline is now sometimes blamed on men like Weinstock for their single-minded cost-cutting.[52] Others have experienced more dramatic falls from public favour. Sir Ralph Halpern of the Burton Group was hailed as a financial wonder in 1987. Self-made and with a flair for the retailing side of the clothing business, he typified the new generation of service-sector managers. Business acumen and sexual virility seemed indistinguishable in Sir Ralph's case. Press reports about his relationship with a young model emerged on the eve of the firm's annual meeting and announcement of record profits, prompting the popular press to dub him 'five times a night Ralph'.[53] Halpern was the first managing director to break the million pound salary barrier, which he justified by pointing to his potency as bread-winner for the Burton Group.[54] But, with a string of poor returns in the late 1980s Halpern faded from favour, along with those other retailing idols of the city, Sir Terence Conran of Storehouse, George Davies of Next, and Gerald Ratner.

Such managers may or may not be responsible for their own downfall. In the case of the fallen industrial idol Sir John Egan of Jaguar, changes in exchange rates, recession, and intensified international competition were trends over which he had limited influence. Yet reduced profits and the eventual takeover of Jaguar identified Sir John as a 'former hero of the Thatcherite revolution'.[55] A symbiosis between masculinity and business endeavour underpinned the cult of the 'new entrepreneur' during the 1980s. Reacting against a postwar version of masculinity which emphasized technical aptitude or experience as the hallmarks of a true man, economists, politicians, and business commentators strove to fashion masculinity around profit-and-loss statements. Historians, too, deeply attracted by this phallic discourse, incorporated it in their vision of Britain's industrial past.

ii. Masculinity and the Changing Regimes of Business

Among men The decline histories illustrate the fact that masculinity is not a unitary category, and that symbols of manly virility may carry a range of meanings, sometimes contradictory. Two images of masculinity were prominent in business during the 1980s. Within manufacturing were the financial managers, ruthless cost-cutters like Weinstock and the younger generation of business-school-trained managers. In the service sector a more effusive and colourful masculinity took hold, exemplified by the retailers who commercialized the 'style revolution' of the later 1980s. The effects of these business regimes on organization men were clearly apparent, for, in contrast to the financial managers and retailers who were fêted during the 1980s, they found themselves increasingly under threat.

The masculine identities which my informants fashioned in the interviews reflected this loss of public esteem. Their life stories can be seen as a reaction against the rise of the service economy and the restructuring of manufacturing. Facing a drive for economic efficiency often spearheaded by younger managers, these organization men responded by asserting experiences and skills which were particular to their generation. Today they present an image of manhood in which practical experience is the principal motif. This is the

2 *'Sir Ralph camps it up'*
The dress-conscious retailing heroes of the 1980s 'enterprise economy'
differed dramatically from the grey suited organizational man. Men like Sir
Ralph Halpern symbolized the advent of a more flamboyant—but still
firmly heterosexual— masculinity in business. Sir Ralph here models
himself *and* his company's products.

Richard Young, *Guardian*, 16 Nov. 1990

one thing to which they can lay claim over the young financial managers, who they tended to dismiss by playing up their book learning. As one man explained, the new recruits to senior management had 'been taught a whole set of techniques and tools in business schools, but really the job was done by earthy, instinctive reactions. "Get stuck in," that kind of thing.' Even the fact of survival in the face of cutbacks and retrenchments was for organization men a sign of superior hardiness.

This image of management by gut instinct contradicted the advent of internal labour markets which tended to reward tacit knowledge less highly than formal education. It also went against the dominant managerial creed within manufacturing which held that profit must take precedence over technical wizardry. The organization man's vision of a 'man's man' played an important role in warding off the criticisms of young accountants from within the firm, or city financiers without. At the same time, while it served as a rallying point of old against young, this image was not all-encompassing. Organization men also measured each other according, as Mr Wright put it, to 'how you shape up as a man'. Differences in family background and education were grounds not just for placing a man by class, but for positioning him between the polar opposites of the ex-apprentice's 'rough' masculinity and the middle-class 'academic type'. Below I will illustrate the range of images of manhood which interviewees displayed to me, and briefly trace their lineage.

The 'earthy, instinctive' masculinity projected by organization men has a long pedigree. It drew its inspiration partly from the nineteenth-century conception of industry as an alliance between gentlemen amateurs and practical men or 'players'.[56] At the same time it inverted the social status of the two figures, the practical man being depicted as more heroic than his social superior. The emphasis on 'hands-on' learning also derived from experiences which were unique to the post-war generation, such as compulsory military service and the practice of moving new recruits around the factory on a 'Cook's tour'.[57] Three-quarters of the men in the sample had undergone national or war service. As we shall see in Chapter 4, they feel that this training made them physically tougher than their successors. It endowed them with the ability to hold their own against men on the shop-floor. Today they still regard this kind of 'man management' as a more effective way of controlling the shop-floor than the sophisticated human-resource strategies peddled by younger managers. Similarly, we shall see in Chapter 4 that the task of acquiring 'hands-on' skills in early career—learning to operate plant, for example—is remembered as a kind of rite of passage between youth and manhood. Conveying this mixture of sexual and managerial maturity, one manager described his first post as mill hand in a steel factory as 'a kind of seminal point'. Fascination for production and products was crucial to the organization man's vision of himself as a man's man. This managerial trait was a legacy of family capitalism and the post-war economic climate to some extent, but took on a new role in late career. Indulgence in technical pleasures now constituted a form of private rebellion against the young upstarts—a means of bucking against the dominant culture of financial austerity.

Despite their tendency to exhibit a kind of practical masculinity akin to that of working-class men, for much of their careers the members of this managerial milieu were in fact deeply split along lines of education and class.[58] Organization men today emphasize the affinities they feel towards others of their generation. Nevertheless, they hold widely varying views about the qualities which constitute manly prowess. Among the university graduates, particularly scientists, academic excellence could take on gender overtones. Graduate managers sometimes ranked each other by recalling a man's ability in his original area of expertise. Intellect and rationality might thus be equated with manliness. On the whole, however, interviewees regarded a background in engineering as a more worthy mark of a man than a university education. Intellectual occupations never had quite the same cachet which could attach to occupations more firmly technological or physical in character. Men who went on to staff posts like personnel or work study felt particularly vulnerable, for, while such functions increasingly held the key to career success, the work itself was prone to the accusation of mere pen-pushing. Arts or commerce graduates often underplayed the mental content of their work, struggling, it seems, to overcome a sense of inferiority.

At the opposite extreme, ex-engineers sometimes displayed their wealth of practical knowledge in a quite aggressive manner. Reacting against the class superiority of academic knowledge, they found a certain enjoyment in bewildering me with technical terms. My lack of comprehension served to reinforce their expertise. Moreover, they cast aspersions on staff functions, seeing them as 'soft'. Accountants and salesmen were, as Graham Turner remarked of the motor-vehicle industry in 1968, 'thought of as lesser breeds of men'.[59] This

valorization of things practical by the ex-engineers reveals, in particular, the tensions between their images of true manhood and the
managerial hierarchy. Ex-engineers could successfully challenge the
virility of the young accountant or salesman, but were often dominated by them on the company ladder. Even the engineers were confronted with a dilemma, for the more senior they became, the further
away they moved from the drama of the shop-floor and the chance to
indulge in things technical. As Cynthia Cockburn has observed, such
men often experienced a kind of 'male menopause' in mid-career, as
they were promoted to just the kind of desk-bound jobs which they
had once dismissed as unmanly.[60]

We might understand the disdain of ex-engineers for intellectuals
in terms of an image of manhood in which those who had proved
their mettle through physical labour or technological expertise were
superior to those who depended on mere brainpower. In the same
vein, the desperate attempts of financiers to introduce a heroic element to their work indicates tension between a masculine hierarchy
in which they are subordinate, and an economic climate in which
they take precedence. Even within one generation and one industrial
sector, there is no simple correlation between masculinity and managerial status. The visions of manhood projected by organization
men varied according to their social background, the traditions of the
industry in which they worked, and the immediate audience they had
in mind. While the ex-apprentice manager in the motor-vehicle
industry might dominate the ex-public-school man, both could claim
a certain superiority over younger, better educated men like myself.

Women and men   While masculinity in its various forms is manifested in the relations between male managers, it is equally visible in
the organization man's normative ideas about the sexual divisions of
labour. To ignore the relations between men and women would be
simply to echo industrial sociology of the 1950s and 1960s. Classics
such as C. W. Mills's *White Collar*, William H. Whyte's *The
Organization Man*, Melville Dalton's *Men Who Manage*, or Cyril
Sofer's *Men in Mid-Career* gave us elaborate contemporary descriptions of the organization man's work culture and occupational identity.[61] Whyte even considered the role of wives in sustaining the
organization man's loyalty to the corporation.[62] And yet these works
did not critically question the assumption that managerial work was
men's work. Sexual divisions of labour were taken for granted.

Studies of gender segregation in 1980s Britain reveal the extent to which men dominate management. In 1985 they occupied three-quarters of managerial jobs.[63] Within the professions as a whole, women were most likely to be concentrated in jobs related to education, health, and welfare.[64] This pattern of horizontal segregation also holds good to some extent within management. Over the past two decades the proportion of women managers has increased most in industries such as financial services, retailing, and catering.[65] Within firms, change has been most marked in staff functions like training, personnel, and finance. Women continue to be particularly under-represented in 'line' jobs (core management tasks) such as general management. So, while in 1988 11 per cent of general managerial staff were women (an increase of just 2 per cent over the 1983 figure), over twice that proportion could be found in professional jobs supporting management and administration.[66] Moreover, Nigel Nicholson and Michael West found in their study of British Institute of Management members that men and women tended to follow different career paths.[67] Men were more often generalists, while women had usually reached senior management on the basis of a functional specialism. While men moved easily from technical posts into general management, women were more often promoted within the one specialism.[68] Finally, alongside these differences in career path and management function, vertical segregation is still pronounced.[69] As Nicholson and West conclude, men 'overwhelmingly predominate in the top jobs'.[70]

Life history makes us question the way in which sociologists have understood these sexual divisions of labour in management. Many approaches distinguish between the structural and ideological dimensions of gender segregation.[71] Occupational segregation refers to the structural location of men and women in different jobs, while sex-typing refers to the designation of particular jobs as 'masculine' or 'feminine'. Sex-typing is seen partly as the product of historical circumstances, reflecting the gender order at the moment when the job concerned first emerged from the division of labour.[72] This emphasis on the structural and historical aspects of labour divisions means that the subjective meanings which people associate with those divisions are not adequately explored. The masculine imagery which both women and men use when describing managerial work is, after all, a product of the imagination. The organization men of the post-war generation were primary beneficiaries in the gender order described above, and agents of its perpetuation. For example, my interviewees often subscribed to what Rosemary Crompton and Kay Sanderson call 'indirect exclusionary practices'. That is, they gauged fitness for management in terms of requirements like career continuity and breadth of work experience, which women often find difficult to meet.[73] At the same time, beliefs like these did not result from a conscious intention to exclude women. Rather, the men's *own* identities as managers were founded on these requirements. We have seen that they resisted the idea of promotion on the basis of formal qualifications, one of the principal means available for women to overcome disadvantage.[74] In the clearly defined bureaucratic ladder, length of service was prized above education as a mark of manhood. As one man explained, borrowing a bar-room metaphor to make his point, 'You don't just suddenly come up like a bubble in a beer glass.' The stress on geographical mobility also reflected their own experiences, which had most often been in the company's operating divisions. Experience 'outside' head office was depicted as a man's prerogative.

The masculine imagery which men employed when describing the work of management reflected a further sexual division of labour—that between paid and domestic work. When managers talked of how they had become hardened by their experiences in line management jobs, this presumed a contrast with other, 'soft', and more homely occupations like personnel. As Joan Acker has remarked, the concept of an 'organizational hierarchy' already contains within it 'the separation between the public and the private sphere'.[75] The organization man inhabited a world which was deeply split between work and home. In a study of managers and their families carried out in the late 1960s—the heyday of the organization man—J. M. and R. E. Pahl found that only 15 per cent of wives had paid employment outside the home.[76] The narratives of the men I interviewed bear ample testimony to this separation of spheres. They described a passage from one male-dominated institution to another, from public school perhaps, to national service, to the corporation. Yet they never saw this culture as being in any way masculine; it was just normal. In contrast, they invariably defined home as a feminine sphere, emphasizing women's special arts in keeping house and mothering.[77]

In the organization man's view, it was the responsibility of wives to provide a retreat from work. Sir John Harvey-Jones, the ex-chairman of ICI, explained in his autobiography that 'creating our various homes' had been his wife's principal life work. While she spent most of her time in the domestic sphere, he regarded their homes as 'treasured havens for us both'.[78] The organization men in this study described their home lives in equally glowing terms. At the same time they found it difficult to strike the right balance between the spheres. A successful career might prove their abilities as bread-winners, but meant that they were not often at home. They loved the excitement of travel but felt guilty about their frequent absences and the continual job changes which had forced wives and children to relocate. They felt that their influence on home life was often negative, as if their presence intruded on the domestic idyll. Paradoxically, home did function as a retreat for them, but only in the company of men could they feel genuinely 'at home'. This split was carried through into the world of work. As with wives, they distinguished the labours of women secretaries or managers by their qualities of emotional support. Yet the men felt profoundly ambivalent about this supposed presence of domesticity in the workplace. Even a skilled secretary might threaten the clear boundaries which they had built up between the nurturing functions of women and their own truly productive work. Travel, technical discovery, and 'hands-on' knowledge were the marks of a true organization man, but also constituted his haven from domesticity. Attention to the way in which men think about their career past can help us to understand the psychic investments which they made in exclusionary practices. Exclusion rarely stems from a coherent strategy. Yet it has sometimes been treated as if it could be traced back to the conscious intentions of men to ensure that women remained in subordinate jobs.[79] In practice, exclusion usually operates in a much more contingent and implicit way than this.

Organization men thought of masculinity in terms of career advancement, and femininity in terms of home-making. However, relations between managers at work might also duplicate that split, mimicking domestic gender relations. The hostility which interviewees sometimes expressed towards women in production jobs reflected what David Collinson, David Knights, and Margaret Collinson aptly refer to as a 'bread-winner ideology', in which men earn the profits for the company while women service their needs in functions such as personnel.[80] Even when men did profess support for women managers, this might be for reasons which simply reinforced their conceptions of femininity and ultimately discouraged free career choice among women. For example, one manager felt that the more caring, 'more relaxed' style of women managers provided a welcome relief from the 'hard-hitting . . . desk-thumping, confrontational' style of men. He was pleased that 'some of these differences come through'. In one sense he seemed to be voicing a protest against the dominance of macho management styles. At the same time, of course, this celebration of women as carers places them at a disadvantage in management structures as currently conceived. We need to know more about the often subtle ways in which men's normative conceptions about gender are reflected in their different treatment of women managers.

iii. Subjectivity: Interviewing Organization Men

If the organization man's masculinity was shaped by the post-war industrial culture and economic climate, it is equally a product of unconscious processes. Life histories have a psychic as well as a cultural content, which emerges quite naturally as a result of the interactions between interviewer and interviewee. In the process of remembering, interviewees impose 'archaic (childhood) images onto present-day objects', as Jennifer Hunt puts it.[81] For this reason it is imperative that I consider whom I represented in the pasts of organization men. What kind of fantasies did my appearance, age, background, and demeanour touch off? The psychoanalytic concept of transference offers a way of approaching this kind of relationship, where the particular past which an informant draws upon relates to whom the interviewer represents at a psychic level. As Karl Figlio notes, in all social transactions, but in an intensified form in interviews, 'past relationships—more particularly the emotion-laden fragments of experience fixed in the psyche—find their way into present relationships, fleshing them out, often bestowing on them what is felt to be real and recognisable'. The analyst or interviewer in this case thus 'becomes part of the internal world' of the interviewee.[82] Far from this being an obstacle to research, it is the study of transference that illuminates the subjective identities of organization men.

In my research I was initially drawn to consider the relationship between myself and my informants because of the emphasis which they placed upon early career. This was a period when the future had seemed to hold all, a perception heightened by the symmetry between youth and the buoyant economic conditions of the 1950s.

Their present dilemma as managers, poised on the edge of retirement or recently retired, perhaps edged out by a younger generation of men, gave a particular poignance to their memories. They described their early triumphs in great detail, reliving the vigour of youth. Engineers recalled their 'dirty hands experience' on the shopfloor, and the master works which had eventually singled them out for promotion. University graduates, many self-funded, talked of their feats in juggling study and work. Fantasies of youthful omnipotence were associated with the absence of domestic responsibilities, as if the two could never be entirely reconciled. As Mr Aldridge put it, 'at 28 it's limitless', whereas at 40 'it's having a family, a feeling that you've got to cope, you've really got to know where you're heading'. Early career symbolized physical prowess and independence: in short, possibility.[83]

This tendency to hark back to early career clearly illustrates how career history may become a forum for airing the satisfactions and discontents of masculinity. But their comments were also shaped by suppositions about me. My position as a single man, a student, and a traveller in Britain stirred in interviewees a strong yearning for the past. I put them in mind of their youth. Sometimes they imagined me as a younger version of themselves, assuming, for example that I too would become a manager. Parting comments might take the form of advice to avoid the pitfalls they had experienced. I stood for the chance they no longer had to explore unrealized ambitions. A personnel manager who had suffered throughout his career with the stigma of being on the margins of 'real' management explained that, if I determined to go into personnel, I should think about industrial relations rather than his own 'soft' job of graduate recruitment. Other interviewees were prompted by my project to reflect on why they had chosen not to go on to postgraduate study. Sometimes the wish to help became confused with the desire to control. One interview foundered completely as the manager concerned, a head-hunter, abandoned his life story in order to set me up with a brief, contacts, and a publisher. He had long wanted to write a history of British business in the 1960s, and thought I might research it. He would invest in my future if I allowed him to 'take over' my enterprise.

I was led to wonder at various points how my Australian nationality influenced their accounts. I always mentioned this in introductory letters and sometimes emphasized the theme of outsider in the interview itself—for example, admitting my ignorance about the traits characteristic of public-school men. Perhaps informants felt themselves to be cultural ambassadors, in line with Britain's Imperial past, playing host to the representative of a daughter country.[84] Some interviewees had worked in Australia, and many firms in the sample had subsidiaries there. Undoubtedly my national status enhanced this aspect of goodwill and made interviewees more secure about the anthropological nature of my endeavour. As a nation, Australia summoned images of youthful promise, a suggestion also evoked by my age and freedom from domestic fetters.[85] It was the young national serviceman serving in the wilds of Malaysia or India, or the trainee manager sent on his first assignment to a company outpost, both cultural ambassadors of a kind, which my presence evoked.

The tendency of interviewees towards fantasies of youthful grandiosity was also signalled by my own reactions during interviews. I often left with a heightened sense of confidence about my career prospects. It was as if I was being invested with the powers that interviewees themselves wished to possess or perhaps recover—a typical instance of countertransference.[86] Moreover, I felt a tremendous sense of being *cosseted* by them. Interviews were often held in the directors' offices, seated in luxurious lounge furniture, with tea or coffee in china cups served personally by a secretary. The men gained considerable pleasure in demonstrating their ability to command the company's resources and 'their' women in this way. They conveyed their power to me through the gift of first-class service.

Their tendency to reminisce at length about older men who had influenced their careers could similarly be explained as a product of transference. Our interview was a psychodrama of their experiences with a mentor, this time one in which they played the older man while I represented the protégé. My role as protégé put a particular complexion on the 'empathy' which is critical to the interview process. As Chapter 3 explains, one way of approaching the narratives is to read them as vignettes of seduction between younger and older men. In the course of the field-work, I realized that the interviews which had 'gone best' were those where I played the part of a younger man and courtier. I found myself steering around controversy and focusing on the moments when informants stressed their competence. I was colluding in a culturally prevalent discourse between older and younger male managers in which, as others have observed, the junior flatters his boss in return for knowledge and opportunities.[87] That process had direct parallels with my asking for information about their careers and possible further contacts in order that I might enhance my own career prospects, whether business or academic. Admiration was exchanged for intimacy. Yet my age and fantasized future managerial career not only brought with it the pleasures of transference from past (youth/protégé) and more recent (father/mentor) relationships. The similarities between me and their protégés also revealed the other side of mentoring: anger at being cast aside by a younger generation. This feeling was exacerbated by the early 1980s recession, in which this generation entered late career. On the one hand, they identified with their one-time mentors, and the satisfactions of appointing an heir. On the other, they were angry at their impending loss of power, and expressed this by mocking the feeble manhood of 'lily-white' young men like me. The relationship between young and old men has its wellsprings in both aggression and desire.

This book is informed by the conflicts and affections which emerged in interviews between me and organization men. Like the young business graduates whom they abhor, I am sometimes critical of them. Perhaps at times I am too eager to condemn them for beliefs which were, after all, partly forced on them: aggression as the key to career success, the necessity to deny stress, and a disavowal of anything 'soft' or unmanly. Recognition of this desire to 'get stuck in' to my father's generation, to live out my own Oedipal drama, is essential, since the tension between parricide and seduction so often underpins succession in management. The psychoanalytic tools of transference and countertransference can help us to understand this dynamic, focusing as they do on the past referents of present fantasies. This work is itself partially the product of countertransference: recognition, however incomplete, of the differences and similarities between my masculinity and that of my father's generation. It reflects the tensions which I experienced in interviews between affection and criticism, sympathy for the burdens of the organization man's masculinity, and an often uncomfortable identification with it.

NOTES
1. The concluding words of C. Barnett, *The Audit of War: The Illusion and Reality of Britain as a Great Nation* (London, 1987), 304.
2. J. Scott, 'Gender: A Useful Category of Historical Analysis', *American Historical Review*, 91/5, (1986), 1053–75.
3. Ibid. 1067–8.

4. K. Purcell, 'Gender and the Experience of Employment', in D. Gallie (ed.), *Employment in Britain* (Oxford, 1988), 158. The question of how we might reread sociological classics on work so as to bring out their 'hidden' stories about masculinity is addressed by D. H. J. Morgan in *Discovering Men* (London, 1992), 49–72.

5. C. Cockburn, *In the Way of Women: Men's Resistance to Sex Equality in Organizations* (London, 1991), 17.

6. This issue is discussed in M. Alvesson and Y. D. Billing, 'Gender and Organization: Towards a Differentiated Understanding', *Organization Studies*, 13/2 (1992), 74.

7. W. H. Whyte, *The Organization Man* (Harmondsworth, 1963), 8.

8. R. Scase and R. Goffee, *Reluctant Managers: Their Work and Lifestyles* (London, 1989), 15.

9. The significance of memory for the study of oral history is explored in P. Thompson, *The Voice of the Past*, 2nd edn. (Oxford, 1988), ch. 5. Two good commentaries on subjectivity and the oral-history method are the introduction to R. Samuel and P. Thompson (eds.), *The Myths We Live By* (London, 1990), and A. Portelli, *The Death of Luigi Trastulli and other Stories: Form and Meaning in Oral History* (New York, 1991), esp. ch. 1.

10. Samuel and Thompson (eds.), *Myths We Live By*, 21.

11. A useful introduction to the use of psychoanalytic methods in interviews is J. C. Hunt, *The Psychoanalysis of Fieldwork* (London, 1989), ch. 3.

12. R. Pringle, *Secretaries Talk: Sexuality, Power and Work* (Sydney, 1988), p. x.

13. Further information on the backgrounds of organization men can be found in Appendix I.

14. Industrial restructuring in the 1980s further threatened the work identities of organization men, as younger women and men, schooled in financial and strategic management, began to exert their influence. Changes which particularly affected the managers in this study included the stripping-away of management levels, which disrupted once-clear career hierarchies, and a reversal of the diversification strategies often pursued in the 1960s, profits being more often maintained through divestment or cost control during the 1980s rather than internal growth. For a summary of these changes, see Scase and Goffee, *Reluctant Managers*, ch. 1, 'The Changing Context of Work, Careers, and Life-Styles'.

15. The phrase is taken from J. McDougall, *Theatres of the Mind: Illusion and Truth on the Psychoanalytic Stage* (London, 1986).

16. *Management Today* (Jan. 1980), 3.

17. Ibid. (Mar. 1983), 53.

18. Ibid. 52.

19. M. J. Wiener, *English Culture and the Decline of the Industrial Spirit, 1850–1980* (Cambridge, 1981; repr. Harmondsworth, 1985). Many thanks to Ravi Mirchandani at Penguin Books for passing on the sales information. He commented that 'the sales compare very pleasingly with those of many other, more general, historical titles we publish' (private communication with the editor, 1 Oct. 1992). The public debates surrounding Wiener's work are discussed in J. Raven, 'British History and the Enterprise Culture', *Past and Present*, 123 (May 1989), 178–204. See also J. Baxendale, 'Martin J. Wiener:

English Culture and the Decline of the Industrial Spirit, 1850–1980', *History Workshop Journal*, 21 (Spring 1986), 171–4.

20. Wiener's thesis had many predecessors. The best is D. C. Coleman, 'Gentlemen and Players', *Economic History Review*, 2nd ser., 36/1 (1973), 92–116. Neil McKendrick has published many articles illustrating the hostility of the British literary establishment to industrialization. See, e.g., his introduction to R. J. Overy, *William Morris. Viscount Nuffield* (London, 1976) and 'Gentlemen and Players Revisited: The Gentlemanly Ideal, the Business Ideal, and the Professional Ideal in English Literary Culture', in N. McKendrick and R. B. Outhwaite (eds.), *Business Life and Public Policy: Essays in Honour of D. C. Coleman* (Cambridge, 1986), 98–137. G. C. Allen, 'The Cult of the Amateur', in D. Coates and J. Hillard (eds.), *The Economic Decline of Modern Britain: The Debate between Left and Right* (Brighton, 1986), 153–9, found particular favour among the business community.

21. Wiener singles out both the inheritor Samuel Courtauld and the 'self-made' managing director of British Leyland in the 1960s, Lord Stokes, as proponents of the gentrification of industry (*English Culture*, 137–45).

22. *Management Today* (July 1981), 19. Wiener's book was my 'brainchild', claimed Barnett.

23. See also *Management Today* (Jan. 1985), 29; (Apr. 1986), 85.

24. Barnett, *The Audit of War*; see, esp., his comments on the role of Victorian and Edwardian public schools in fostering disdain for industry (p. 14).

25. Ibid. 221.

26. Allen, 'Cult of the Amateur', 154.

27. Barnett, *Audit of War*, 13.

28. The phrase is used by C. Heward in her study of Ellesmere College: *Making a Man of him: Parents and their Sons' Education at an English Public School, 1929–1950* (London, 1988).

29. Wiener, *English Culture*, 19–21. Maternal images are also used by Barnett, who describes Oxbridge as the 'nursery of the intelligentsia' (*Audit of War*, 222), and by Allen, who refers to public schools as the 'nursery of political leaders and administrators' ('Cult of the Amateur', 153).

30. Barnett, *Audit of War*, 214.

31. Wiener, *English Culture*, 24. The same contrast between domestic comforts and rugged industrialists is evident in analyses of why Britain lagged behind its competitors in technology investment; e.g. D. C. Coleman and C. McCleod argue that British business men prefer a 'quiet, technically conservative life' to 'persistence in innovating' ('Attitudes to New Techniques: British Businessmen, 1800–1950', *Economic History Review*, 2nd ser., 39/4 (Nov. 1986), 606).

32. Wiener, *English Culture*; the theory of 'domestication of the industrial revolution' is described on many occasions (e.g. pp. 10, 30, 158).

33. The thesis of Britain as a nation made economically impotent by the continued dominance of its aristocracy has appeal on both the Left and the Right. P. Anderson, for example, approvingly quotes Marx's remark of 1861, that the aristocracy's monopoly over foreign affairs since the Glorious Revolution of 1688 had 'emasculated the general intellect of the middle-class men by the circumscription of all their energies and mental faculties within the narrow

sphere of their mercantile, industrial and professional concerns' ('The Figures of Descent', *New Left Review*, 161 (Jan.–Feb. 1987), 23).
34. Quoted in A. Sampson, *The New Anatomy of Britain* (London, 1971), 570.
35. S. Pollard, *The Development of the British Economy, 1914–1980*, 3rd edn. (London, 1983), 281. Included within the service sector are distributive trades such as insurance, banking, finance, and business services; professional and scientific services; and public administration and defence.
36. The term was coined by R. B. Reich. Quoted in H. Perkin, *The Rise of Professional Society: England since 1880* (London, 1989), 502–3.
37. Wiener, *English Culture*, 158.
38. D. F. Channon, *The Strategy and Structure of British Enterprise* (London, 1973).
39. Ibid. 221.
40. Ibid. 42, 234, 242.
41. G. Turner, *Business in Britain* (London, 1969).
42. Ibid. 325. Turner himself is a great admirer of Weinstock's aggressive financial manipulations. He recounts Weinstock's life history in terms of the number of firms which he managed to turn around, citing profit margins as proof of the man's greatness. Weinstock succeeds in uprooting the engineer-dominated management at GEC, in which the strategy had mistakenly been based on production of 'goods which measure up to a standard of perfection'. In their book on GEC, R. Jones and O. Marriott heap similarly lavish praise on Weinstock, calling him a 'living advertisement for capitalism' (*Anatomy of a Merger: A History of GEC, AEI and English Electric* (London, 1970), 14).
43. Turner, *Business in Britain*, 309.
44. Turner's admiration for 'ruthless' Weinstock can be compared to his disparagement of 'blood and guts merchants' like Sir Roy Dobson. 'Production men' who had come up from the shop-floor in engineering industries and who managed by 'hunch' are yesterday's heroes, their status eclipsed by men of superior 'rationality' (*Business in Britain*, 306–9).
45. Wiener, *English Culture*, 158.
46. Quoted in P. Morris, 'Freeing the Spirit of Enterprise. The Genesis and Development of the Concept of Enterprise Culture', in R. Keat and N. Abercrombie (eds.), *Enterprise Culture* (London, 1991), 29. Morris charts the development of the concept through a close analysis of speeches by Lord Young. However, the gendered nature of enterprise metaphors is ignored.
47. The metaphor of dependence is explored well by R. Keat, 'Introduction: Starship Britain or Universal Enterprise?', in Keat and Abercrombie (eds.), *Enterprise Culture*, 4–5.
48. Barnett, *Audit of War*, 304.
49. Morris, 'Freeing the Spirit of Enterprise', 32.
50. We can also observe this gendering of the profit motive in the ambiguities which today surround the term 'entrepreneur'. In its strict sense the word describes founder–owners. Yet, as P. S. Florence points out, over the course of this century the word has come to embrace those engaged in taking risks with other people's capital as well as those who bear that risk (*The Logic of British and American Industry: A Realistic Analysis of Economic Structure and Government* (London, 1972), 196, 337–46).
51. 'Strategies for Battle', *Management Today* (Nov. 1987), 5.

52. C. Huhne, 'The Public Issues that Lie behind the Private Deals, *Guardian*, 11 Jan. 1989, 15.
53. *Guardian, Financial Times*, 27, 30 Jan. 1987; *Guardian*, 16 Nov. 1990. At the annual meeting a shareholder declared Sir Ralph to be 'England's second greatest man this century—after Winston Churchill', adding that his sexual activities were 'his own business, and if I was up to his standard I would do exactly the same' (*Financial Times*, 30 Jan. 1987). As the *Guardian* observed, the mythologizing of Sir Ralph's virility must be seen in the context of 'Mrs Thatcher's elevation of the entrepreneur to social hero' (*Guardian*, 30 Jan. 1987).
54. *Financial Times*, 20 Jan. 1987.
55. R. Cowe, *Guardian*, 17 Mar. 1989, 19.
56. For a commentary on this tradition, see Coleman, 'Gentlemen and Players'.
57. For a more detailed explanation of the 'Cook's tour', see Ch. 4, sect. iii.
58. Contemporary evidence of this is provided in the report of the Acton Society Trust, *Management Succession: The Recruitment, Selection, Training and Promotion of Managers* (London, 1956), 5–19.
59. Turner, *Business in Britain*, 301.
60. C. Cockburn, *Machinery of Dominance: Women, Men, and Technical Know-how* (London, 1985), 193–6.
61. See M. Dalton, *Men Who Manage: Fusions of Feeling and Theory in Administration* (New York, 1959); C. W. Mills, *White Collar: The American Middle Class* (New York, 1951); C. Sofer, *Men in Mid-Career: A Study of British Managers and Technical Specialists* (Cambridge, 1970); Whyte, *The Organization Man*.
62. W. H. Whyte, 'The Wives of Management', *Fortune* (Oct. and Nov. 1951), quoted in J. M. Pahl and R. E. Pahl, *Managers and their Wives: A Study of Career and Family Relationships in the Middle Class* (London, 1971), 181.
63. H. Bradley, *Men's Work, Women's Work: A Sociological History of the Sexual Division of Labour in Employment* (Oxford, 1989), 13, table 1.1a, taken from *Labour Force Survey* (1985).
64. Ibid. 13.
65. N. Nicholson and M. West, *Managerial Job Change: Men and Women in Transition* (Cambridge, 1988), 185; M. J. Davidson and C. L. Cooper, 'Women Managers: Their Problems and what can be Done to Help them', in C. L. Cooper and M. J. Davidson (eds.), *Women in Management: Career Development for Managerial Success* (London, 1984), 32.
66. V. Beechey, 'Women and Employment in Contemporary Britain', in V. Beechey and E. Whitelegg (eds.), *Women in Britain Today* (Milton Keynes, 1986), 87, table 5, taken from *EOC Eighth Annual Report, 1983*, 80, fig. 3.4; Davidson and Cooper, *Women in Management*, 32; M. J. Davidson and C. L. Cooper, *Shattering the Glass Ceiling: The Woman Manager* (London, 1992), 11.
67. Nicholson and West, *Managerial Job Change*, 192.
68. See ibid. 190. Confirming this pattern, the Hansard Society found that, of 43 women executive directors on subsidiary boards, 19 occupied posts in finance or related functions, while 13 were in operations or general management (*Women at the Top*, App. 3, 100).

69. A recent survey of the CBI top 100 companies found that 6.7% of senior managers were women (*Women at the Top*, App. 2, 96).
70. Nicholson and West, *Managerial Job Change*, 205.
71. For a comprehensive survey of this literature, see Bradley, *Men's Work, Women's Work*, ch. 1.
72. R. Crompton and K. Sanderson, *Gendered Jobs and Social Change* (London, 1990), 45.
73. Ibid. 102, 114.
74. Ibid. 34.
75. J. Acker, 'Hierarchies, Jobs, Bodies: A Theory of Gendered Organizations', *Gender and Society*, 4/2 (June 1990), 149.
76. Pahl and Pahl, *Managers*, 126; their sample included 86 couples.
77. Most interviewees paid tribute to a wife's skills in these areas. Similarly, in his autobiography, Sir John Harvey-Jones—the ex-chairman of ICI and one of Britain's best-known organization men—praises his wife for her home-making abilities. He explains that 'from our earliest times together I had reaped the benefits of her tremendous talent for producing tasteful comfort out of very little' (*Getting it Together: Memoirs of a Troubleshooter* (London, 1991), 273).
78. Ibid. 356.
79. See S. Walby, *Patriarchy at Work: Patriarchal and Capitalist Relations in Employment* (Cambridge, 1986). Walby identifies two main strategies of patriarchy: the complete exclusion of women from paid employment, and their confinement to jobs which are graded lower than those of men (p. 244). As Crompton and Sanderson remark, it is important to recognize that exclusion may be systematic. However, the assumption that men as a category oppress women robs us of potential for change (*Gendered Jobs*, 17).
80. D. L. Collinson, D. Knights, and M. Collinson, *Managing to Discriminate* (London, 1990), 86.
81. Hunt, *Psychoanalysis of Fieldwork*, 25–6.
82. K. Figlio, 'Oral History and the Unconscious', *History Workshop*, 26 (Autumn 1988), 122. Joyce McDougall, *Theatres of the Mind*, provides particularly fascinating examples of how transference and countertransference operate in psychoanalysis. See also Hunt, *Psychoanalysis of Fieldwork*, ch. 4. 'Transference and Counter-Transference in Fieldwork'.
83. D. J. Levinson also points out that middle-aged men, particularly those forced into reassessing personal or career options, often dwell on memories of early career (*The Seasons of a Man's Life* (New York, 1978), 91).
84. This was certainly the case with the local Rotary Club, which invited me to one of its meetings as an act of international goodwill.
85. Media representations of Australia often feature images of youth and virility. These were particularly prevalent at the time of interviewing, because of the approaching bicentenary, the aggressive acquisitions of Australian entrepreneurs in Britain, and the release of the Crocodile Dundee films. Media like this portrayed the Australian man as particularly rugged and independent, his success in business reflecting a gauche disregard for gentlemanly traditions, supposedly born of egalitarian bush traditions. Whether capitalist or bushman, like the nation itself he was essentially youthful. These images worked their

way into my interviews, interviewees sometimes quoting Australian slang like 'G'day', or joking about the macho types featured in beer advertisements or Crocodile Dundee.
86. Figlio, 'Oral History and the Unconscious', 123–4.
87. This exchange of flattery and assistance is described in R. M. Kanter, *Men and Women of the Corporation* (New York, 1977), 181; Sofer, *Men in Mid-Career*, 19. In his discussion of protégés, C. W. Mills quotes Balzac, who wrote that 'it was his duty to flatter and advise, to give advice in the guise of flattery, and flattery in the form of advice' (*White Collar*, 96).

2

The Eclipse of Family Capitalism

....

> The change-over from a family firm to a managerial corporation is a recurring drama of our time.[1]
>
> Anthony Sampson, 1965

The generation of managers in this study began their careers just as the slow decline of family capitalism in Britain began to accelerate. During the post-war years industrial capital became more concentrated, as smaller, often owner-managed firms merged or were taken over, to become publicly owned enterprises run by salaried managers. While the 100 largest companies in 1970 accounted for 45 per cent of manufacturing output, in 1948, just twenty years earlier, they had accounted for 21 per cent of output.[2] A succession of merger waves beginning in the 1920s meant that, by the end of the 1960s, the ownership of capital had become well and truly separated from managerial control. Where managers had once funded their businesses largely with personal or family capital, by 1969 the chairmen of the top 100 British firms owned a mere 2 per cent of equity in the firms they managed.[3] Career managers had succeeded entrepreneurs and inheritors.

In *The Rise of Professional Society*, the historian Harold Perkin describes this transformation in terms of two ideal types. The inter-war years in particular witnessed a 'battle of ideologies' between the entrepreneurial ideal and the emerging professional ideal. In the nineteenth century the ideal citizen had been 'the self-made man, the entrepreneur who had made his way to success and fortune by his own unaided efforts'.[4] During the twentieth century, however, the

47

managerial style characteristic of family capitalism—passionate belief in the free market and a 'dynastic desire' to hand the business on to heirs—gradually waned. In the professional ideal which replaced it, the motor of economic growth was the professional man's desire for 'further expansion of managerial power' rather than competition or the wish to secure financial independence for successors.[5] Managerial authority was increasingly based on educational qualifications, as succession by inheritance gave way to selection by merit. The career manager's tools of management control were rationalization and scientific management rather than paternalism. Perkin's analysis helps us to understand the industrial milieu in which organization men spent their careers. In common with other business historians, he points out that the rise of professional management was a long-drawn-out process in Britain.[6] The first wave of industrial concentration occurred in the 1920s. Yet many of the management practices associated with family capitalism persisted through the post-war period, alongside new service industries like management consultancy and education. Perkin neatly sums up the 1960s with the comment that 'Britain's industrial managers . . . had undergone a revolution, but a reluctant one'.[7]

This chapter explores the legacy of family capitalism in post-war Britain, and the rise of professional management as it influenced organization men. Just as the economy was betwixt and between two epochs in mid-century, so, too, were the post-war generation of industrial managers. Their educational backgrounds reflect the split between academic and vocational qualifications which economic historians have identified as typical of pre-corporate capitalism in Britain.[8] The typical social background of senior managers in this period—middle class and public-school educated—also indicates that, despite the march of professional management, the market for managerial skill was far from meritocratic.[9] When we turn to the accounts of organization men themselves, we see not only overlaps between family and corporate capitalism, but contradictions between them. On the one hand, organization men represented the nascent generation of professional managers. They helped implement what Robert Locke calls 'the new paradigm' of management science: organizational innovations such as the multi-divisional structure, or the new management tools of operations research, work study, performance appraisal, and sophisticated finance systems.[10] On the other hand, they upheld many of the traditions of family capitalism, particularly its twin cult of the benevolent 'gentleman amateur' and the technically trained 'practical man'.[11] Like gentlemen amateurs, they honoured their company's history and its founders, but, like practical men, they took delight in technical achievement. Organization men were thus the *vanguard* of what Perkin correctly calls a 'reluctant revolution', as Britain underwent its transition to a professional society. Yet Perkin sheds little light on why the career managers of the post-war generation should have clung so tenaciously to the culture of family capitalism, particularly since it sometimes actually disadvantaged them in career terms. Below I explore Perkin's two ideal types—the rugged individualist and the professional man— as gender images. The problem with most accounts of professionalization is that they describe a change in the kinds of masculine images that operate in business, but without ever making gender the analytical focus. As a result, they simply mimic the self-ascriptions of the men they study.[12] The images of 'gentleman amateur', 'practical man', or 'professional man' are more than class images.[13] They are representations of authority based on certain normative assumptions about what it means to be a 'man'. Viewed from a gender perspective, the triumph of professional society over the horizontal solidarities of class becomes a rather complicated process.[14] For a generation inducted to management through military service and practical experience in the firm, the prospect of becoming a desk-bound professional held little appeal. The post-war generation valued its knowledge of products and company routines more than its formal qualifications. It shunned the professional ideal in favour of a work identity which combined the rough masculinity of the 'player' with the gentleman inheritor's loyalty to the enterprise. Looked at from a gender perspective, it is the continuities rather than the breaks between family and corporate capitalism that are most notable.

i. Historical Time: The Rise of the Corporate Economy

Whereas in the United States the 'managerial revolution' occurred quickly and dramatically at the turn of the century, this was not the case in Britain.[15] Family capitalism endured well into the twentieth century, its contribution to productive output being overtaken by public firms only in the early 1960s. This shift wrought a transformation in business structures and practices. As Leslie Hannah concludes, 'in the 1960s and 1970s the managerial enterprise began to replace the personal and entrepreneurial enterprise as rapidly as it had done fifty years earlier in the United States'.[16]

One way of measuring the consolidation of the corporate economy is by analysis of merger activity.[17] There were two significant periods of merger activity in Britain. The first was the 1920s, which saw the formation of at least two industrial giants.[18] Whilst Hannah claims that the merger wave of the 1960s was no more significant than that of the 1920s in terms of accelerating concentration, nevertheless it marked a departure from the relative quietude of the immediate post-war years. In the fifteen years after 1948, 25 per cent of firms listed on the stock exchange were acquired by other firms, whereas 38 per cent were taken over in just ten years between 1957 and 1967.[19] The 1961 bid by ICI for Courtaulds, while ultimately unsuccessful, brought the second merger wave to public attention. As a result, Courtaulds itself embarked on an unprecedentedly aggressive campaign of acquisition, buying up smaller, often family-managed firms.[20] Encouraged in the later 1960s by the Labour government and its Industrial Re-organization Corporation, there were also a number of mergers between large firms. Among them was Weinstock's take-over of AEI (1967) and English Electric (1968) to form the conglomerate of GEC; the creation of British Leyland from Leyland Motor Corporation and British Motor Holdings, and the creation of the computer company ICL.[21] By the mid-1970s Britain had firmly entered the era of the large bureaucracy. Its largest 100 firms then held 91 per cent of the total share in capital assets, a rise of more than 30 per cent over the figure just eighteen years earlier.[22] Its manufacturing sector was among the most concentrated in the world.[23]

While not all mergers involved the demise of family firms, the overall trend towards concentration inevitably diluted family control. Where over half of Britain's ninety-two largest firms were still controlled by one family in 1950, that figure had fallen to 30 per cent by 1970.[24] At the same time, the transition to a managerial economy was a far from uniform process. A majority shareholding still remained with the founding family in some of the largest firms in the post-war period, particularly in the retail sector. Manufacturing enterprises such as the glass manufacturer Pilkington also continued with a majority shareholding in the family.[25] Even where families no longer held the balance of financial control, their members might nevertheless continue to dominate the board. This was true, for example, of the electronics firm Plessey and the sugar refiner Tate and Lyle in the

1960s. A 'hidden' influence over management styles might thus continue to be exerted in public companies, since family members often retained a significant financial and managerial interest.[26] Contemporary public debates about business reflected this, with frequent discussion about how family traditions could be maintained in publicly owned firms.[27]

More significant than the presence of individual inheritors was the endurance of family forms of organization long after mergers or public flotation. Up to the middle 1950s the holding company structure was still the norm. Subsidiaries remained 'virtually autonomous', with the holding company controlling investment but little else.[28] Merged family companies often preferred to maintain their separate dynasties under the umbrella of loose federations like this. As one interviewee explained of his employer who merged with another family business in 1966, 'It was just a sort of nominal merger of the two. Financial merger at the top of the boards, the equity and that kind of thing were merged. But the operations were not at all.' Until well into the 1960s even diversified companies often retained the kind of loose-knit structure characteristic of family enterprises.[29]

In Britain the 'managerial revolution' was spread over a comparatively long period, from the First World War on. What particularly distinguished the years after 1945 from earlier periods, however, was the concerted drive towards professionalization. This was reflected in the restructuring of bureaucratic hierarchies, further specialization of management functions, and the growth of management education. While management practices continued to exhibit characteristics of the entrepreneurial past, the institutions of the corporate economy began to flourish. In the largest British firms, departmental or holding company structures were often dropped during the 1960s in favour of a multi-divisional structure, a crude indicator for business historians of successful transition from family to corporate organization.[30] Only eight of the top 100 British companies were organized along divisional lines in 1950, but nearly three-quarters had adopted this structure by 1970.[31] In a multi-divisional firm the head office concentrates on strategy and co-ordination, leaving the more product-directed work to divisions.[32] The move to divisional structures has tended to coincide with a greater emphasis upon profit and financial criteria within middle management, as divisions attempt to make 'what can be sold at a profit' rather than selling what is made.[33] In Britain it has also been accompanied by the expansion of

3 'The British father of professional management'
Lyndall Urwick, the 'evangelist' who introduced F. W. Taylor's principles of scientific
management to Britain. Urwick founded the consultancy firm of Urwick and Orr in 1934. He
was instrumental in the establishment of business education after the war in Britain, and
became vice-chairman of the British Institute of Management on its foundation in 1947.

Lydall Urwick, cover illustration from *The Manager*, Jan. 1957 'in-house' functions like personnel, marketing, and strategic planning,[34] and of specialized supplier services such as management consultancy, 'head-hunting', advertising, and accountancy.[35]

The emergence of management as a profession was also clearly signalled by the founding of new regulatory and educational institutions. In 1947 the British Institute of Management (BIM) was formed. Soon afterwards it began sponsoring publication of the weekly business journal, the *Manager* (subsequently *Management Today*), and a Diploma of Management Studies for middle managers at Henley Staff College, which had opened in 1945.[36] Management education mushroomed in the years following the establishment of the BIM. In 1961 there were 200 students attending post-graduate management courses in British universities.[37] The 1963 Robbins and Franks reports proposed two schools—one in London and one in Manchester.[38] By 1969 no less than thirty-seven business schools and university management departments, five independent colleges, forty-five polytechnics, and 150 technical colleges were offering management courses.[39] Postgraduate business programmes were being attended by 2,300 students, while a further 125,000 managers were enrolled in 'post-experience' courses.[40] At London Business School, the two-year Master of Business Administration included courses in organizational behaviour, finance and accounting, economic analysis, and business policy.[41] The new generation qualified for management on the basis of their expertise in general management rather than by virtue of technical or firm-specific knowledge. As R. Whitley, A. Thomas, and J. Marceau comment, formal qualifications gave these MBAs 'legitimate authority over the technical specialists'. It equipped them for management in multi-divisional firms, with their profit centres and more complex head office functions.[42] It was not until the 1980s that MBAs really began to make their presence felt at senior levels in manufacturing industries. For most of the period covered by this study, the partial emergence of Perkin's professional society showed itself in the kinds of educational qualifications possessed by its managers. Around half the managers in Britain's largest 100 companies in the late 1960s were university trained, typically in science or arts rather than management.[43] As Robert Locke argues, in contrast to the situation in the United States, it remained common for British managers to enter the profession on the basis of generalist qualifications.[44]

Class distinctions also cut across the emerging professional ideal.

Senior management in the post-war period was staffed largely by men with middle-class family backgrounds. In a study carried out in the late 1960s, Michael Young and Peter Willmott found that 83 per cent of managing directors had fathers who were also in professional or managerial jobs.[45] A similar class bias emerges when we look at educational qualifications. R. V. Clements concluded in his 1956 study of Midlands manufacturing firms that around half the managers born in the inter-war years—the generation of organization men—had been educated at a public school.[46] Little had changed twenty years later. John Fidler found in the late 1970s that over half Britain's 'top businessmen' had attended a public school.[47] In comparison to sectors such as the civil service, management in the manufacturing sector was relatively open to men of working-class origin. A third of managers in Clements's survey had a working-class background and had been promoted from the shop-floor.[48] But within management itself there were pronounced vertical cleavages according to class and educational background. Mainly engineers, the 'self-starters' were concentrated in junior and middle management, works-related posts.[49]

In terms of provision for industrial education, the post-war picture was of a corporate economy still operating to some extent within the dual tradition of 'gentlemen and players'. Different class traditions attached to pure and applied education.[50] According to Locke, who perhaps overstates his case, potentially relevant management subjects such as economics remained rather abstract in content, while economics graduates showed a preference for non-business careers in the city, civil service, or universities.[51] Scientific training, while firmly based in the universities, was internally differentiated. The superior status of pure science created a problem for industry, since the best graduates tended to opt for university research.[52] This split between pure and applied knowledge was sometimes replicated within the institutions of management. ICI's research establishment, Winnington Hall, has often been singled out as an example of this, because of the upper-class and gentlemanly aura which it cultivated.[53] Other firms placed less emphasis on creating a managerial aristocracy for their science graduates. Furthermore, such traditions were partially undermined by the 'insatiable' demand for industrial scientists in the post-war years, scientists of working- and lower-middle-class backgrounds being attracted by the pay and promotion prospects.[54]

If post-war science sometimes continued to be biased towards 'pure' research, the reverse was true of engineering. As late as the 1960s it remained a firmly apprenticeship-based, practical kind of training. The provincial universities were the first to offer graduate engineering degrees, but enrolments lagged for most of the twentieth century. In 1950 90 per cent of mechanical engineers were not university educated.[55] Engineering training was closely identified with nineteenth-century British entrepreneurship. Joseph Locke, James Nasmyth, and Joseph Whitworth were all celebrated for inventions conceived on the shop-floor. The apprenticeship system replicated this heroism of practical knowledge, as formal education took place at night school with the major emphasis on workshop experience.[56] The class-specific character of engineering education sometimes engendered a kind of reverse snobbery which manifested itself in an unwillingness among engineering fraternities to admit the utility of academic education.[57] In post-war firms the legacy of this culture was still apparent. Engineering industries demonstrated continued reluctance to recruit graduates; Tube Industries took on only a dozen graduates in 1959, while Plessey took on five in 1960.[58] At the British Motor Corporation there was a preference for managers who had served apprenticeships.[59] Production functions often remained separate from sales or marketing. Exaggerating perhaps, Graham Turner claims that the product development in engineering firms was more often inspired by technical challenge than market needs. Certainly the seller's markets of the post-war period produced no pressure to divert efforts from 'that technical excellence which had always been an important part of the British engineering tradition'.[60]

The picture surrounding post-war British industry in every sphere then—from the structure of firms, through the education infrastructure, to the social backgrounds of managers—is of transition between eras. While the paraphernalia of a managerial economy was being set in place, the structure and practices of many public firms shared much with the family enterprises from which they had evolved. There was a slight opening of management to men of working- and lower-middle-class backgrounds, accompanied by sustained attempts to introduce more relevant management training by narrowing the gap between pure and applied education. But, while the emerging professional ethic seemed to hold promise of a more egalitarian future for men, the educational system and class origins of the incumbent managers reflected a continuing middle-class hegemony.

The post-war generation of managers enacted many of the contradictions which were apparent in the movement towards professionalization. In a visit to a Midlands automotive firm I listened to ex-engineer managers criticizing the superior social status of City financiers while we luxuriated in the gentlemanly atmosphere of the directors' dining-room.[61] Conversely, middle-class, university-educated arts graduates occasionally showed off their technical knowledge to me, as if they were 'practical men' who had worked their way up from the shop-floor. In the accounts of historians like Perkin, Wiener, and Locke, the persistence of gentlemanly traditions in management is seen to constitute the main brake on professionalization. Yet the class and masculine hierarchies operated in different ways. The 'hard' masculinity associated with a working-class background and an apprenticeship was particularly admired by the men I interviewed. Middle-class managers more often imitated their inferiors in class terms than the reverse, emphasizing their practical experience as a way of shaking off the effete image of the pen-pushing professional. In the masculine hierarchy, players dominated bureaucrats and gentlemen. However, if class and gender images cut across each other, both were equally shaped by the traditions of family capitalism.

ii. Generational Time: Organization Men and the Legacy of Family Capitalism

The managers I interviewed were witnesses of and active participants in the momentous changes in industrial organization which took place during the post-war period. Of the twenty-eight who began their managerial careers in Britain in the 1950s, half did so in firms where the family retained a majority shareholding. Yet, at the time of interviewing in 1987–8, only two still worked for a firm in which either financial or managerial control still resided primarily with the founding family. Their careers must be seen in the context of this shift. For the most part, the managers in this study were bureaucrats who began their careers on the basis of technical or academic skills rather than nepotism.[62] Only three were actually inheritors, but even those managers who had spent their whole careers in publicly owned firms upheld a management ethos characteristic of family firms. Family capitalism exerted its influence on career managers and inheritors alike.

Business historians frequently neglect the lived experience of economic change. Thus, while they have depicted the rise of the corporate economy in terms of changes in educational provision or in the qualifications held by managers, their primary interest lies in how performance was affected. When the generational dimension of such change is considered, it is in simplistic terms; young against old, merit against privilege, efficiency against liability. The post-war cohort of managers helped bring about the professionalization of management in the 1960s but also represents its confusions. In their accounts, tensions between paternalism and managerialism, between loyalty to the firm and loyalty to the profession of management, are everywhere evident. Below I portray some of the features common to management in family firms, for this helps us to understand the contradictory pull which the post-war generation experienced between two historical eras. Why were they such 'reluctant' agents of professionalization? How do we explain the persistence of a seemingly outmoded cult of amateurism? What kinds of gender images were summoned by the ideal types of gentleman manager, practical man, or rational bureaucrat?

The work of sociologists in the 1950s indicates the strong nexus between inheritor–managers, the public school, and the Establishment universities such as Oxford and Cambridge. Clements found in his 1958 study that no less than 89 per cent of inheritors had a public-school education.[63] They looked to their schooling as the primary source of management training, emphasizing its role in cultivating 'habits of responsibility, the exercise of initiative, the appreciation of teamwork and the power of leadership'. While a slightly higher proportion of inheritors than of managers overall attended a university, Clements found that they did not regard further education as a necessary preparation for business.[64] Inheritors emphasized the experience which they had acquired on the job, perhaps through a management trainee scheme in the family firm.[65] Inheritors sometimes began their careers in a company outpost or another firm.[66] There they would be taken under the wing of a father's friend, relative, or trusted junior manager, whose responsibility it was to oversee their progress. Mr Briar worked with his uncle at the Briar and Peacock refinery, whilst at Fisher Electronics Mr Van Hoffen's father delegated a career manager to supervise him. Replicating the public-school passage from fag to senior, early career in the family firm involved fostering independence through rapid promotion from

4 'The inheritor'

Here the Midland Bank trades on Britain's heritage of family capitalism. William Stuart of Stuart Crystal proudly presents his company's glassware to the viewer. The product combines beauty, quality and a grand family lineage.   *Management Today,* Aug. 1971 manual work on the shop-floor to manager. Inheritors would typically do the rounds of the whole firm, learning about the various products, production processes, and making their presence visible to employees.[67] What they lacked by way of formal knowledge in the management disciplines of production, personnel, or finance, inheritors compensated for by their detailed knowledge of the firm. Past traditions and future directions seemed indistinguishable. At the London School of Economics seminar series on 'Problems in Industrial Administration' which ran during the 1950s and 1960s, inheritors frequently presented elaborate company histories.[68] Rather than addressing contemporary problems, they stressed their role in perpetuating the founder's original strategies.[69] A special relationship to the objects being manufactured was also important. Like the company history itself, their goods reflected a grand family lineage. Inheritors would speak about products as material embodiments of family traditions. Here is Mr Briar describing quality control at Briar and Peacock, for example:

> I tasted the golden syrup every day like my uncle before me. And if the flavour was off, 'Why?' During the war we had to change the process because of a shortage of something or other. And my cousin came back from the war and said, 'The flavour has altered. You've altered it!' And we said, 'Yes.' and he said, 'Don't f—— about! Bloody well go back to the original process.' 'It'll cost more.' 'It doesn't matter. Go back to the original recipe.' And he was right. Only way to maintain the standard.

'Hands-on', proud amateurism characterized management not just in family firms but in the British economy as a whole. Abstract knowledge was distrusted, and faith was placed instead in what one manager, speaking in 1959, referred to as 'intuition or good judgement . . . factors which cannot be taught'.[70] Thirty years later traces of this emphasis on innate practical ability still remain. An ex-career manager who subsequently started his own electronic components firm explained that he rarely visited the plant in Wales, but spent most of his time tinkering with new designs in the attic of his London home. Unhindered by the stresses of day-to-day management, which he left to his partner, he was free to indulge in 'hands-on' invention. Among career managers this family ethos manifested itself in a strong emphasis on firm-specific knowledge. Like their employers, they strongly identified with the family and its products. Indeed, as

59

Chapter 5 explains, the satisfactions afforded by pride in the product to some extent compensated career managers for the fact that they lacked a financial share in the business.

Like inheritors, career managers in family firms also celebrated family traditions. Liberal policies on labour relations or employment benefits might be mentioned as evidence of the employers' generous spirit. At Hill Components, the chairman continually emphasized the beneficence of the founding families. They had established extensive training schemes in the inter-war years for engineers, managers, and clerical staff. Profit-sharing schemes were implemented, along with advanced medical facilities, and machinery for negotiating with trade unions. They had a 'social conscience', he concluded. Career managers at Jennings Windows made similar claims about the founding families' good record in employee welfare. They had set up medical and dental services, and in the 1930s had established a village to house workers from the north. The Jennings managers had mixed feelings about the impact of public ownership. On the one hand, they sometimes resented the fact that their perks had not been competitive with colleagues in publicly owned firms. On the other hand, they valued the job security. In the face of yet another take-over, they remembered with great pleasure the feeling that 'the governor's going to look after you and you're alright'.[71] They longed for a return of the 'two-way loyalties' which had existed between owners and career managers.

Domination of the board by family members of course ultimately constrained the mobility of career managers. As Baker, the contracts director of Jennings Windows, put it, 'You get a realization at a certain point in the company that the management stops at middle management.'[72] So, on the one hand, paternalism implied informal management, an 'organic' structure, symbolized in the tradition of knowing all the staff by their first name. On the other hand, it implied perpetual dependence of all on the owner/parents. That reinforced the social distinctions between family and career managers. Sitting in his office in the directors' suite, Baker recalled that, when he was a lad, 'I never came down this corridor. . . . It was the Holy Land, the Mecca.' Public ownership had made this Holy Land accessible to him, yet Baker lamented the end of family control.

For inheritors, the demise of family firms could be extremely fraught. They sometimes continued on as executive directors, hoping to preserve the family history and welfare of employees.[73] All three inheritors in this sample stayed on, but two were eventually retrenched by new owners. It was not only the founding families whose position was threatened by these 'palace revolutions', but also the career managers who served under them.[74] For the most part, the post-war entrants did not possess the formal skills in finance or human resources needed to manage the restructuring after takeovers. Only 13 per cent of my sample possessed formal qualifications in finance, a proportion which is broadly in agreement with previous studies of this cohort.[75] Nevertheless, some did take advantage of the growing market for management services during the 1960s. They entered fields like personnel or consultancy on the basis of their 'hands-on' experience in managing industrial disputes or implementing work-study projects. As we shall see, this kind of switch could enhance immediate career mobility, but eventually placed them at a disadvantage against younger, better-trained entrants.

The shift towards cost efficiency as an overarching measure of corporate success has been particularly difficult for this generation to swallow. It undermined the importance which engineers and scientists alike placed on development of new products. The transition from product to profit was experienced as a battle between generations. As Mr Dolan explained of the reorganization which followed the take-over of Jennings Windows: 'The new men were dreadful; wet behind the ears, very unpleasant . . .'

Reorganization in the electronics and motor vehicle industries in the 1960s—two of the industries studied here—involved particularly dramatic swings from engineering and production to financial control. This was most detrimental to engineer managers. Their original skills had sometimes become outdated because of technical change, while their subsequent management experience often did not extend beyond the one firm. Not surprisingly, three of the four managers in this sample who were made redundant in the early 1980s were ex-engineers. Science and arts graduates were more secure, but still faced pressure in an environment where profitability was increasingly important. After all, the Jennings manager quoted above was a Cambridge arts graduate, not an engineer. The cult of the practical man also influenced graduates, who, in engineering firms in particular, recalled feeling embarrassed about their academic qualifications, and being taunted about their lack of 'dirty-hands' experience. In such firms, the Cook's tour ensured that graduates became competent with the machinery of production and could hold their own on the shop-floor. As one of the senior executives of Vickers is reported to have said of graduates, 'My attitude was "let the buggers learn the hard way."'[76] Like their engineer brothers, graduates of this generation often came to celebrate a version of masculinity which revolved around mechanical aptitude, intimate knowledge of products, and experience working with men on the shop-floor. By late career they too could assert that their knowledge had been gained from years of work in the industry, man and boy. The commonly perceived threat from younger, formally trained managers tended to unite managers of diverse social backgrounds. It encouraged emphasis on their superior practical knowledge and intensified their allegiance to products—precisely the traits which have traditionally been ascribed to family capitalism.[77]

Industrial concentration undoubtedly helped shift the basis of managerial skill from amateur knowledge to formal expertise. This has been perceived as part of a growing meritocracy in management.[78] It is arguable whether the post-war consolidation of the corporate economy challenged the domination of management by middle-class men. Moreover, the ethos of professional management was not whole-heartedly welcomed, either by middle-class managers or by true meritocrats. Organization men were the messengers of a new managerial order, but often aligned themselves with the gentlemen and players, fighting shy of the professional image.

iii. Individual Time: Masculinity and the Professional Ideal

It is often argued that the rise of professional society during the twentieth century has involved the gradual casting aside of the entrepreneurial ideal under pressure of industrial concentration, and its replacement by the ideal of management as a formally acquired skill. Yet, when we look at the life stories of the post-war generation, business history no longer appears in terms of a long march towards the rationally structured bureaucracy. Organization men switch backwards and forwards between the two ideals, between a conviction that, as one man put it, 'a manager is a natural', to a present context in which formal management training is the key to promotion.

We might understand this fondness for the entrepreneurial ideal in functional terms as the defensive response of a generation which lacked professional training. However, this does not explain the fervent desire to give up the life of an organization man, and return to the state of an independent, self-willed man. Almost a quarter of the men in my sample had chosen to leave a bureaucracy for self-employment, literally making the transition back from organization man to entrepreneur. The remainder—perhaps thinking ahead to retirement—often expressed feelings of anonymity or regret at having served without leaving their mark. This was particularly apparent with men who had spent their careers in large multi-divisional companies, the kind noted by historians as furthest down the evolutionary path from family or entrepreneurial enterprises. Organization men strove particularly hard to demonstrate that they had not been smothered by the bureaucracy. Promotions from divisional level to headquarters, a sign of having finally opened a path to senior management, were experienced in an ambivalent way. Control over products and men in the operating divisions had provided great personal satisfaction. However, organization men often recalled a sense of unease about their work at company headquarters. Inside head office they felt a certain insecurity about themselves as men, which threatened to outweigh the pleasure at promotion. Below I want to explore this unease further through the life stories of three organization men in British multinational firms. Their comments illustrate the complexities between a movement in historical time from entrepreneurial to professional capitalism, and individual men's fantasies about breaking the professional mould and proving themselves by becoming entrepreneurs.

In the Introduction I explored the life story of Sir Peter Aldridge, to show how, despite the authoritative, rational image which he projected, he felt a persistent sense of inadequacy as a man. His career narrative, highlighting the hardships he had endured as a child and in early career, was in part a defence against this self-perception. Aldridge's desire to fashion an image of himself as a practical, resilient man is significant, given the slightly dismissive descriptions which his juniors gave of him. To them he had appeared a little bumbling. He was an academic type: 'Peter, he was not a man of action really. Not a practical man. He would go away for weeks and lock his door, and then write something which was pretty thoroughly researched and compelling reading, but Meadows [then chairman] would read it and say, "It's of no practical use."' A gentle put-down was intended, one which hinged on the contrast between Aldridge's solitary mental endeavours and the acquisitive, combative spirit of his predecessor.

Aldridge sought to slough off a studious, over-rational self-image in our interview. It ended with him in a more vivacious mood than I had observed hitherto, as he told me about one occasion when he had felt able to escape the bureaucratic fetters:

> We'd put a million pounds of our pension-fund money into one of these secondary banks. It went bust in the end, but by that time we'd made a few million pounds. And this bloke—because I'd made it my business to know this bloke, because I realised my reputation was at stake . . . So this man Grey, he said to me one day, 'We talk about you. We just wonder why you, and Chemtex, should have taken the risk of backing us. We've decided that at heart, you're an entrepreneur, and you wanted to prove it to yourself before it's too late.' And then he went on to say, 'Of course, you'll be chairman, you know.' I said, 'What, me?' He said, 'Just look at the competition!' [laughs]. That was about 1966-ish, first time I realized that I might be in the running for the chair.

There are two separate events prompting Aldridge's memory at this point. One concerns his appointment to the board in the mid-1970s, while the other concerns his successful investment some ten years earlier. While in terms of his formal career history the earlier event is only a 'side issue really', in Aldridge's mind it is the more important moment. It was then that he earned the right to the chairmanship. Aldridge presents the investment as a rash act, somewhat out of character with his usual prudent image. The financial gains it yielded are less important to Aldridge than deliberately having placed 'my reputation . . . at stake'. By extreme risk-taking with his career, Aldridge justifies his accession to the chairmanship. Independent action, breaking the bureaucratic mould, is the hallmark of a man, whether salaried or self-employed. A further important twist to this tale was the fact that it was Aldridge himself who had caused the secondary bank to 'go bust'. He had withdrawn all the pension funds at once, making a further profit of three to four million pounds. So, not only does Aldridge renounce his reputation as a safe investor; he causes the downfall of the very men who had complimented him on his financial acumen. The story proves Aldridge's ability to be totally ruthless.

The passage to senior management did not bring this kind of compensation for two men from Swan Oil. Ex-chemists, they had both been promoted from general-management posts in oil refineries to Swan's head office in late career. Mr Greenwood had enjoyed his time as a refinery manager in Malaysia, first 'getting the damn thing off the ground properly . . . the whole distribution thing going, the markets sorted out, the training . . .'. During his time at head office in industrial relations he missed this sense of action. Life there seemed too passive. He was in danger of no longer being his own master:

> GREENWOOD. At times you wonder whether you shouldn't have stayed on in the general management stream totally . . . Because, towards the end, I was tending to become the influencer rather the the up-front man.
> MSR. What was good about being the up-front man?
> GREENWOOD. Because you're up front. The buck stops here. It's great in the decision-making mode, because you think it through and then you decide what you're going to do, and then you start doing it. Whereas when you're the influencer, you've got to come at it a different way . . . you've got to convince and persuade to get results. I'm not so sure that isn't true in the world generally today. I think maybe those days, the pioneer-type days that I'm talking about, are over for ever.

In Mr Duncan's story, this sense of power lost, of becoming the man behind the 'up-front man', takes a more explicit gender framework. Duncan had been very unhappy in his role as a personnel director at Swan head office. He continually emphasized the contrasts between this job and his previous post at one of Swan's British refineries:

> I had expressed interest in getting back to what I considered the front line . . . I had no patch, you see. Here I was, a person . . . I had a division with a number of graduates, etc., answering to me, but it was unlike refinery work, [or] at the research laboratory or anything like that. I couldn't kind of put my hands in my pockets, and kind of wander around and say, 'What are you doing today?', because I was now in another personnel manager's patch. Because each of the various divisions had their own personnel managers. I felt that you kind of got cut off.

For Duncan the promotion through the multi-divisional structure had involved a double kind of removal. As a personnel manager at the refinery, his job had been to resolve industrial disputes with the shop-floor workers, dealing out and 'being given a basin full'. The mixture of excitement and challenge he experienced is conveyed in the military metaphor of being in command at the 'front line'. At Swan Centre, he was not only removed from the point of production, but was managing mere graduates. Swan managers had enhanced their masculinity by pitting themselves against 'hard men' on the shop-floor. Removed from the daily task of proving their prowess as practical men, they felt drained of power as managers. In what he later described as the 'effete, artificial atmosphere' of Swan Head Office, Duncan's feelings of impotence took a bodily dimension. He was unable to relax, to put his hands in his pockets and claim the space of headquarters as his. He felt 'cut off' as a man and a manager.

Looked at from the perspective of historical time, the post-war period certainly did mark the triumph of professional society. Even at this level, however, overlaps between entrepreneurial, family, and corporate capitalism were apparent. Traces of the culture and business methods of pre-corporate capitalism remained, even within those firms at the forefront of professionalization. At the level of generational time, the historical themes are echoed. The post-war cohort of managers often began their careers in family firms, but most ended up as managers in publicly owned enterprises. Their views of management as an amateur pursuit, and of management skill as an innate quality honed down by practical experience, reflected the legacies of entrepreneurial and family capitalism. When we look at the patterns of individual time, focusing on how managers constructed their career narratives, the historical theme of progress towards the rational bureaucracy is reversed. We find career managers acting out fantasies about the entrepreneurial ideal type, seeking to demonstrate their aggressive, acquisitive instincts. This cannot be adequately understood as the detritus of the historical past, a work identity which is fast disappearing with the passage of modernity.

Rather, there are ongoing tensions between the private desires of organization men for truly independent action, and their location in bureaucracies. Even the most senior career managers are ultimately servants of their shareholders. As C. W. Mills explains in *White Collar*, 'he is always someone's man, the corporation's'.[79] Post-war innovations like the multi-divisional structure reinforced the organization man's feeling that he was not his own man. He preferred production to planning, but power in the bureaucracy lay increasingly with the strategy-makers in head office. Doing had become subordinated to thinking. The anxieties felt by organization men have been noted by various commentators.[80] In 1956, for example, the US business journalist William H. Whyte published *The Organization Man*. This exciting polemic was driven by a profound fear for the future of American capitalism. Where would the will to profit come from, now that the 'rough and tumble days of corporation growth are over'?[81] Society had been overtaken by yes-men, who clung to the creeds of 'belongingness', 'togetherness', and 'scientism'.[82] Future prosperity would depend on top executives who could still stand alone from the crowd:

Of all the organization men the true executive is the one who remains most suspicious of The Organization. If there is one thing that characterizes him, it is the fierce desire to control his own destiny and, deep down, he resents yielding that control to the Organization, no matter how velvety its grip. He does not want to be done right by; he wants to dominate, not be dominated.[83]

Whyte here rouses his business audience through a language of masculine conquest. His hero shrinks from the secure, almost homely atmosphere of corporate life. Sexual virility is the subtext, for 'fierce desire' is the engine of business. The potent organization man does not need to be mollycoddled, to 'be done right by'. He demands but he does not yield. In order to achieve mastery he must shun the tempting feminine 'velvety grip' of the organization.

The 1980s creed of the enterprise culture in Britain rested on a strikingly similar set of fantasies. Its advocates also levelled accusations at the organization man, accusing him of nestling too comfortably within the bureaucracy. As we have seen in this chapter, organization men themselves experienced similar tensions between their historical position as the harbingers of the corporate age, and their identities as men. They were ever anxious lest their role as servants of the corporation meant that they appeared 'effete'. In their fantasies they might play out the role of ruthless Victorian entrepreneur, or seek ritual confirmations of their masculinity through confrontations with practical men, perhaps by breaking strikes or demonstrating their proficiency in technical matters. The passage from the entrepreneurial ideal to the professional ideal was fraught with contradictions. At a psychic level, the passage may go the opposite way, so that the modern professional man seemingly idealizes a bygone era. These complexities are not appreciated in the 'modernist' interpretations which have dominated business history, such as Perkin's *The Rise of Professional Society* or Chandler's *The Visible Hand*. Such accounts erect cast-iron divisions between the public and private spheres, and concentrate only on the former. Among the post-war generation, the ideal types of the professional man or entrepreneur also conveyed certain gender images. Organization men did not easily integrate their masculine and professional identities. We cannot trace the rise of professional society simply by following the emergence of new management institutions, or changes in capital ownership, business structures, and educational provision. As the next chapter explains, the spirit of family capitalism did not disappear with the emergence of new 'scientific' management methods during the inter-war period, but simply became embedded within them.

NOTES

1. A. Sampson, *The Anatomy of Britain Today* (London, 1965), 532.
2. L. Hannah, *The Rise of the Corporate Economy*, 2nd edn. (London, 1983), 1; H. Perkin, *The Rise of Professional Society: England since 1880* (London, 1989), 292.
3. Ibid. 296.
4. Ibid., p. xiii.
5. Ibid. 297–9.
6. R. Locke, in a book published just after Perkin's *The Rise of Professional Society*, advances a very similar thesis. His view is that the 'new paradigm', the application of science to managerial problems, did not begin to influence British management until well after the Second World War (*Management and Higher Education since 1940: The Influence of America and Japan on West Germany, Great Britain and Japan* (Cambridge, 1989), 195).
7. Perkin, *Professional Society*, 301.
8. Locke, *Management and Higher Education*, 5.
9. A good survey of the social backgrounds of British company directors is J. Fidler, *The British Business Élite: Its Attitudes to Class, Status and Power* (London, 1981).
10. Locke, *Management and Higher Education*, esp. ch. 1.
11. D. C. Coleman, 'Gentlemen and Players', *Economic History Review*, 2nd ser., 36/1 (1973), 102–3.
12. A similar observation is made by A. Witz in her work on health-care professions (*Professions and Patriarchy* (London, 1992), 3).
13. I have concentrated my criticisms here on Perkin, but a host of business histories make use of the gendered distinction between gentlemen, players, and professional men. See the discussion above in Ch. 1, sect. i. Notable examples are M. J. Wiener, *English Culture and the Decline of the Industrial Spirit, 1850–1980* (Harmondsworth, 1985); R. Locke, *The End of the Practical Man: Entrepreneurship and Higher Education in Germany, France and Great Britain, 1880–1940* (London, 1984), and his *Management and Higher Education*; or the work of N. McKendrick, 'Gentlemen and Players Revisited: The Gentlemanly Ideal, the Business Ideal, and the Professional Ideal in English Literary Culture', in N. McKendrick and R. B. Outhwaite (eds.), *Business Life and Public Policy: Essays in Honour of D. C. Coleman* (Cambridge, 1986), 98–137. S. Lash and J. Urry, *The End of Organized Capitalism* (Cambridge, 1987), while it

breaks with the modernist leanings of most business history, still leaves the masculine character of the 'professional man' unexplored.

14. Perkin's argument is that, in contemporary society, professional allegiances— e.g., to free enterprise in the case of private sector managers, or to state expansion in the case of public sector professionals—cut across the horizontal ties of class (*Professional Society*, 1–3).

15. The classic account of this process in the United States is A. Chandler, *The Visible Hand: The Managerial Revolution in American Business* (Cambridge, Mass., 1977). Chandler argues that the rise of the modern business enterprise, specifically the multi-divisional structure, brought 'managerial capitalism' with it (pp. 1–14). The 'appurtenances of professionalism—societies, journals, university training and specialised consultants' thus followed in the wake of family capitalism (pp. 464–8).

16. L. Hannah, 'Business Development and Economic Structure in Britain since 1880', in L. Hannah (ed.), *Management Strategy and Business Development: An Historical and Comparative Study* (London, 1976), 46. S. Pollard concurs in this judgement; by 1970, he remarks, 'the large British firms allowed, if somewhat belatedly, the Chandler pattern of diversification, as they also advanced further along the road from family control to control by professional management' (*The Development of the British Economy, 1914–1980*, 3rd edn. (London, 1983), 302.

17. Hannah adopts this approach, discounting internal growth as a significant contributor to concentration (*Corporate Economy*, 166).

18. ICI was created in 1926 from three family enterprises, Nobel Industries, Brunner Mond, and British Dyestuffs, whilst Unilever was formed in 1929 through a merger of Lever with Unie (Hannah, 'Business Development', 45).

19. Hannah, *Corporate Economy*, 166.

20. D. C. Coleman, *Courtaulds: An Economic and Social History*, iii. *Crisis and Change* (Oxford, 1980), 241–323; Sampson, *Anatomy of Britain Today*, 536–7; G. Turner, *Business in Britain* (London, 1969), 399–416.

21. R. Jones and O. Marriott, *Anatomy of a Merger: A History of GEC, AEI and English Electric* (London, 1970), 11; Turner, *Business in Britain*, 82–5.

22. L. Hannah and J. Kay, *Concentration in British Industry* (London, 1967), 85, 96, quoted in Perkin, *Professional Society*, 293.

23. Small firms employed only 2% of the work-force in 1963, prompting Perkin to remark provocatively that 'concentration in private industry could hardly go any further without becoming outright monopoly' (*Professional Society*, 293).

24. Pollard, *British Economy*, 302.

25. Perkin, *Professional Society*, 296; Turner, *Business in Britain*, ch. 8, 'Families on the Mat'. Among the retailing firms were Sainsbury, House of Fraser, and Great Universal Stores.

26. Hannah, 'Business Development', 12. Economic historians are sometimes too keen to attribute the persistence of family modes of control to the continued influence of inheritors; see, e.g., B. Elbaum and W. Lazonick, 'An Institutional Perspective on British Decline', in B. Elbaum and W. Lazonick, *The Decline of the British Economy* (Oxford, 1986), 5. At Courtaulds an inheritor supported the recruitment of scientists and other meritocrats to the board, spearheading the drive for professionalization in the face of resistance by career managers (Coleman, *Courtaulds*, iii. 139).

69

27. A good example is the London School of Economics seminar series, Problems in Industrial Administration. The theme of how to balance family with outside control is discussed in *Development and Organisation of the Simon Engineering Group* (195; 20 Nov. 1956); *Development and Organisation of Rowntree and Co.* (203; 19 Feb. 1957); *Development and Organisation of Fisons Ltd.* (204; 26 Feb. 1957); *Development and Organisation of Booker Bros., McConnell and Co. Ltd.* (248; 24 Nov. 1959).

28. D. F. Channon, *The Strategy and Structure of British Enterprise* (London, 1973), 3. R. Scase and R. Goffee point out in *The Entrepreneurial Middle Class* (London, 1982) that a holding-company structure often provides a means of preserving the status quo in family firms while giving the appearance of democracy (p. 158).

29. Channon, *Strategy and Structure*, 75.

30. Channon claims that, of the top 100 companies in the 1960s, a third called in management consultants to revise the administrative structure (*Strategy and Structure*, 239).

31. Channon, *Strategy and Structure*, 67, table 3–2.

32. R. Whitley, A. Thomas, and J. Marceau, *Masters of Business: The Making of a new Élite?* (London, 1984), 18.

33. Ibid. 25.

34. Pollard observes that the 1960s in particular were notable for development of in-house management functions (*British Economy*, 302).

35. Little work has been done on the rise of management consultancy in Britain. Its notable characteristic was the American influence. McKinsey engineered the reorganization of Shell, Dunlop, Courtaulds, and ICI during the late 1950s and 1960s (Sampson, *Anatomy of Britain Today*, 509–10). Other management services such as head-hunting continue to reflect a strong North Atlantic presence.

36. Locke, *Management and Higher Education*, 156.

37. Turner, *Business in Britain*, 93.

38. M. Wheatcroft, *The Revolution in British Management Education* (London, 1970), 98.

39. Turner, *Business in Britain*, 93; A. Sampson, *The New Anatomy of Britain* (London, 1971), 591–2.

40. Turner, *Business in Britain*, 93.

41. Wheatcroft, *Revolution in British Management Education*, 76, table 6.1; Locke, *Management and Higher Education*, 177.

42. Whitley, Thomas, and Marceau, *Masters of Business*, 27.

43. *Management Today* (Mar. 1967), 62–5.

44. Locke, *Management and Higher Education*, 5.

45. M. Young and P. Willmott, *The Symmetrical Family: A Study of Work and Leisure in the London Region* (London, 1973), 242. In their 1971 study of directors covering the period 1900–1970, P. Stanworth and A. Giddens found that only 14% of directors were of working-class origin; two-thirds had attended public school, and, of the university-trained directors, two-thirds had attended Oxford or Cambridge (see 'An Economic Élite: A Demographic Profile of Company Chairmen', in P. Stanworth and A. Giddens (eds.), *Élites and Power in British Society* (Cambridge, 1974), 82–3).

46. R. V. Clements, *Managers: A Study of their Careers in Industry* (London, 1958), 189, app. 2, table 38. The Acton Society Trust found in its study of 1956 that, compared to the figures for the general population, public-school-educated men had ten times the average chance of becoming managers (*Management Succession: The Recruitment, Selection, Training and Promotion of Managers* (London, 1956), 8).
47. Fidler, *British Business Élite*, 84.
48. Clements, *Managers*, 76. The Acton Society also noted the comparative openness of management compared to other professions (*Management Succession*, 9).
49. Clements, *Managers*, 76–80. Over 50% of managers in works departments had fathers in lower-middle-class or skilled manual occupations (*Managers*, 132).
50. R. Locke, *The End of the Practical Man: Entrepreneurship and Higher Education in Germany, France and Great Britain, 1880–1940* (London, 1984), 58.
51. Locke, *Management and Higher Education*, 98–101, 146–50.
52. M. Sanderson, *The Universities and British Industry, 1850–1970* (London, 1972), 339–59.
53. W. J. Reader, *Imperial Chemical Industries: A History*, ii (Oxford, 1975), 70–2; A. Pettigrew, *The Awakening Giant: Continuity and Change in Imperial Chemical Industries* (Oxford, 1985), 128; Wiener, *English Culture*, 149. Winnington Hall has been variously described as resembling a gentleman's club or an Oxbridge college.
54. Sanderson, *Universities and British Industry*, 349–55.
55. Locke, *End of Practical Man*, 58. Engineer–managers in this sample reflect the post-war generation's position in the midst of initiatives to restructure industrial training. Some had done only apprenticeships but two went on to obtain university qualifications as well. For them, as for the economists or personnel managers, there was a strong sense of pride in being at the start of a new development.
56. Locke, *End of Practical Man*, 30.
57. Locke concludes that 'German engineering fraternities welcomed engineering graduates: the British had a deep prejudice against the university man—the useless theoretician' (*End of Practical Man*, 58).
58. Turner, *Business in Britain*, 308.
59. Ibid. 304 (the chairman of BMC Lord Stokes had begun his career as an engineer).
60. Ibid. 301. See Jones and Marriott for similar comments on the heavy-electrical industry (*Anatomy of a Merger*, 13).
61. See Ch. 3, sect. iii.
62. At the same time, even the sons of career managers might occasionally benefit from a kind of nepotism. They might be offered a post in the same firm as their father, or gain a post in another firm through his contacts.
63. Clements, *Managers*, 174, app. 2, table 3.
64. Ibid. 31–4. Of those who went on to further education the majority were Oxbridge graduates (ibid. 174, app. 2, table 3).
65. Whitley, Thomas, and Marceau, *Masters of Business*, 27.
66. On completion of his schooling, for example, Mr Briar was sent to a subsidiary

of the family firm in the West Indies to learn about primary production of sugar cane.

67. Briar worked night shift for three months—part of a family tradition of toughening sons before they took up a managerial post.

68. The series was initiated by Sir Ronald Edwards and Mr Harry Townsend shortly before the Second World War. Many leading industrialists gave detailed papers at the seminar on the growth and development of their organizations, some of which were subsequently published elsewhere. For further information, see Channon, *Strategy and Structure*, 18 n. 21.

69. A good example is Lord Simon's account of his career in the family engineering group. Appointed chairman in 1910 at the age of 29, he saw his role as being to carry out his father's intentions for the firm. Although his father had died in 1899, as late as 1956 Simon was moved to write: 'I believe that the business methods and outlook of my father were outstandingly good, and that his descendants respect this tradition and do what lies in their power to maintain it' (*Organisation of the Simon Engineering Group* (Problems in Industrial Administration, 195; 20 Nov. 1956), 29).

70. Sir George Dowty, *Development and Organisation of the Dowty Group Ltd.* (Problems in Industrial Administration, 245; 19 May 1959).

71. Scase and Goffee make the point that, in competing with larger, often better-paying public firms for skilled labour, family firms may emphasize the benefits of greater job security (*Entrepreneurial Middle Class*, 156).

72. Scase and Goffee also mention the limits which family ownership places on the mobility of career managers (ibid. 164).

73. This is the reason given by Brown for Mr Jennings's decision to stay with Jennings Windows after its take-over in 1968.

74. 'Palace revolution' was the phrase used by Chemtex Textiles managers to describe a major management reshuffle in the mid-1960s.

75. See Clements's figures for the 1950–5 entrants (*Managers*, 187, app. 2, table 34). The Acton Society Trust found that the proportion of non-technically trained graduates was on the increase; however, only 5% of its sample had qualifications in accounting or secretarial qualifications, compared with 9% in engineering (*Management Succession*, 12, 16).

76. Turner, *Business in Britain*, 304.

77. The oral-historian Paul Thompson makes the point that in 'threatened' communities, 'memory must above all serve to emphasise a sense of common identity, so that episodes of division and conflict slip into oblivion' (*The Voice of the Past*, 2nd edn. (Oxford, 1988), 145). This process appears to have occurred among the post-war generation of organization men, who today underplay differences of class and industrial culture and assert their generational affinities instead.

78. Coleman concludes that the dichotomy between educated amateurs and practical men may at last be giving way to a less class-bound, more meritocratic management style. Perkin—more accurately, I believe—claims the reverse; that, since the Second World War, the public schools and Oxbridge have attracted increasing numbers of business people's sons, and sent more of them into business (Coleman, 'Gentlemen and Players', 111; Perkin, *Rise of Professional Society*, 372–3).

79. C. W.-Mills, *White Collar: The American Middle Classes* (New York, 1951), p. xii.
80. As Mills describes the 'little man' in *White Collar*: 'He is more often pitiful than tragic . . . living out in slow misery his yearning for the quick American climb' (p. xii).
81. W. H. Whyte, *The Organization Man* (Harmondsworth, 1963), 128.
82. Ibid. chs. 3, 4, 5.
83. Ibid. 143.

Part Two

Among Men

3

'Family Romances': Management Succession and the Older Man

A lot of people discount paternalism but everybody yearns for a father-figure.[1]

Lord Stokes, chairman of British Leyland, 1969

For Max Weber, the exclusion of emotion from public life accompanied the transition from pre-industrial to industrial organization. The specific nature of bureaucracy, he wrote, 'develops the more perfectly the bureaucracy is "dehumanized", the more completely it succeeds in eliminating from official business love, hatred, and all purely personal, irrational, and emotional elements which escape calculation'.[2] Just as mechanized production had replaced hand labour, so the dispassionate authority of the bureaucratic machine had gradually supplanted the personal authority of feudal times. Experts schooled in the science of organization had taken the place of 'the master of older social structures, who was moved by personal sympathy and favour, by grace and gratitude'.

The key figure in Weber's modern bureaucracy was the 'detached and strictly objective *expert*', who could be trusted to conduct business according to clearly established rules and without regard to personal sentiment.[3] The bureaucracy, with its efficient routines and increasingly specialized functions, enabled the triumph of rationality over emotion.[4] Weber's conception of modern organizations has a remarkable hold over us still. As we saw in the previous chapter, Harold Perkin's *The Rise of Professional Society* charts a transition

77

from the nineteenth-century entrepreneurial ideal to the twentieth-century ideal of management expertise applied without regard to 'family sentiment or loyalty'.[5] Similarly, in his Pulitzer prize-winning book *The Visible Hand*, Alfred Chandler depicts the US 'managerial revolution' in terms of the increasing efficiency of management structures.[6]

Weber's thesis of a shift from subjective to rational modes of action pervades not only the field of business history, but also—not surprisingly—the management sciences. Organization studies, too, have often replicated Weber's model by splitting rationality off from sentiment and dismissing the latter as outside the field of study.[7] In this literature, the post-war generation of managers are commonly depicted as exemplars of bureaucratic rationality.[8] Yet the organization men in this study tell a different story, one in which the divisions between emotion and managerial work were extremely indistinct. On the one hand, they spoke the language of bureaucratic rationality. They separated their private feelings from their public role in business. They argued that the personal favouritism which had characterized management in family firms had now largely disappeared. While sympathetic in some ways to that way of managing, their own authority rested on formal qualifications in arts, science, or engineering. Moreover, in later career they had often helped to standardize recruitment and promotion procedures, introducing such practices as formal interview schedules, career-planning schemes, and performance evaluation. In all these ways they acted as 'objective experts', supposedly limiting the exercise of power for subjective motives. On the other hand, as the perceptive Lord Stokes noted, the longing for father-figures persisted. This chapter turns Weber's interpretation on its head. Instead of looking for a process of increasing rationality in management, it argues that relations between men in the modern bureaucracy function through the arousal of highly subjective fears and satisfactions. As I argued in the previous chapter, the basic structure of succession mimics Weber's pre-industrial patrimony, where power is passed on from father to son. Management succession involves the playing-out of emotional dilemmas between older and younger men.

In an essay called 'Family Romances' Freud offers a way of exploring the authority relations between men. He points out that social progress as a whole can be understood in terms of opposition between generations. Liberation from the authority of parents

78

involves an often painful recognition that they are not 'incomparable and unique'.[9] 'Family romances' concern the rich imaginative life which attends the process of achieving independence. Freud notes that children's day-dreams often revolve around the rejection of real parents and their replacement with altogether 'grander people', perhaps socially superior figures such as emperors or empresses. Such fantasies may also have an erotic component, involving 'secret love-affairs' with mothers; and the simultaneous exaltation of fathers alongside Oedipal motives of 'revenge and retaliation'.[10] All these features can be found in my interviewees' stories about older men. Their narratives were romances in which older men might be endowed with the features of an ideal father, supremely confident and multi-skilled, his authority unchallengeable. Yet alongside these emperors were other men, perhaps standing in for real fathers and their failures, upon whom scorn was poured. Organization men veered back and forth between the idealization of older men and a wish to unseat them. But their stories have a richer life even than this. Inverting the heterosexuality of family relations, management succession may take the form of love-making between men. Mr Wright explained that a 'good' relationship between younger and older men was just like a love-affair, where 'high levels of energy' flowed from 'the chemistry being right'. Power in the bureaucracy is not handed down in dispassionate ways. Rather, the affective relations between men are concealed within the image of bureaucracy as a machine.[11]

In the management literature, relations between junior and senior managers are often described in terms of 'mentor/protégé', with the mentor's task being to shepherd, educate, and encourage younger managers. For example, in her path-breaking work *Men and Women of the Corporation*, Rosabeth Moss Kanter illustrates the different ways in which mentors may extend opportunities to protégés. They might enable younger managers to take short cuts through the formal promotion hierarchy, or act as a source of 'reflected power', allowing the protégé to act with the backing of more powerful resources.[12] Mentoring is often recommended for women managers, because it seems to offer a quick route to seniority.[13] Kanter argued that mentors, while 'important for the success of men', were 'absolutely essential for women', and that the relationship should therefore be institutionalized.[14] Echoing Weber, Kanter trusted that formal mechanisms would overcome patrimonial power, with all its arbitrary features. Authority in the bureaucracy could ultimately be exercised in an objective manner, and thus without regard to sex.[15] As Kanter explained it, 'power wipes out sex'.[16]

Closer attention to the relations between younger and older men in management reveals the difficulty of separating the nature of their psychic identifications with each other from their hold over power in the bureaucracy. As Kanter herself confessed, mentor relationships between men frequently operate through the younger man's affinities with an older man.[17] Woman have particular need of 'sponsored mobility', but the emotional complexion of mentor relationships discourages that. With the eclipse of family capitalism, mentors have replaced fathers, but the male lineage remains. Below I explore the kinds of emotional investments which organization men made in their relationships with older managers. These reveal important links between family and work which are usually broken in studies of management. Like their entrepreneur predecessors, organization men view career progress as a passage from the dependence of youth to the independence of manhood. Authority in the family and organization also confirm each other, there being a symmetry, for example, between marriage and first management post, and between fatherhood and mentoring. Moreover, succession is imbued with father–son metaphors, as the common substitution of the name 'godfather' for 'mentor' suggests.[18] This anchorage in family relations gives mentoring between men its exclusive quality. At an institutional level, the mode of empowerment is father to son. At the psychic level, however, the guise of the father is only one in a range of childhood and adolescent dramas in which the older man becomes a protagonist. The intensity of mentor relationships has often been noted,[19] but the Weberian split between rationality and emotion obscures its operation. Succession is not just an issue of who possesses power and how the structure of organizations can be put right to achieve parity. It takes the form of a family drama in which women and men play different and unequal parts.

Interviewees tended to represent the older man in two ways. Sometimes he was depicted as a father-figure whose task was to take younger managers 'under the wing', as one man put it, assisting their passage from boyhood to manhood. In Section i of this chapter I shall outline some of the perceived stages in this passage and consider how these interlocked with domestic relationships. It is partly because older managers often stood in for real fathers, that they subsequently became the lead characters in career histories. Yet, as

Section ii explains, the psychic theatre surrounding succession entails more than the restaging of father–son relationships.[20] A complex of sexual fantasies emerges in the narratives, the older man being depicted perhaps as a experienced lover, or as a mistress seduced by the younger man. Interviewees commonly drew on the language of heterosexual intimacy to describe these kinds of affections. At the same time, as the final section illustrates, older men were frequently also the object of rivalrous feelings. The organization men in this study portrayed a managerial world which was deeply divided between idealized and despised figures.

i. Sons and Fathers

Most of the men I interviewed did not enter the work-force until their mid-twenties, but in retrospect they view this as their youth. 'I started as a boy,' explained Mr Sorrell of his life-long career with the Turner Motor Works, even although he was a 23-year-old graduate at the time. Narratives of early career depict an all-engrossing single man's culture. First posts replicated the fraternal and competitive worlds of the public school or the armed services, in which many had spent their early adulthood. These various all-male institutions functioned in similar ways. As Mr Jones put it, 'I joined Swan Oil in the same sort of way you might have joined the army . . . As an unmarried single bloke, yes, it was rather good. It was rather like going on with university, or a bit like army life. There was a gang of blokes there and we had a lot of fun!'

Like these institutions, first posts often demanded commitment to a total way of life in which the boundaries between work and leisure were fluid. Sometimes young managers were assigned to company outposts. Two managers in my sample began in the Middle East, two in Africa, and two in the Far East. The remembered excitements of travel and work are inseparable. In continuous process industries such as oil or steel, graduate recruits might be assigned to shift work or placed 'on call' to the plant. This kind of work often involved frontier technology as well as frontier locations, particularly in the rapidly expanding oil and chemical industries. Youth, and the feeling of being in on 'something new', went hand in hand. The dominant sense is of men working together, completely absorbed by their new discoveries, just as perhaps they had been absorbed by science experiments at school.[21]

81

Promotion to management was often via a trainee programme, which could last up to two years. This would entail a tour of the company's various plants, often working in manual jobs. In the style of 'fagging' at public school, or basic training in national service, such posts were intended to make 'hard' men of prospective managers by putting them through a kind of crash apprenticeship. As we shall see in the next chapter, middle-class men were particularly proud of having worked on the shop-floor. The arts graduate Bannerman recalled his traineeship with great excitement, the more so because, through the experience, he had earned a place among the boys:

> What was very good is that it didn't make any concessions to your ulti-
> mate status, in the sense that I was starting work at half past seven in
> the morning and working in the tube mill as a member of a mill gang.
> One had a certain amount of artificial progress, in that you became a
> sort of charge hand and inspector, but nevertheless you also worked in
> the gang.

In Bannerman's account the attainment of his 'ultimate status' as a manager is seen to stem from his success in performing men's work. He proved that he could cope with a physically demanding job, and possessed technical talents as well. Whilst on the mill gang Bannerman became fascinated by the process of steel-tube drawing. Although he had no formal engineering qualifications, his enthusiasm led him to discover a way of improving the process. On this basis he was able to move into methods engineering, launching himself on to a much more satisfying career path. Completion of a first project like this often forms a rite of passage in memory. Successful first posts signified a double passage from a boy's to a man's world and from 'the gang' to management.

A first performance like Bannerman's is only successful in effecting the passage from underling to manager if it captures the attention of senior managers. Early career reminiscences are often woven around the moment when an older man was persuaded to 'take notice'.[22] If, at one level, early career entails a kind of personal liberation, at another it is marked by extreme dependence. Paradoxically, it is through subjection to father-figures at work that this much vaunted independence is achieved.

Like fathers, older men combine protection with the otherwise mutually exclusive quality of discipline. As Arlie Hochschild remarks in *The Managed Heart*, in the case of men in management, 'the capacity to wield anger and make threats . . . is delivered over to the company'.[23] Managerial authority hinges partly on the ability to use aggression for corporate ends. The post-war generation learnt this ability by being subjected to an older man's aggression. Perversely, perhaps, being given a rough time by an older man was an advantaging mechanism. As Mr Stewart, now deputy chairman of Chemtex Textiles, described his mentor Lord Meadows:

> I saw him reduce one of my colleagues to tears—literally—at the meeting. He just tore him apart. He was a formidable bugger, but he was also an exciting man to work for . . . The great thing about him was that he was always supportive. The only thing that really used to enrage him was if you didn't do something. If you did it and it turned out wrongly, he would curse and shout at you, but he would often end up saying, 'Well, better luck next time. Don't make the same mistake again.' So you felt quite supported. And you had a lot of freedom.

Another ex-employee made an even closer association between Meadows's anger and his support when she remarked that those men who had escaped his wrath seemed also to have been deemed by him to be unworthy of promotion: 'a sort of joke between us all was that you weren't any good unless you'd been sacked at least once by Ron Meadows. And reinstated, we hoped, next morning!' So mentors are not only protective figures, but also act in somewhat tyrannical ways towards younger men. As Mr Tinsley commented of his mentor, he was a 'slave-driver, did me the world of good'. Voicing a similar elision between punishment and reward, Mr Wright commented of his mentor that 'one could talk to him, one could work with him, he could bawl the living daylights out of you . . .'. There was a widespread belief that career advancement—and, by extension, manhood—was secured by the successful negotiation of challenges presented by an older man. Memories of challenges successfully endured were sometimes accompanied by painful recollections of failure. Like naughty boys, at such times they were fearful of annihilation at their fathers' hand. Good mentors were men like Meadows, who taught lessons that his boys never forgot but who simultaneously supported them. The seeds of 'freedom' lay in the capacity to survive a father's rage.

Marriage forms a further rite of passage in the managerial transition to manhood. All the men in my sample married, most a few years after being appointed to management.[24] Memories of 'freedom' in early career are thus associated with being unattached.[25] We saw above how Jones began his description of the first post by stressing the absence of domestic ties: 'As an unmarried single bloke, yes, it was rather good.' Camaraderie fed into a work culture which emphasized the unhindered development of skills. The engineer Mr Tinsley recalled that he had spent his twenties in self-improvement, doing a postgraduate engineering course, and becoming involved in the Production Engineers Institute. Activities like these involved competing with others for office and academic results. Bachelorhood made single-minded pursuits like this possible. For Tinsley the satisfaction of meeting 'a lot of young chaps of my own age with similar ambitions' was only possible because 'of course I was single, so I could spend as much of my spare time on it as I wanted'.

Yet by the time a man reached his thirties and mid-career, marriage was expected. Cynthia Cockburn observes in her study of print workers that after a certain age an unmarried man was 'an outcast in a social world organised around the nuclear family'.[26] Managers in my sample also saw men who had remained unmarried as marginal figures. They were recalled by reference to this supposed lack, identified at first mention as 'the bachelor'. A work culture based on fraternity gave way in mid-career to one in which family men were advantaged. Marriage was frequently an informal prerequisite for promotion. While the single man's culture had been so central to Mr Jones's early early career at Swan, promotion to a staff position at the age of 39 was contingent on marriage:

> I don't think I would have been made staff manager of Swan UK if I hadn't got married, because I always remember going and telling the old boy who was personnel director of Swan UK. I used to pass their office, and I just sort of popped in early [one] morning on my way through and said, 'By the way Mr Billings, I've just got engaged.' He said, 'Good for you. That's marvellous.' And within a week I was down there and they were thinking of me as the next staff manager of Swan UK.

Memories of mid-career highlight a paradoxical relationship between work and home. The most demanding jobs went to married men, but prevented them from spending more time at home. Moreover, while men's work duties took them away from the domestic domain, families and particularly wives might become increasingly 'incorporated' in the company's business. This was particularly true with overseas postings, as Sonya Tramayne has observed. At Shell, for example, 'Shell cousins' are deputized to introduce new arrivals, and the managerial hierarchy is replicated in the social networks formed by wives.[27] Even where the company was not at the centre of community life, as was the case with overseas posts, wives were nevertheless incorporated. Interviewees frequently referred to their role in recruitment, perhaps helping to vet new employees or being the object of corporate scrutiny.[28]

This merging of company and family in mid-career is reflected in the men's ways of perceiving work. The transition from single to married was accompanied by a shift in narrative motifs. The early career emphasis on freedom gave way to metaphors of fatherhood; work was depicted in terms of responsibilities rather than as a source of independence. Added to the young manager's concern with the acquisition of power for himself came a preoccupation with how power over others should be exercised. Where they had once depended upon an older man to provide opportunities, in mid-career they were involved in learning to father others.[29] Corporate fathering remains fundamental to their understanding of management succession. As Mr North expressed it,

> I've always believed that a person's responsibility in a company like Chemtex is to train and help other people around them, and put them in positions where they can gain experience. When we were recruiting for the financial network in Chemtex over the years, I always tried, when I took somebody on, to place him under a mentor, almost like an apprentice, and say to [the mentor]. 'Now you like him. Make sure you get on well together, appreciate one another.' And then make that man responsible for bringing on the new recruit so he didn't lose his way. I think that's just doing what was done to me, really.

The institutional function of the mentor is to bring forward a new generation of managers. This is how North, in his capacity as senior manager, perceives its importance. At the same time, the images which he associates with mentoring—protection, appreciation, education—pertain to fatherhood. The task of directing younger managers involves a metaphoric holding of the child's hands, so he didn't 'lose his way'. North sees himself in the context of a corporate dynasty in which power is passed down from managerial fathers to their sons. He acknowledges that his own prominence is due in part to the older men who mediated his passage to manhood. He had merely 'stumbled along' like a child before becoming a 'disciple' of the chief accountant at Chemtex. Typically, North's acquisition of mentor status at work dovetailed with parenthood. The fact of being a father was often cited as a spur to career success, encouraging the desire to secure a good education and standard of living for children. The awakening of North's ambition was associated with the fact that 'I'd been married, and started to have a family'.[30] As bread-winning became a central career motivation, so the tasks of management became more and more akin to those of fatherhood.

The incorporation of wives into the enterprise, the adoption of managerial sons, and the notion of family as the principal motivation for work, coincided with a reduced presence of men in the home. In a study carried out in the 1960s, J. M. Pahl and R. E. Pahl pointed out that male managers experienced tensions between home and work commitments as they entered mid-career.[31] Among men in my sample there was a continuing sense of guilt at having played a limited role in the early years of parenthood.[32] Accounts of mid-career often began with thanks to a wife for having taken the major responsibility of parenting. The work environment thus co-opted the relations of domestic life whilst discouraging men's involvement with their actual families. Mentoring reflects this generation's displacement of emotional energy from the nuclear family, and its relocation in the corporate family.

In late career, questions of succession preoccupy this generation. The present entails a contrary pull between personal desire for immortality and an obligation to conform to patrilineal traditions, which demand that older managers stand aside in favour of their heirs. Sometimes older men were pushed aside: four interviewees in my sample were made redundant in management reshuffles initiated by a younger generation. Most have made way for younger men, however. Mr Grainger explained proudly that he had spent two years in a failing computer business, trying to protect his more promising managers from possible redundancy by finding them jobs elsewhere in the company. He accepted his own redundancy without question, and obtained immense satisfaction from following the subsequent career successes of his protégés. As he explained, 'They're still there and they're doing well. That was good, and they were worth the company hanging on [to]. I didn't mind fighting for them.' Such actions involve the sacrifice of personal ambitions in favour of younger men, but also place the older man at the pinnacle of the gender hierarchy. Senior managers are distinguished by their powers to confer opportunities on others. Both their organizational status as mentors and their familial status as fathers depend on their capacity to provide. In the act of resigning power, managers in late career also perpetuate their presence, for the men whom they choose as their successors are moulded in their image. Organization men gain a kind of immortality through shepherding their managerial sons to manhood.

ii. Fathers and Lovers

The older man's prominence in career histories results partly from the fact that emotional dilemmas—dilemmas which arise entirely outside the work world—are projected on to him. In the 1970s and 1980s the so-called 'men's movement' stressed the need for men to rediscover their emotional selves, rejecting the instrumental, calculative roles which they had learnt to play so successfully.[33] The middle-class manager is frequently depicted as the classic example of men's alienation from their feelings. Thus, in an American study, Richard Ochberg points to the numerous ways in which middle-class men attempt to control the realms of emotion by presenting a façade of cold rationality. He sees the problem as being that 'men's private experience of themselves has been submerged beneath their experiences of themselves as public actors'.[34] Such a view is based on a misconception of what work means to men like this. It was the emotional content of managerial work that made it enjoyable for organization men. Management provided a forum for playing out the pleasures and discontents of masculinity. This psychic theatre was fixed with particular intensity on the mentor–protégé relationship, which was weighted with sexual and emotional significances.

Some of my interviews reflected indirectly on sexual conflicts and desires. Seemingly 'instrumental' acts were narrated through a sexually charged language, clearly illuminating the psyche. For instance, in the previous section we viewed Mr Bannerman's shift into methods engineering primarily as a managerial rite of passage. We might equally interpret his description in terms of its reawakening of adolescent sexual dramas. Bannerman's career move also announced a turning-away from his mother and her occupation, teaching, and a move towards his engineer father. After leaving grammar school at 17, on his mother's suggestion Bannerman did an arts course at university. In the subsequent search for a possible career, however, he began to fear that his education had been decidedly effeminate, that it might only have equipped him to 'go into something soft, like administration or personnel or whatever'. At the steelworks Bannerman began to resolve his dilemma:

> Although I wasn't an engineer I found that I was solving one or two problems that engineers hadn't solved. [Pause.] It might be interesting just to illustrate it. If you're drawing a tube, you have to make a small piece at the front of it; you have to hammer it down so that it will go through the die so that it can be pulled through. Clearly, if you hammer it down too far, it closes up and you can't let acid flow through it to clean up the bore of the tube. If you don't knock it down far enough, you have to keep knocking it down and knocking it down. So that getting it done in one job is crucial. And, on a rather empirical basis, I spotted that if you theoretically made the tube solid; you calculated its cross section area this way [gestures], because there was a certain amount of stretch as it went through the machine, it left a hole. I tested that formula out—I was a kind of acting charge hand then—and it seemed to work. [Pause] As far as I know, they're still using it.

Bannerman's discovery of a new method of tube-drawing clinches his switch from humanities to work that 'appealed' because of its technical character and its similarity to his own father's interests. In conquering the production process Bannerman helps resolve his adolescent gender confusions. Fascination with tube-drawing perhaps also has a more fantastic quality, however, akin to a adolescent's preoccupation with the new abilities of his penis. He secured his manhood when he 'theoretically made the tube solid'. His narrative at this point possesses intense energy, as he describes the labour of tube-making. Drawing, hammering, pulling, 'knocking it down and knocking it down', 'getting it done', are onomatopoeic, clearly evoking the virility required to perform the job. In Bannerman's account the various management functions are also endowed with sexual significance. He considers that making the tube solid is 'hard', i.e. men's work. In contrast, the thought of going into a 'soft' function like personnel management made him anxious that, 'My God, I seem to have cut myself off here.' Bannerman's passion for production is partly represented in sexual terms, the men's work of production enhancing his potency.

For others, work has not permitted the resolution of psychic conflicts so much as simply providing a stage for their continued exhibition. In this stage the older man is a key player. Stories about senior managers may serve as occasions for re-enacting family dilemmas. Here Mr Grainger furnishes an interesting contrast to Mr Bannerman. His father had been a regular soldier, and Grainger had spent his early life in English army communities overseas. At 15 he and his mother returned to England, and, on his mother's advice, Grainger began an engineering apprenticeship. 'If my father had been there, I might have gone towards the army,' he explained, 'but it was this drive of hers to make sure I'd never be an infantryman.' Grainger's conflict between personal ambition and his mother's wishes continued into later career and adulthood. At 20 he got married, and shortly afterwards did national service. Tension again resurfaced between his dreams and the perceived demands of women around him. He was offered a commission and the chance to stay in the army, but 'my wife hadn't sort of been brought up in the army, so I sort of came back'. As he explained, 'a large part of me still, when I get fed up I think, "Did I do the right thing?"' It was not so much the army itself as the world of men—the world represented by his father —whose loss he laments. Even in later career he tends to contrast fantasies about freedom with the responsibilities of domestic life.

The figure who has come to represent autonomy in Grainger's life is his long-standing friend and mentor, David Moss. Moss and Grainger first met in the early 1960s when they were working for Winwood Appliances in Peterborough. When Moss was appointed general manager of the North Wales plant in 1965, he called Grainger over to take up a job as production manager. Five years later Grainger took up Moss's offer of a post on a management consultancy team. In 1974 Moss left Winwood to become managing director of Dealex Audio, and, once again, Grainger followed him over. This time, however, the move was disastrous. Moss soon left to start up his own business. Later that year Dealex Audio was taken over, and Grainger, left unprotected, was made redundant.[35]

Moss represents the archetypal hero with supernatural powers. He is rational and mechanical man rolled into one, since he holds both engineering and accountancy qualifications. He has 'a hell of a memory' and a keenly developed business instinct. Most importantly, 'he's just got that charisma'. In Grainger's mind the figures of his wife and Moss conflict. It was his wife, Grainger explained, who counselled him not to take up Moss's offer of a job in Dealex Audio. And yet there is something irresistibly attractive about Moss. Grainger was seduced into the job, not only against his wife's wishes but against his own better judgement: 'So again, he gets on the 'phone, "How about coming down to join me?" And, of course, I fell for it! And, of course, if I'd done my homework and gone into [it]. [Pause.] Massey had taken them over six years previously, and they'd gone through, I think, four MDs. It needed a hell of a lot of work.' After he was made redundant Grainger spent five years moving from job to job trying to re-establish his career. He has eventually settled for a post—albeit a demotion—with his old firm, Winwood. Despite the trauma caused by the redundancy, Grainger continues to dream of a partnership with Moss. Once again, however, it is his wife's voice which awakens him:

> I've sort of reconciled myself to the fact now that I'll be a production engineering bloke for the rest of my life. The big problem I have to face, and I keep resisting it like hell, my old MD has set up on his own; he's fairly keen for me to join, and he's got lots of jobs overseas and everything else. But I promised my wife, I says 'No overseas.'

Moss is depicted here as an intensely alluring figure, overpowering Grainger with his 'keen' desires and attractive propositions. The nature of their relationship is indicated by the term 'Svengali', which Grainger coins to describe his mentor. Grainger places himself in the role of a younger woman, a Trilby being seduced by the sexually experienced man. Unlike Trilby, however, Grainger never outgrows the older man's influence. Moss is still able to stir potent passions in him, perhaps even threatening his family life. Grainger must keep resisting such desires 'like hell', so he has not contacted Moss, despite having considered the possibility—again like the obsessed lover—time and time again. A rendezvous with him might jeopardize the 'promise' (and vow) he had made to his wife: 'I don't want to go back to him just for old pal's sake. I've been silly the other way; I just won't get in touch with him. At times when you get a bit low and you're sort of fed up, you think "pick up the phone and . . . " [pause]. But it would be the wrong thing to do. The couple of moves that I had with him didn't work out.'

There is a strong element of unfulfilled desires in Grainger's memories of his seducer. He fantasizes about a relationship with another man which is beyond the reach of mothers or wives. The strength of these desires distorts his memory, so that, although their 'moves' had harmed his career, still 'you only remember the good times and the fun'. At the very end of the interview Grainger again set out the unresolved tension between his youthful, unconsummated lusts, and an older man's responsibilities: 'Ever since I was a kid I've had a wander-lust. If this old boss of mine phoned me up now, if I could ignore the family and everything else, I'd be off like a shot, I'd be on the other side of the world doing something crazy.'

The attempt to reconcile conflicting desires between family life and bachelorhood, heterosexual and homosocial love, forms an underlying thread in Grainger's narrative. He has settled in favour of security in career and family, but presents these as choices borne out of loyalty to women. While his fate seems dictated by family responsibilities, fantasies of an 'escape' with Moss retain their tantalizing hold. He had established a career which was independent from the admired older man, but in his dreams, as Grainger himself noted, 'I keep coming back to him.' To own such fantasies fully would entail confronting not only homoerotic desires but also his lost youth. At a psychic level the older man is thus polymorphous. In Grainger's case he is both a lover and a father. Moss's charisma rests on his ability to give younger men a 'good time' but also on his ability to maintain control, to be a 'real bastard'. Typically, in the older man both qualities are combined. Remembrance of the heavy hand, the temper which could make you 'shit scared of him', goes with ritual seduction. As Grainger remarks, the older man is the object of 'a sort of a love–hate relationship'.

It would be mistaken to interpret stories about succession solely in terms of domination by an older man, even though mentors do wield considerable institutional power. There is a strong element of play at work in mentoring. Dramas between senior and junior managers might involve the reversal of sexual and status hierarchies. The visible structure of emotional relationships thus coexists with a radically different erotic life—what R. W. Connell calls a 'shadow structure'.[36] Domination and subjection are not fixed categories at the level of fantasy; indeed there is considerable room for reversals of the power order.[37] Part of Grainger's delight in working with Moss can be attributed to the continually shifting character of their relationship. Moss might occasionally relinquish the whip hand:

> He . . . was so bombastic . . . He would tackle anybody on their own
> sphere and they would back down. And he was good as long as he had
> someone like me to come along behind and pick them up. We used to
> work as a team often like this. There was a firm in Germany who used
> to supply a lot of machine tools and he used to purposely go out there
> and upset the managing director.

> We used to have great fun planning this out, and try and screw this chap for about 5 per cent discounts. This would go on until about 8 o'clock at night. Mossy would storm out of the office and this German would say, 'I'll do nothing for him but you can have the 5 per cent.' And it was a game. We all knew what was going on, but it went on for years, this bloody thing. Sometimes we swapped around, but usually I was the good guy and he was the bad guy.

Once again we see here how relations between older and younger men may mimic the form of a heterosexual union. The two men act out feminine and masculine identities. Grainger usually plays the healer and manipulator, while his *alter ego* acts out the rampaging bastard. Yet little is fixed in the role-play: as Grainger recalls, they sometimes cross-dressed for a bit of light relief. Amidst these reversals the only constant is the intimacy between the two men. Business here provides an occasion for playing with the post-war scripts of complementary sex roles.

iii. Despised and Idealized Fathers

So far we have observed a tendency in the succession narratives to idolize and fear older men, relieved by the kind of identity-swapping just described. The 'shadow structure' of this is the identification of other managers who were incompetent, and whose replacement was therefore justified. This duality is constantly played out in accounts of career mobility. The managerial world is populated by men who are either grossly inferior and must be replaced, or those whose powers (and jobs) are unattainable. As Freud observed, family romances concern revenge and idealization.[38]

Grainger again provides a good example of this split between the potent and the castrated father. Like others, his career progress consisted of defeating men who stood above him, and so establishing his own authority as a manager. His first major promotion at Winwood, from production engineer to production manager, had occurred when Moss offered him a job at the North Wales factory in 1965. In his new role Grainger was confronted with a shop-floor culture with long traditions of national solidarity. He was an outsider by virtue of being both English and boss. Recognition of his managerial status depended on the demonstration of shared norms, the most important of which was masculinity:

But I was lucky. Every year they used to run a boozy trip to Ireland. It was a tradition. And I'd only been there a couple of months and this came up. And the previous manager who'd organized this came along as well. But what I didn't realize, I was on trial the whole damn weekend. And it was a boozing competition. And the tricks they played on me and everything else! We ended up on the Sunday afternoon in some pub way out the back of Dublin or something, and I mean I can't take drink normally, but something must have been on my side and I managed to drink this old boss under the table. And he actually slipped under and made a mess of himself [chuckles].

And it was a strange thing, but the fact that I'd put up with all this messing about and got the sort of feel of them, and no sooner we got back to work and it was different. But they were strange buggers, they really were.

Here the shop-floor workers set the parameters of the contest, suspending the ordinary work codes. They pit their previous manager against Grainger, the 'old' against the 'new'. Grainger enters the contest as a child, seemingly without choice, and fearful of yet another trick being played on him. His victory turns on a reversal of status between the older and younger man. The 'old boss' is reduced to infancy—on all fours and unable to control his bodily functions. It is Grainger who emerges clean and still standing, very much the man amongst men. His boss had 'slipped' as man and manager. Involving at one level the attainment of adulthood, at another level this narrative again invokes primal fantasies. The childhood world is populated by 'buggers' who play with each other in strange ways. 'All this messing about'; getting 'the sort of feel of them', fascinates Grainger as well as being slightly embarrassing through adult eyes. It provides the kind of wonderment of the infant playing with his bodily excretions or embarking upon taboo sexual explorations. It is perhaps not just the boss who reverts to childhood here. The work environment as a whole thrives on regressive fantasies.

Other interviews confirmed the explanation of career progress in terms of the destruction or eulogizing of older men. The admired older man often becomes an object of homoerotic desire. Status or age differences are commonly expressed as sexual differences. When managers recall their early career, they cast themselves in the role of 'virgins' in the business world, readily seduced and eager to learn. In the rest of the chapter I shall explore through two further examples the nuances which inform the young manager–admired older man relationship.

I interviewed four senior managers from Chemtex Textiles, including Sir Peter Aldridge, whose life story I outlined above.[39] They all talked at length about Ron Meadows, chairman from the mid-1960s. It was the extraordinary intensity of their feelings about him (rivalry in the case of Aldridge, admiration in the others) which first alerted me to the wider significance of mentor relationships. Meadows had come to prominence at Chemtex in the early 1960s, when he led a group of 'rebels', among them my interviewees, in a 'palace revolution' where they pushed aside the incumbent directors. Class and generational tensions combined. Where my interviewees saw themselves as meritocrats, grammar-school boys who had done well, their establishment elders had achieved prominence by nepotism. The metaphoric killing was justified because their fathers had been pompous and ineffectual. From being the outsider in the 1950s, Meadows became synonymous with Chemtex during the 1960s. He dispensed with the 'Gentlemen of the Bedchamber' approach of his predecessors, and set the company on an aggressive course of expansion. Meadows operated by cultivating 'a group of loyal supporters', younger and often relatively junior men whom he promoted rapidly. Among them were Mr Stewart and Mr North. Trained as an accountant, North became indispensable in Meadows's new regime, arranging the funds for his acquisitions. As we saw earlier, for North this job signified a new-found adulthood. And yet, along with the other protégés, he was locked into perpetual dependence by his omnipotent father. Whilst they had been granted the privilege of custodianship over Meadows's power, these protégés could never appropriate that power. As North expressed the dichotomy, 'I was Meadows's right-hand man. I wielded, in a sense, his power.'

Meadows fostered loyalty partly by seduction. Like Moss, he became a kind of sugar-daddy. But, whereas there was always something dangerous about Moss's propositions, Meadows's underlings luxuriate in memories of their seduction. North and others surrendered themselves wholly to him:

> Meadows was a great mentor. He was a man. [Pause.] Meadows was a very clever man, a man of some genius. He had a great ability with people. He bawled them out terribly. His bark was terrible; worse than his bite. He didn't actually sack people, he sacked them theoretically. He opened doors for you and excited you, and drove you and expanded you. But also he was very appreciative. He had a marvellously common

94

touch to make you feel ten feet tall. He made you feel much better than you actually were, so that you could conquer things.

. . . I had flu once, and couldn't come in, and had to send an apology to him because he wanted me for some reason. And within an hour his chauffeur was around at the door with a crate of champagne, and a little note from him saying, 'Take one three times a day after meals.' I wasn't anything much in those days, but he had that sort of touch. And therefore . . . alternately, he could crush you and make you feel dreadful, or he could lift you up. It was part of his technique.

North's eulogy to Meadows is strikingly similar to Stewart's (quoted above). They both describe the older man keeping his juniors in subjection through a fearsome temper. Yet censorship and encouragement, toughness and nurturing, were two sides of the same coin. In this passage North also describes a kind of seduction. It is Meadows who makes the amorous advances, who 'wanted me', whilst North is the object of his love. The two men do not have fixed roles. Sometimes Meadows plays the older man while North is the young woman being courted. Meadows opens doors for 'her' and sends little notes and gifts. At such times North's pleasure came from how the experienced lover 'drove you, and expanded you'. At other times Meadows represents an older, sexually mature woman. He has what North later describes as a 'feminine touch'. In the role of the younger man he recalls the exquisite intensity of sensation aroused by Meadows. With his expert 'technique' or 'touch' he could not only 'lift you up', he could 'make you feel ten feet tall'. Playing the traditionally feminine role, Meadows vicariously boosts North's self-esteem, confirming his masculinity. Sexual metaphors provide North with a means of expressing the older man's profound influence on him. Meadows awakens his potency and cures a deep-seated (here identified as feminine) lovesickness. The images which North employs are always heterosexual, but they convey homoerotic desires. These strains between homosexual love and a heterosexual work culture are characteristic of mentoring between men. Management revolves around extreme conformity, a conformity which is signified largely through the adherence to heterosexuality. Yet, while the open expression of affections between men is proscribed, business thrives on homoerotic encounters.

The staffing of the managerial mind by gods and frauds remains a tableau of succession in the age of professional management. Whereas the reminiscences of a man like North or Grainger partially concern the generation above him, they also speak of the present, in which they have themselves become objects of a younger generation's dislike or adoration. Acts of corporate parricide have gained a great deal of support in Britain over the past decade. It was not only socialist initiatives like nationalization that were blamed for Britain's poor economic performance before 1979, but also the incompetence of its industrial managers. They failed to keep the unions under control, encouraged anti-competitive practices such as cartel agreements, and did not pay sufficient attention to market needs. As we saw in Chapter 1, this criticism became a growth industry during the 1980s.

Organization men were thus held responsible for Britain's economic failures in the post-war period. Given this context, it is not surprising that they suffered heavy casualties in the management reshuffles of the early 1980s. As one retrenched director explained, 'Quite a lot of people are just hanging on trying to make the sixty mark.' Even those whose jobs were secure faced a difficult task. With their own poor record prominent in the public mind, they felt unequal to the task of mediating the ambitions of a younger generation, heavily armed with business theory. Whilst theirs was a new battle, it was essentially the same old war, only this time they had become defendants rather than aggressors. As North perceived, the tensions which racked Chemtex in the early 1980s had their parallel in that 'palace revolution' a generation earlier:

NORTH. They were pretty arrogant and they also took up a tremendous amount of time. The younger chaps—how old are you, by the way?
MSR. Twenty-seven . . .
NORTH. Yes, well, you see, a chap like you, would come out [of] business school, about your age, and you'd have done terribly well, and you'd have all these new-found tools, and you'd come to a company like Chemtex, wasn't doing very well possibly at the time, and you're itching to get stuck in with all this theory. And you'd see a person like myself as being an obstacle . . . or at least the management as an obstacle, because they were doing silly things just like their fathers had before them. And you'd want to conquer the whole world in no time flat. Very difficult to handle, because you'd be putting people's backs up left, right, and centre. They'd all look at you and think, 'Here's a kid who's trying to teach me my job . . . He's come from business school as if it's Mars or something . . . thinks he can put me right but I've been doing the job this way for years.
So there was a personality problem and an adjustment process

which meant that people like myself had to spend an awful lot of time with younger men, teaching them how to behave with their elders, and, as their elders thought, betters. So there were tears and storms and all that. And when the younger man got into a position of responsibility very early in his career and was then responsible for older men in their fifties, he wanted to sweep them out of the way, and retire them early and all that sort of thing. [Pause.] I'm not saying there's anything wrong with that, but the whole process of demoralization that spreads out as a consequence of that is bad.

In North's account the wheel of succession comes full circle. Where the 'rebels' of his generation had dispatched the gentlemen managers, now the young men get 'stuck in' to them. With the older man's wisdom he can see that succession always takes the character of a battle between fathers and sons. There is nothing 'wrong with that', he explains, it is just the way business operates. Each generation is fired by the belief that the previous one was 'doing silly things just like their fathers had before them'. Younger men, convinced by the utility of the 'new-found tools' they acquired at business schools, cannot appreciate the wisdom of their elders, and seek instead to 'sweep them all out of the way'. Succession takes the character of a family romance in which managerial sons turn their fathers into objects of despisal.

If the accession to power of younger men has a parricidal character in the organization man's eyes, it also retains its flirtatious aspect. The men I interviewed were equally as often the objects of adoration by younger men. I had an opportunity to observe a seduction scene in some detail. This was in late 1987, at a lunch in the directors' dining-room of a Midlands vehicle-components firm. Before lunch I interviewed the chairman, Mr Dowell. He explained that one of his first tasks on taking over the chairmanship in 1983 had been to reorganize the ageing and inefficient board. He had selected men of different ages, in the belief that qualities of youth needed to be balanced with the experience of older men. So he recruited one man in his forties from outside, and internally promoted two men in their late thirties, one an ex-engineering apprentice who had 'come up from the shop-floor'. Their 'whole-hearted commitment to the place' would be moderated by himself and another man of his age (60), whom Dowell had brought in from outside. Together they would 'bring through the two . . . younger managers to the point [where], when we retired, we would have stabilized out senior management'.

Dowell was proud of his hand-picked successors, and the lunch was a way of showing them off. One was an ex-public-school boy, polite and reserved, whilst the other, bright-eyed and enthusiastic, was the ex-apprentice whom Dowell had talked about. They, two other men, and myself stood around the sherry cabinet for a drink, and then we sat down at a massive dining table large enough to seat twelve. We were waited on by a woman who stood at Dowell's side. Dowell himself sat at the head of the table, with me on his left and the two younger directors on his right. We talked about my future career, the chances of a return to the cabinet by Cecil Parkinson and Jeffrey Archer, and about a conference which the ex-apprentice had recently attended. The lunch involved a complex shifting and regrouping of allegiances. Dowell did not speak much, but his comments were taken as definitive. For most of the time he was the object of seduction by the younger men. As with North's tribute to Meadows, heterosexual images formed the context of a homosocial encounter. Discussion of the Tory ministers' sexual indiscretions prompted a barrage of innuendo jokes from the younger directors. This banter was quick and competitive, presumably reflecting on the teller's own virility. It was essentially a younger man's sport, designed to capture Dowell's attentions. Dowell gained obvious pleasure from the tale told by Mr Grey, the ex-apprentice, of his trip to Brussels for a conference. The young director was trying hard to recapture the hilarity of a folk night which delegates had attended at a local restaurant. Halfway through the event, he explained, bread rolls, later dipped in beer, had begun sailing across the room, bringing the organized performance to a halt. He and a fellow sales representative had capped the moment by dressing up in tablecloths and napkins as Arabs, stealing off to the kitchen, and commandeering basketfuls of rolls which they pelted at the others. Once again Dowell was being seduced. Brown's story drew on the traditions of the schoolboy prank. It had elements of misogyny and racism, being directed partly against the waitresses and caterers, and it had climaxed in rough play between the boys. Brown had played upon his youthful charm, and we all, especially Dowell, who chortled loudly throughout, did indeed find him irresistibly attractive.

Brown's tale and the response of his audience brings us back to the question of how masculinity operates in business. It suggests that succession is not dependent upon formal skills alone, but that it also involves the cultivation of intense intimacy between men. This intimacy has sexual undercurrents, but these are rarely overt. Much of the socialization for management consists of homosocial play. Among the post-war generation, the public school, the services, and early career provided many forums for the staging of such 'family romances'. Family romances at board level typically have a dual plot, one part involving flirtation between young and old, the other centring on the younger generation's struggle to overthrow its oppressors. Relations between men in senior management are deeply split between loved and hated fathers.

Mentoring between women and men would, I suspect, have a different emotional complexion. Women's sexuality is highly visible in the monoculture of senior management. Questions of how to dress, how to present oneself in front of a largely male audience, are complex ones for women managers because of the heightened perception of their femininity. As Deborah Sheppard remarks, for women managers, being 'sexual' and being 'organizational' are seen as opposite qualities.[40] In contrast, the men I interviewed cultivated sexual relations of a kind among themselves, but these were hidden by the costume of the grey suit and the aura of bureaucratic rationality. Furthermore, as Chapter 7 explains, when they spoke of mentoring younger women, they presented a family drama of an entirely different kind. Their images of women managers were, like those of the older man, split between good and bad objects. Organization men expected a heady mixture of competition and veneration from younger men, but imagined younger women as gentle dependants. They described helping women returners into junior management posts as acts of courtesy, and wondered whether, perhaps, they had been too helpful, too 'soft'. They tyrannized their managerial sons, but could not see that, in a culture which exploits aggression, this was a way of grooming the men for succession.

Men remain the principal heirs to management positions in the corporate culture, just as they were in family firms. Given the tenacity of this lineage, it is not surprising that mentoring has become an issue in attempts to redress inequalities. In the wake of Kanter's 1977 study there have been a host of calls to formalize mentor–protégé relations so as to assist women.[41] But this raises many potential problems. Since most senior managers are men, it is likely the relationship will be cross-gender. Recognizing this, the management literature warns of the dangers of 'sexual innuendo'.[42] David Clutterbuck and Marion Devine explain that it may be difficult for the mentor and protégé to ward off assumptions that the two are 'motivated by sexual interest'.[43] Advice like this conspires in the over-determination of women's sexuality.

Mentoring among men is certainly motivated by sexual interest, and yet the management literature perpetuates the myth of the asexual professional man. An important basis of power among men is thus left unobserved and unchanged. Furthermore, studies which attempt to define more clearly what women want from mentoring often end up reproducing the instrumental–affective gender stereotypes promoted by organization men. Surveys generally find that women are more likely than men to want emotional support from a mentor, while men value the career development aspects of the relationship.[44] Thus the assumption is perpetuated that male managers are closer to the ideal type of bureaucratic rationality.[45] Many questions are left unanswered by approaches which focus solely on the institutional means through which women in management are disadvantaged. Limiting the agenda to equality of access, they risk overlooking the psychic dimensions of succession. Mentoring is part of the process through which gender hierarchies in management are reproduced. It exploits the particular emotional complexion of relations between men, rather than being simply 'an important training and development tool'.[46]

NOTES

1. Quoted in G. Turner, *Business in Britain* (London, 1969), 433.
2. M. Weber, 'Bureaucracy', in H. Gerth and C. W. Mills (eds.), *From Max Weber: Essays in Sociology* (London, 1948), 214–16.
3. Ibid. (emphasis in original).
4. For a critique of Weber's separation of rationality and emotion, see R. W. Bologh, *Love or Greatness: Max Weber and Masculine Thinking—A Feminist Inquiry* (London, 1990), esp. intro and ch. 8. Accounts which address organization studies specifically are G. Burrell and J. Hearn, 'The Sexuality of Organization'; and R. Pringle, 'Bureaucracy, Rationality and Sexuality: The Case of Secretaries', both in J. Hearn, D. L. Sheppard, P. Tancred-Sheriff, and G. Burrell (eds.), *The Sexuality of Organization* (London, 1989), 1–29, 158–78. R. M. Kanter includes a brief but useful discussion in *Men and Women of the Corporation* (New York, 1977), 22.
5. H. Perkin, *The Rise of Professional Society: England since 1880* (London, 1989), 288.
6. A. D. Chandler, *The Visible Hand: The Managerial Revolution in American Business* (Cambridge, Mass., 1977).
7. A good summary of neo-Weberian approaches to sociology of organizations is

in P. Thompson and D. McHugh, *Work Organisations: A Critical Introduction* (London, 1990), 13–22. The notion of the rational bureaucracy, they argue, is merely 'an ideology masquerading as science' (p. 14).

8. e.g. R. Scase and R. Goffee, *Reluctant Managers: Their Work and Lifestyles* (London, 1989), 1–17.
9. S. Freud, 'Family Romances', in *On Sexuality: Three Essays on the Theory of Sexuality and other Works*, trans. J. Strachey (Harmondsworth, 1986), 221.
10. Ibid. 223–4.
11. M. B. Calas and L. Smiricich argue a similar point in relation to the leadership literature in organization studies; it uses sexually charged language to describe the role of senior managers, but in a way that serves to reinforce the antithesis between leadership and seduction (M. B. Calas and L. Smiricich, 'Voicing Seduction to Silence Leadership', *Organization Studies*, 12/14 (1991), 567–602.
12. Kanter, *Men and Women*, 181.
13. British studies are reported in J. Marshall, *Women Managers: Travellers in a Male World* (Chichester, 1984), 106–7; D. Clutterbuck and M. Devine, 'Having a Mentor: A Help or Hindrance?', in D. Clutterbuck and M. Devine (eds.), *Businesswoman: Present and Future* (London, 1987), 92–107; and V. Arnold and M. J. Davidson, 'Adopt a Mentor—the New Way Ahead for Women Managers?', *Women in Management Review and Abstracts*, 5/1 (1990), 10–19. Reviews of the literature on mentoring are provided in R. A Noe, 'Women and Mentoring: A Review and Research Agenda', *Academy of Management Review*, 13/1 (1988), 65–78; D. M. Hunt and C. Michael, 'Mentorship: A Career Training and Development Tool', *Academy of Management Review*, 8/3 (1983), 65–78.
14. Kanter, *Men and Women*, 183, 279.
15. Ibid. 73–4.
16. Ibid. 200. Rosemary Pringle points out the limitations of Kanter's approach in understanding the position of secretaries in bureaucracies. Kanter sees the relations between bosses and secretaries as an anachronism, a hangover from the patrimonial past. Yet, as Pringle argues, this completely ignores the issue of sexuality (*Secretaries Talk: Sexuality, Power and Work* (Sydney, 1989), 84–9; and 'Bureaucracy, Rationality and Sexuality', 160–1.
17. Kanter quotes one of her women informants, who described the older man's attitude towards a male protégé in this way: 'he sees himself, a younger version, in that person . . . Who can look at a woman and see themselves?' (*Men and Women*, 184). In his study of British technical specialists, C. Sofer drew similar conclusions; sponsors regarded 'the appointments and disappointments of their protégés as indicative of their own status and influence' (*Men in Mid-Career: A Study of British Managers and Technical Specialists* (Cambridge, 1970), 19–25). C. W. Mills also emphasized the importance of mentoring for ambitious young 'new entrepreneurs' in US public corporations; promotion was won by these 'adroit climbers' through the art of flattery (*White Collar: The American Middle Classes* (New York, 1951), 96).
18. Hunt and Michael, 'Mentorship', 476.
19. See, esp., D. J. Levinson, *The Seasons of a Man's Life* (New York, 1978), 98–101; Levinson points out the ambivalent nature of the relationship, wherein 'becoming one's own man' involves overthrowing the mentor in some way (pp. 147–9).

20. The concept of psychic theatre is taken from J. McDougall, *Theatres of the Mind: Illusion and Truth on the Pscyhoanalytic Stage* (London, 1986). See, esp., 'Prologue: The Psychic Theatre and the Psychoanalytic Stage'.
21. Duncan still enthuses over his first discovery, while building a 'Cat. Cracker' in Trinidad:

    We had a situation where we created an emulsion which just went solid. And you could turn this thing up in a beaker, and it was just absolutely solid. So we couldn't pump it out [pause] it was almost as if we'd have to take the top off and dig it out! And could we break this?
    I remember being absolutely fascinated by this. I found out that Shell Tipol, the detergent—the opposition!—worked amazingly well. You would put in just a little bit of this, and it would immediately break into two levels. You couldn't believe it. You would do this demonstration in the laboratory and show how, just by putting a few drops in a beaker, this solid stuff, which you had standing upside down, would just break into water and oil. And the oil, the black oil, would float to the top and the water, a bit cloudy and dirty, but nevertheless [water would] stay at the bottom.

22. Thus Stewart claimed that success at Chemtex was generally secured through acts 'that brought you to the attention of a wide range of senior managers'.
23. A. R. Hochschild, *The Managed Heart: Commercialization of Human Feeling* (Berkeley, Calif., 1983), 164.
24. The average age at first management post was 24.6, whilst the average age at marriage was 27.
25. See Ch. 6, sect. i, for further discussion of the tension between 'domestic ties', and 'freedom'.
26. C. Cockburn, *Brothers: Male Dominance and Technological Change* (London, 1983), 202.
27. S. Tremayne, 'Shell Wives in Limbo', in H. Callan and S. Ardener (eds.), *The Incorporated Wife* (London, 1984), 123.
28. These issues are discussed further in Ch. 6, sect. ii.
29. If early career is characterized by the learning of practical skills, mid-career involves the acquisition of mentoring skills. Stewart recalls that the two went hand in hand:

    When I became deputy head of the lab., I well remember the research director of the company—who was a very god-like being to me in those days—came to see me in the lab. and said, 'Whatever else you do, make sure you move people about. Don't let people stay in one job too long.' And I thought at the time, 'Well that's not a very profound piece of advice,' but he'd put his finger on something that was necessary in the outfit. Of course I got to know him quite well after that. So he took notice.
    Here Stewart describes making the passage from boy to man, protégé to mentor. He was beginning to take responsibility for promotion of other staff but remained extremely anxious to attract 'notice' from 'god-like' superiors. He implies that youthful arrogance prevented him from realizing the wisdom of his mentor's comments. Now in late career himself, Stewart sees that the task of assisting the mobility of juniors is vital.

30. Later North explained that he also felt 'driven by my wife to some extent, I suppose'. Confirming his comments, J. M. Pahl and R. E. Pahl observe that a wife's ambition for her husband is often cited as a spur to career success (*Managers and their Wives: A Study of Career and Family Relationships in the Middle Class* (London, 1971), 60). In my sample this kind of vicarious influence was less often voiced than the pleasure taken in being a good provider. Consider Tinsley's account, for example, in which the death of his daughter removes the point of career ambition:

> TINSLEY. It really threw me for six—you'd expect it to—and objectives which seemed important to me before then suddenly didn't matter then.
> MSR. Was it because you felt that you were partly always working for your family, do you mean?
> TINSLEY. Yes. I mean, one of my objectives was, I wanted to take the kids to Disneyland. And do all sorts of other things. I, I, I. [Pause.] Which meant that I had to do well in my career and had to keep on going. Had to earn more, had to make more progress . . . But once she had died, that didn't seem . . . there didn't seem to be any point to it, somehow. And, as I say, even after eleven years—it's eleven years since she died—I'm still not sure to what extent that influenced my get up and go. It took me about three years before I really began to get my old fire in the belly again.

31. Pahl and Pahl remark that the tension between 'conflicting value systems' of home and work, family and career, provides 'the dialectic social reality for the middle-class' (*Managers and their Wives*, 107).
32. Nash blamed himself for a rebellious son: 'One of the main reasons why he has developed the way he has, has certainly been partly the fact that I haven't given him as much time as perhaps I should.' Other managers passed similar comments.
33. See, e.g., A. Metcalf, 'Introduction', in A. Metcalf and M. Humphries (eds.), *The Sexuality of Men* (London, 1985).
34. R. L. Ochberg, 'The Male Career Code and the Ideology of Role', in H. Brod (ed.), *The Making of Masculinities: The New Mens' Studies* (Boston, 1987), 190.
35. Sofer correctly points out that the advantages for the protégé are often tempered by the fact that obstacles encountered by a mentor invariably rebound on the protégé as well (*Men in Mid-Career*, 25).
36. R. W. Connell, *Gender and Power: Society, the Person and Sexual Politics* (Cambridge, 1987), 114–15.
37. J. Benjamin argues that the tendency towards 'erotic transgression' results partly from the opportunity it provides to 'express what is ordinarily denied' (see 'Master and Slave: The Fantasy of Erotic Domination', in A. Snitow, C. Stansell, and S. Thompson (eds.), *Powers of Desire: The Politics of Sexuality* (New York, 1983), 294–5).
38. Freud, 'Family Romances', 224.
39. See Introduction.
40. D. L. Sheppard, 'Organizations, Power and Sexuality: The Image and Self-Image of Women Managers', in J. Hearn, D. L. Sheppard, P. Tancred-Sheriff, and G. Burrell (eds.), *The Sexuality of Organization* (London, 1989), 144–6.
41. Marshall, *Women Managers*, 107; Clutterbuck and Devine, 'Having a Mentor',

93; Arnold and Davidson, 'Adopt a Mentor', 10; Hunt and Michael, 'Mentorship', 476; Noe, 'Women and Mentoring', 65. Noe passes the cavalier remark that 'without a mentor women are unable to understand the reality of the male-dominated business culture.' In doing so he reconstructs the ideal of a helping father who interprets the outside world (the organizational 'reality') for his dependants.

42. Clutterbuck and Devine, 'Having a Mentor', 101–4; Noe, 'Women and Mentoring', 70; Hunt and Michael, 'Mentorship', 481.
43. Clutterbuck and Devine, 'Having a Mentor', 104.
44. See, e.g., the pilot study conducted by Arnold and Davidson, 'Adopt a Mentor', 13; unlike some others, this study is sensitive to the problems involved in men mentoring women, and the fact that they had sometimes tried to block women's career development (p. 16).
45. Esp. H. M. Reich, 'The Mentor Connection', *Personnel* (Feb. 1986), 54; Reich reports that women rate 'the emotional factor' of mentoring much more highly than men; they stress its 'caring, nurturing, teaching' aspects rather than its 'professional nature'.
46. Hunt and Michael, 'Mentorship', 475.

4

The Cult of Toughness

In the traditional Thorn culture, if you weren't running around hitting bits of iron with hammers or wielding a spanner, then you weren't a man.[1]

Thorn/EMI senior manager, describing management in the 1960s

Established manufacturing industries such as motor vehicles, steel, and shipbuilding have generally been recognized as the 'bastions of culturally "male" employment'.[2] The statistical record certainly demonstrates a high concentration of men in these industries. In 1983 women constituted under 15 per cent of the labour force in the motor vehicle, mechanical engineering, oil processing, and metal industries.[3] It has been argued on the basis of this segregation that the sex-typing of jobs as 'masculine' reaches its fullest form in such industries. Yet what it is that makes employment in heavy manufacturing industries 'culturally "male"' remains unclear. Moreover, while we might expect the managers working in this sector to be the best advertisement for its masculine ethos, they were decidedly ambivalent. The 'hard' men who work in manufacturing rarely feel that they measure up to its exacting standards.

The masculine image of jobs in heavy industry does not mean that 'the feminine' disappears from view. In fact, quite the reverse was true among organization men in this sector. For them, failure to make it as a 'hard' man was experienced in terms of effeminacy. Their vision of 'men's work' was shaped by both feminine and masculine imagery. Some industries within manufacturing were designated more macho than others, staff jobs held less kudos than production-related functions, and men who possessed formal

105

qualifications were considered less hardy than those who had begun their careers on the shop-floor. It seems that the more sex-typed an occupation, the more images of sexual difference are invoked. The character of male-dominated occupations is not defined solely in terms of masculine imagery.

Paul Willis has written compellingly about the cult of toughness among shop-floor workers in northern manufacturing industries. He points out that unskilled and semi-skilled work in manufacturing is often described as a battle of individual endurance against the odds.[4] To the working-class man, the opponent is the machinery of production. His identity as a man and worker rests on his ability to master noisy, dirty, often unsafe conditions. More than this, however, the masculine mystique is a central emblem in working-class culture as a whole.[5] Even in more highly mechanized industries where the burden of heavy physical work has all but disappeared, the heroic associations of shop-floor work remain. As Willis explains, 'The metaphoric figures of strength and bravery worked through masculinity and reputation still move beneath the more varied, visible forms of workplace culture.'[6] These comments raise questions about the image of the manager in the traditional manufacturing industries. The shop-floor worker's mechanical competence and physical labour earns him a special place in masculine mythology, as both Willis and Cynthia Cockburn have pointed out.[7] However, it is not just working-class men who construct a masculine hierarchy in which physical labour is at the summit. In the sector as a whole, practical work is valued above book-learning. This poses managers with a particular dilemma, for, while they possess formal authority over manual workers, for the most part their work takes place well away from the factory floor. Managers cannot claim the kind of heroism which male shop-floor workers do through their daily confrontations with the machinery of production. This renders the managers' position somewhat precarious—capable of subversion through jokes, taunts, or flagrant disobedience.[8] As David Collinson and Margaret Collinson observed in their study of a truck factory, shop-floor workers felt a certain sense of superiority to the 'yes men', and often ridiculed them 'as effeminate'.[9]

Even men who had been promoted from the shop-floor might face difficulties on entering management, having to give up the very qualities which had previously singled them out in order to take up a desk job. As Cockburn has aptly remarked, where the ex-engineer's masculinity had once rested on 'running down the desk bound intellectual', in mid-career he might find himself transformed 'into one of these suspiciously unmanly creatures himself'.[10] For the middle-class men who dominated post-war industrial management, however, the problem was somewhat different. They lacked even the shop-floor experience possessed by ex-working-class managers. Mere 'boys' in the hard culture of the factory, they felt a particular need to prove their masculinity.

The managers I interviewed described a constant struggle to quell suspicions that they were unmanly or 'soft'. At the same time, they made frequent use of hard–soft dichotomies when describing company life. They graded management hierarchies according to the level of aggression required to perform at each level, represented the staff–line split as a distinction between feminine supportive and masculine productive jobs, and ranked different industries according to how masculine they were. For example, among motor-vehicle suppliers, electrics or plastics were considered less heroic than braking, suspension, or engine components. Despite the common tendency for men to endorse the cult of toughness in these ways, they often felt that they had failed to assert a sufficiently 'hard' masculinity. Qualities which they experienced as feminine kept resurfacing, hampering the will to power. Management was a constant struggle to keep fear at bay and hide sensitivity to others. As Lynne Segal remarks of the author Ernest Hemingway, the quest for a 'pure' masculinity

> depends upon the perpetual renunciation of 'femininity'. No one can be that male without constantly doing violence to many of the most basic human attributes: the capacity for sensitivity to oneself and others, for tenderness and empathy, the reality of fear and weakness, the pleasures of passivity—all, of course, quintessentially feminine. So while the feminine may be dispatched in the insouciant bravado of masculine endeavour, it will always return to haunt the conquering hero.[11]

Among organization men, this rejection of and haunting by feminine qualities occurred in various ways. Section i of this chapter looks at how this 'insouciant bravado' might be literally enacted in the appearance and movements of managers. Section ii explores the narratives of war and national service. These illustrate just how unsteady is the balance between bravado and fear. The men praised their military training for having given them a sure footing in management. They promoted a myth of military service as the foundation stone of self-sufficiency, but also recalled their fears of failure. Section iii illustrates how the ethos of battle extended through to careers within the company. The Cook's tour in early career introduced graduates to factory life, and so played an essential part in the transition from book-learning to 'man management'. By demonstrating competence among men and machines on the shop-floor, graduates earned the right to manage. Metaphors of struggle are especially prominent in mid-career narratives, as Section iv explains. Managers were often appointed to deliberately difficult posts, designed to test their mettle against rival managers or a recalcitrant work-force. These critical posts were semi-institutionalized as a means of 'separating the men from the boys' on the path to senior management. Failure revealed the personal burdens of this desire for pure masculinity. Many of my interviewees had ended up in jobs which they considered soft, and laboured under the stigma of being unmanly.

Managers of all levels in manufacturing industry were anxious to demonstrate their toughness, but this quest was riddled with contradictions. It was the muscular culture of the shop-floor which provided a paradigm for combat within management, but this meant that managers rarely felt themselves to be the equals of those they were meant to be governing. Although it seemed to them that they never won the battle, in fact they often ran roughshod over those who posed even the slightest threat.[12] Battles between hard and soft raged fiercely within the minds of men, but also determined real courses of action.

i. Embodiments of 'Hard' Masculinity

The cult of toughness does not confine itself to the language which industrial managers use to describe their work; it is also conveyed in posture, gestures, facial expressions, and movements. These dimensions of masculinity accompany speech and are thus largely absent from the transcripts of life stories. Yet it is the bodily living-out of masculine identities which often provides the clearest indication of what R. W. Connell calls 'the structure of power in gender relations'.[13] As he remarks, 'the social definition of men as holders of power is translated not only into mental body-images and fantasies, but into muscle tensions, posture, the feel and texture of the body.

This is one of the main ways in which the power of men becomes "naturalized", i.e. seen as part of the order of nature.'[14] At the same time, the correspondence between social power and physical 'machismo' is not direct. Despite the popularity of 'hard' masculinity in manufacturing, those managers seemingly most successful in flaunting their aggression were not necessarily the most successful in career terms.

This physical living-out of the cult of toughness was very apparent in my interview with Reg Johnson, the managing director of Bridgend Motor Parts, a small (100 employees) automotive components firm. A secretary showed me into Mr Johnson's office. My first impression was of his size. He had a large head with close cropped hair, and he was seated in a high-backed chair which he completely filled. I was accustomed to an initial exchange in which managers would stand up on my entry, move forward to shake my hand, motion me to a chair, and ask me about my trip. But Mr Johnson just sat watching me. He shook hands from behind his desk with a grip that completely engulfed mine. Unsure what to do next, I searched for a place to put my coat and sit down. Silent and still staring, he waited until I had found a seat before asking, 'Well, what do you want?'

The tape recording confirms my memory of feeling unnerved. It reveals a succession of hesitant, half-finished questions on my part, my confidence fading in the face of his monosyllabic replies. He had agreed to an interview, and yet remained somewhat taciturn. My first line of questioning was about the significance of having recently become the firm's owner–manager, but he kept stressing that it was irrelevant to ask him this because there were other shareholders. He briefly mentioned that he had been in the navy boxing team. Since this seemed to shed light on his physical appearance and my feeling of being personally dominated, I tried to get him to talk about whether boxing had contributed to his subsequent career. He also denied any connection there. The influences which were initially most apparent to me—self-employment and his fighting past—were the ones about which he was most defensive.

During the rest of the recording he would throw out the occasional comment, but dismiss my follow-up questions. I found it frustrating that I seemed unable to establish any positive empathy with him. After about forty-five minutes I turned the tape recorder off and began to pack my things, convinced that he wanted me to go but would not tell me directly. When I stood up he also rose, but then he would not let me go. He began to talk about his childhood and his management training. As he talked he began to move from foot to foot in a nimble, almost elegant way, quite astonishing for a man of his size. He would occasionally draw back into a defensive posture, become silent, and then, with a burst of energy in hands and feet, he would relate another memory. His dance revealed the logic of our exchange. Sitting opposite me he had been intent on frustrating my ambitions for a 'good' interview. But once I had admitted a kind of defeat, and had signalled my intentions to leave, he became anxious that I should stay. Even then, he could only talk if he was on his feet, and able to protect himself from the consequences of the information he was giving me. By physically going through the motions of sparring, he relaxed into the telling of life history. At the same time, his performance provided ample warning to me of his physical powers, so protecting him from harm.

Business itself seemed like a kind of boxing match to Mr Johnson. He was not unaware of the effect which his aggressive manner had on others, but he felt ambivalent about it. His threatening manner helped ensure that people would carry out his orders. Moreover, in physical terms he was the equal of any man on the shop-floor, so he could share a joke with them and not risk compromising his authority:

> I don't go down there every day. I don't go down there as the benevolent boss, to be looked at that way as if 'he does lower himself by coming down and talking to us'. But I go down there and I'll have a joke with them. [Pause.] Or in passing—I make sure it's never seen as going down there specifically—I go down there and say 'hi', and maybe pull their leg or whip back at them; repartee. I think they all know me. Some of them are frightened of me, I know that.

Mr Johnson's physical supremacy provided him with a way of gaining the respect of men on the shop-floor. Yet 'repartee' and fear often became confused. This was particularly true of his relations with fellow managers. Insecurity had often led him to act the tyrant with them:

> Some of my staff are [frightened of me] too. I suppose I can be overpowering at times. I can, I accept that. I don't wish to be; I don't think that's a very nice thing to say, but, as my brother might have said to you, I can be overpowering at times. I tend to be a bit domineering at times, which I've tried hard to [pause]. I don't think it's a good characteristic.

By his own admission, Johnson's coercive style isolated him from his fellow managers. He felt that he did not utilize them properly, preferring to oversee everything personally. He always had to resist a tendency towards 'not trusting or not believing them'. Johnson recognized that this need for control prohibited the company from growing, because, in order to expand, he would have to delegate power. At the same time it was difficult to shake off the habits of a lifetime, which had shown him that he could get what he wanted by inspiring fear.

Our interview ended with Johnson talking about how he had been 'left somewhat on my own at 15', following his parents' separation. The navy had offered him a secure home, and, through boxing, a skill which others did not possess. Since fighting had provided Mr Johnson with a measure of financial and emotional security, it is perhaps not surprising that he adopted an adversarial style in business. Yet this had also left him in some ways a lonely man, with a broken marriage and a self-admitted difficulty in 'getting close' to people. He struggled between feeling vulnerable, a prisoner of his past, and resisting vulnerability through aggression. These contradictions were reflected in his philosophy of life. He believed that people should 'only live in the present', but that 'things mould your life at a very early age, I think'. Mr Johnson's life history, from his childhood to his management career, seemed dictated by the need to conceal emotional needs. He must continue to exhibit 'complete and utter dominance', because, as he had learnt in adolescence, life 'was a matter of whether you succeed or go under. One or the other.' Mr Johnson's example reminds us that the cult of toughness does not guarantee managerial success, despite the fact that managers of all kinds use combative language when they portray management. As with many entrepreneurs, one might argue in Johnson's case that the further growth of his firm is constrained by his inability to relinquish control.[15] 'Hard' masculinity dovetails with a management style in which there is no compromise, no middle ground between enforcing one's will and personal humiliation. Not only does this inhibit business; it places untold burdens upon the tyrants themselves.

ii. The 'Short, Sharp Shock' of Military Service

The organization men's view of management as a form of battle needs to be seen in the light of the historical circumstances in which they reached adulthood. It was perhaps not surprising that they held so strongly to warlike metaphors, for military service was 'a fact of life' among male managers of this generation.[16] In his 1977 study John Fidler found that around two-thirds of chief executives had done national service or served in the war.[17] An even higher proportion of men in this sample, three-quarters, did military service. A third underwent their mandatory two years' national service, while the remainder—those born before 1927—served in the war for between two and six years. Of those who completed military training, almost 60 per cent were commissioned. The Army, Navy, or RAF provided a training ground in management as well as in the cult of toughness, so it is important to understand more about their place in the organization man's life history. Even Mr Johnson, who denied that there was much connection between his business style and his time in the Navy, in fact revealed a strong link. The skills necessary for boxing—aggression, strong defences—were ones he had honed as a navy boxer, and which he continued to rely on as a manager.

Military training provided this generation of managers with a unique claim to authority. It set them apart from younger managers, who, while they might possess formal management training, had little practical experience of 'man management'. As Mr Baker put it, 'That's the best education I had. It gave me total realization of what command and responsibility and achievement was all about.' Beneath this view of military service as a form of management education lay a belief among the post-war generation men that they were superior *men* by virtue of their training. The physical hardships and discipline of the military had educated them in the cult of toughness. Masculinity was won through having been 'battered into a bureaucracy', having learnt 'what discipline meant'. Interviewees gave the appearance that military service revolved entirely around the masculine relations of command. Yet military service did not stand apart from the wider net of gender relations, despite the fact that the forces are often regarded as 'all-male' institutions. Men portrayed their experiences in the RAF, Navy, or Army in terms of contrasts with home life. Masculinity was sustained by ritual purgings of the 'feminine' parts of themselves.

Military service typically brought the first prolonged absence from home for all bar the public-school boarders.[18] Authors such as David Lodge have emphasized this way in which the physical separation might also force an emotional rift between relations with women and the new-found solidarities between men.[19] Military service—particularly the rigours of basic training—announced the successful achievement of manhood: there could be no going back to the comforts of home. In his history of national service, Trevor Royle describes basic training as a process of 'dislocation'.[20] Christine Williams makes a similar point in her study of women in the US marines. The *raison d'être* of basic training, she argues, is to 'separate masculinity from femininity'.[21] The rift between women and the masculine sphere of the services was more closely defined as between mothers and sons.[22] Basic training forced the replacement of maternal ties with camaraderie among men. In his memoirs of national service, the sociologist David Morgan recalls being told by the NCO at his first training session that 'The first thing is this; you won't have your mothers there.'[23] Middle-class men had similar memories. For them, too, it was the leaving behind of mothers that intensified the 'short, sharp shock' of basic training. But organization men concealed their feelings of loss, stressing instead the beneficial role which the services had played by forcing them to become independent.

For example, Mr Duncan paid tribute to the services for helping liberate him from a 'very close family'. Until entering the Army his escapades away from home had consisted of little more than prolonged sessions in the science laboratory. Army life was a rude awakening:

> DUNCAN. In many ways the army was very helpful to me, because otherwise I would have been very closeted in my outlook. [Pause.] I've always looked back on going into the army as very much part of my [pause] it built a lot of experience into me and made me much more able to stand on my own two feet.
>
> MSR. Was it a tough thing in a way?
>
> DUNCAN. Oh, the stories I tell! Going in for food for the first time, this was when I was a private. [Pause.] My mother was very hygienic. We weren't allowed to buy sweets in Woolworths because they were open and people coughed over them, and we'd be stricken with the most horrible diseases, you see. So that was absolutely forbidden. And everything was cleaned and polished goodness knows how many times. And I went in there and this chap dished up this cabbage on the plate in front of me, and it was swimming in water, and he just picked it up and squeezed it out, and then put it back on the plate and carried on . . .
>
> Well, 18 years old and never having seen that before, I was

absolutely appalled! I soon got all that knocked out of me. I had to sleep in some pretty awful places. In the end I think it helps to form you as a person.

Duncan's narrative involves two personas: boy–son and man–soldier. Reliving his feelings as a son, he describes the pollution of domestic routines in the army. The NAAFI was the antithesis of home in every respect. Duncan was deprived of the comforts of a clean, soft bed, and forced to sleep in 'awful places'. The domestic regime of obsessive cleanliness was dispensed with; men's hands replaced the polished cutlery of home. The once rigid boundaries between nourishment and dirt were transgressed. Duncan illustrates the point by comparing the trivial abuses noted by his mother, the display of unwrapped sweets, with the horrors of the NAAFI. The mother in Duncan recalls feeling assaulted by the brutality of the culture into which he was thrown headlong.[24] Speaking as an ex-soldier, Duncan makes his mother the butt of jokes. Her standards are ridiculous, her influence confining. Through a man's eyes he can see that it was essential that he have the mother-dependence 'knocked out' of him. Indeed, at this level the tales are a testament to his manhood. Duncan presents them in a before-and-after format, as evidence of just how competent he has become in the world of men. Today he stands solidly—thanks to the services—'on my own two feet'.

In the standard work on national service, *The Best Years of their Lives*, Trevor Royle illustrates these kinds of connections between leaving home and solidarity among men. Royle himself subscribes to the view that national service facilitated the healthy development of manhood. He remarks that, 'instead of having to conform to the demands of the family, men found themselves detached from the network of domestic relationships and the constraints of their teenage years'.[25] Echoing the sentiments of his interviewees, Royle is here articulating the cult of toughness. It is a view which holds that manhood is stifled by motherhood, and that military life was beneficial because it offered an escape from the 'constraints' imposed by women.[26]

The cult of toughness fostered by military service thus operated through the rejection of femininity and things domestic. However, relations *between* men in the services were described in terms of similarly stark contrasts between 'masculine' and 'feminine' qualities. Divisions between officers and men, for example, might also be understood in terms of sexual difference; for example, between the 'hard' attributes needed for successful leadership and the weaknesses shown by lesser men. This was particularly apparent in the accounts of working-class men who had served in the war. For them, a 'good war' had often resulted in a commission, so marking a turning-point in career terms.[27] Mr Dowell, the son of a mechanical engineer, explained that he had benefited because the pressures of war meant that the services had 'put responsibility on to people'. He felt unable to communicate to me just how exciting his time in the navy had been. Superlatives rolled off his tongue; 'It was super . . . a tremendous period . . . a super time . . . I remember it with great affection . . . a tremendous experience.' Similarly, in Mr Greenwood's tales about his first assignment as an officer, the theme of mobility through the discovery of leadership skills is uppermost. A child of lower-middle-class parents who had struggled to put him through grammar school, Greenwood revelled in his new-found powers. Twice in the interview he told a story about being 'given as a young officer, three or four hundred square miles of territory and that was mine. I ran the law, I ran the mail, fed everybody, kept the transport going, the lot.'

Anxiety frequently stirred beneath this release of ambition, however. Where middle-class men emphasized the necessity to survive without domestic comforts, ex-working-class managers hinted at their fears of failure. They were not accustomed to the conventions of the commissioned ranks, and felt their social inferiority most keenly. They were fearful of 'slipping back' to the non-commissioned ranks, yet any expression of apprehension in their new role was inadmissible.[28] One of the first lessons which Mr Wright learnt on becoming an officer was that he must never show fear. It was a lesson which he has carried through to management:

> I suppose to some extent this stemmed from the war. When you're the leader, boss, manager, call it what you will, there's one most important thing. Never let the blokes below you see that you're bothered. They are looking to you to set an example. And if you ever give them the impression that you're worried, or you don't know what to do, then, of course, it's like a disease. If you're going to keep up the morale of a bunch of people, then you've got to keep your own morale up. Even if it's a bit superficial.
>
> If you're in an aircraft and things start going wrong, then you mustn't panic. You mustn't let other people see that you're panicking. If you're in an industrial situation and there's threats of strikes and things, you

mustn't let the people below you ever get any idea that you feel you can't cope.

Wright's working-class background makes him particularly aware of social hierarchies in the services. His mental world remains split in two: the leaders and the led, exemplars and followers, those on top and those 'below'. Like other men of his background, Wright learnt in war that he must suppress fear. Leaders must demonstrate a solid, unyielding masculinity to those below. Even today, this lesson maintains its ability to haunt Wright. Worry is more than just worry; among weaker men it becomes 'like a disease'. Wright deals with his feelings of weakness by repressing them, acting confident. He stresses the importance of 'impression' and the need to avoid letting men in the ranks 'see' how he felt. Behind the 'superficial' façade of confidence, Wright's own feelings of panic threaten, like a 'disease', to make him succumb.

Similar confusion between the enhancement and the negation of masculinity surrounds the overall distinction between a 'good war' and a 'bad' one. The excitement of a good war arose from being in the 'real thing', but not too close. As one man explained, a 'good war' was one where a man had neither 'fired a shot in anger or got fired upon'.[29] It involved camaraderie and the excitement of leadership but not physical danger: 'all the fun and glory, but none of the action . . .' All the ex-servicemen in this study described a 'good war', except Mr Jones, who had been a prisoner of war in a Japanese prison camp. As a colleague remarked, Jones 'had a bad one'. Paul Fussell has observed that war poets like Robert Graves or Siegfried Sassoon felt an immense gulf separated them from soldiers who had not seen action.[30] Jones seems to have felt a similar sense of alienation from fellow managers who had a 'good war'. They were able to draw on their military training in later life, but Jones could not. A bad war made it difficult to sustain the distinction between play and bloodshed, bringing an ongoing mental struggle by its victims to distance the violent past. Jones's only direct reference to the war bears witness to a sense of disablement in a work culture which exploits the language of combat: 'When I hear people say "I like a good fight", I often want to say "have you ever really been in one? Because I was, and believe me . . ." I mean, I had about three weeks in Sumatra in the war, and we were fighting, and no thank you.'

The notion of management as combat persists today, despite the ending of national service. For example, it is incorporated in the language surrounding take-overs, which are often described as 'battles' led by 'corporate raiders' in which 'defence strategies' must be formulated. So, too, the links between management and military training persist in things like outward-bound or 'management-by-combat' courses. The recruits on such courses plan sorties instead of corporate raids, and use dye pellets rather than financial cunning as their ammunition. The underlying philosophy is that business, like war, involves a combination of 'strategy, organisation, and leadership skills'.[31] Such schools perpetuate the potent cultural associations between masculinity, combat, and management. The courses mimic a 'good war', providing all the perceived benefits of physical challenge, discipline, and the exercise of authority, but without the danger. The kind of training which is offered to the up-and-coming generation of managers simulates the compulsory passage to manhood of their fathers.

iii. Early Career and the Cult of Toughness

Early career brought different dilemmas for working-class and middle-class men attempting to hold their own amidst the macho culture of manufacturing industry. The prevailing ethos was that managerial credibility could only follow from mechanical aptitude and 'hands-on' production experience. This is what the Thorn/EMI manager meant by the remark quoted in the epigraph to this chapter that, 'if you weren't running around hitting bits of iron with hammers or wielding a spanner, then you weren't a man'.[32] In one sense this worked in favour of the working-class men. They had the advantage of familiarity with the rough and tumble, joking and taunting, through which masculinity was asserted. At the same time, reflecting the problems of working-class men who rose from the ranks in military service, they lacked confidence as leaders. Graduates assumed that they would wield authority, but felt easily undermined. Lack of shop-floor experience made them nervous in their dealings with men on the shop-floor. So, while the graduate managers feared rebellions from below, it was the threat from above which technically trained managers had to overcome. Both groups felt a certain weakness in their position in a culture where class and gender hierarchies pulled in opposite directions.

Five men in my sample entered management from semi-skilled or skilled jobs, most on the basis of engineering qualifications. They had struggled to rise above the camaraderie of the shop-floor, and prove their abilities in management. Having achieved that, they felt they now possessed a potent combination of practical experience and leadership. In his interview, Mr Tinsley emphasized just how extensive was his armoury of managerial skills. He possessed the intellectual arts of the middle-class man *and* 'six years dirty-hands experience' in a steel factory:

TINSLEY. I'd worked on the machinery; I'd taken it apart, I'd repaired it, I'd put it together again. I'd worked with all sorts of men: fitters, toolmakers, electricians. I'd literally swept up the shop-floor as a youth, I'd made the tea. I'd done all the things you have to do in a factory. And the value I place on that is at least as great as the value I place on the study I was doing.

MSR. Why was that important?

TINSLEY. Basically because it gave me an understanding of what goes on in a business at every level. When you're an apprentice you have no status. People expect you to move around from one department to another. And each department was different in some way. It was a reflection of whoever was the foreman or superintendent of that department.

I suppose it was then that I first developed some interest in the way organizations tick, and the ways in which people react. Years later I studied that as part of a postgraduate study . . . in the field of psychology and organization study, which was the theoretical aspect of it. In my view, there is no substitute for having got your hands dirty yourself, and having used tools and machinery and equipment, and having rubbed shoulders with people who are still doing that. . . . It means that now, in my present field, I feel as much at home talking to the chairman or managing director, or in my present role, to the VC of a university . . . I feel as at home talking to them as I do to the cleaners or the porters, or the technicians or the mechanics or the gate men.

In this passage Tinsley demonstrates his repertoire of personal and management qualities. He turns his humble beginnings to advantage by stressing his credentials as a practical man. His narrative presents a contrast to the middle-class Mr Duncan, who recalled the horror of seeing dirty hands in the NAAFI. Here Tinsley extols the manly virtue of getting 'your hands dirty yourself'. In so doing he turns his socially inferior background into a qualification for management. At the same time he is anxious to demonstrate that he can hold his own

118

with middle-class academic men, the vice-chancellors of this world. Tinsley attempts to resolve the tension between class and masculine status, between academic and practical skill, by claiming all-round competence. He is equally 'at home' exhibiting his theoretical knowledge of organizations in the boardroom, or his 'hard' masculinity to men on the factory floor.

While Tinsley here perpetrates the myth of an easy crossing from manual to managerial work, this process was not without its difficulties. Like the other skilled men in the sample, he had worked hard at self-improvement.[33] Conspiring against his efforts was an ingrained feeling that his superiors in the workplace were somehow naturally more intelligent. His mental image of a hierarchy in which authority lay with the gentlemen proved difficult to erase. He was easily 'overawed by them': 'To talk to a managing director meant that you stood to attention and you had to be very respectful.' A similar timidity had dogged Mr Grainger in his attempts to gain a commission in the army, and later to break into senior management: 'It took me a long time to sort of build up confidence and go for the bigger jobs. . . . From the positions that I had at one time, I really could have got managing director of any company, but there was this lack of confidence that was deep in there. You'd think "that's a hell of a job, managing director. I could never aspire to that."' Grainger attempted to move from production management to consultancy, but felt uncomfortable in this role and has once again become a production manager. In his present job he spends most of his time on the factory floor with the production engineers. His office was a cubicle in one corner of the plant, amidst the din of the process machinery. His desk was cluttered with electronic equipment, new and in need of repair, and our interview was constantly interrupted by younger engineers wanting advice.[34] In this environment Grainger, although a manager, is not required to take on the garb of the gentleman. In the production function, class divisions are over-ridden by the shared enjoyment of things technical. As he explained, 'As far as I'm concerned we're all manufacturing blokes.'

The class-based dichotomy between 'hard' experience and 'soft' academic knowledge created the opposite problem for the graduate management trainees. They also had to become familiar with the production process, although they were assisted in their passage by formal mechanisms. The Cook's tour was the principal means through which graduates were introduced to production.[35] In some

119

respects it replicated an apprenticeship. Trainees would begin in a menial job and after six weeks or so might take on the role of foreman in that division.[36] They were sometimes allocated to shift work or put on call to the plant. Middle- and upper-middle-class recruits regarded the Cook's tour in much the same light as they had their schooling or national service. It prepared them for leadership by subjecting them to discipline and making them fight their way—albeit in protected conditions—from the bottom up. As Mr Bannerman explained, the Cook's tour 'made no concessions to your ultimate status'.

Just as basic training enforced the close quartering of future officers with their inferiors, graduates 'rubbed shoulders' with workers while on their Cook's tour. They felt that it had helped them to establish their 'ultimate status' as managers. 'Hands-on' experience reduced the dangers of being duped by production workers. Mr Sorrell's period as a trainee at the Turner Motor Works had alerted him to the fact that they 'would try it on, a young personnel officer still training . . . So you had to be reasonably tough and recognize that you were part of management and that your loyalties lay primarily with the management objective.' The inheritor Mr Briar recalled a similar outcome from his Cook's tour. Through it he gained an understanding of the production process and learnt not to be manipulated by men on the shop-floor. As he explained, 'You had to know something about all the departments and what they were doing, and know enough not to be bamboozled. The foreman could say, "Well, I don't think we can do this", and you had to be able to say, "I think we probably can."'[37] The Cook's tour introduced graduates to the cult of toughness. Middle-class men felt that it had boosted their stature among men on the shop-floor. At the same time, they never felt entirely confident that they could resist if the production workers did 'try it on'.

iv. Mid-Career Contests

After the Cook's tour there generally followed a period where graduates would 'prove themselves' in specialist functions—perhaps research and development, production engineering, finance, personnel, or sales. Mid-career frequently brought a move across to general management. Studies of career mobility have pointed out that these transitions from specialist functions to general management are

What have you got to lose if you choose the wrong computer?

In business today, the effectiveness of accounting and management information, of stock and production control and even of cash flow, can all depend on the right choice of computer system. An unwise choice may not only be an embarrassment, but could put your company's administrative and information systems on a disaster course. TSB Computer Services has developed techniques which put the process of selection on to an objective basis. "Computer Choice" is a comprehensive guide with detailed check lists and evaluation profiles for the selection of large systems, micro-computers, data communications equipment, terminals and supporting services. It describes in plain English, how the techniques can be used to ensure that technical requirements and economic constraints are fully met. "Computer Choice" can save you time and money, more importantly, it can assist you to make that major decision without the risk of embarrassment.

For further details of "Computer Choice" and our supporting services just clip this coupon to your letterhead and mail by Freepost to Manager, Consultancy Division, TSB Computer Services Limited. FREEPOST, Wythenshawe, Manchester M22 7QE.

Name _____

Position _____
No Stamp Needed.

T S B TSB Computer Services Limited

---

5 *'What have you got to lose if you choose the wrong computer?'*
This advertisement plays upon the theme of failure as sexual humiliation. Its caption makes explicit the sub-text of castration. *The Director, Dec. 1980*

more typical for men than for women.[38] The men I interviewed often described them in gendered terms, as rites of passage in which the solidarities between men of equal rank gave way to competition. Their memories crystallized around 'critical posts' which they felt had been specifically designed to test their toughness. Managers working in staff functions might be assigned to line jobs, so utilizing the 'man-management' skills which they had learnt in military service or the Cook's tour. Those in head-office jobs might be asked to take on difficult assignments 'outside', in one of the company's divisions. During the take-over boom of the 1960s, for example, some were promoted to the boards of newly acquired firms. Images of toughness entered the men's stories of mid-career in a variety of ways. First, both relations with male shop-floor workers and between managers might be represented through battle metaphors. Shop-floor conspiracies threatened to wreck the hopes of an ambitious manager, but so might a tussle with a fellow manager. Secondly, these challenges were often not of the manager's own making, but might be plotted by an 'older man' in his attempt to test the courage of a protégé. Thirdly, the outcome of the battle was decisive. There was only ever one victor. While the successful challenger went on to senior management, losers described being 'stuck' thereafter. Finally, the distinction between victors and vanquished had a sexual dimension. The successful completion of a critical post was seen as proof of manly virility, while managers who were shunted off into 'soft' jobs such as personnel experienced this as a kind of castration.

Many of these features are illustrated in the career narrative of Mr Stewart, the deputy-chairman of Chemtex whom I introduced in the previous chapter. He recalled two critical postings in his late thirties, both in newly acquired companies with 'powerful cultures of their own'. The moves were suggested to him by his mentor Ron Meadows, who wanted him to leave his post as head of R&D and prove that he could succeed as a commercial manager. Stewart was offered the choice between a staff post in the commercial department of the head office, and a general management job in Lancashire. Acknowledging the rules governing such appointments, he opted for the more difficult job: 'I wanted to be where the action was.' He had felt the need to prove he could operate away from head office, without protection from the older man, in an atmosphere where 'nobody wanted me'. After a harrowing six months, Stewart explained, he managed to subdue the recalcitrant managers. Typical of such confrontations, his was a narrow escape: 'They very nearly got rid of me, but not quite.' Stewart's second post again shows the role of the older man in setting the parameters of battle. Lord Meadows had appointed Stewart chairman of Northern Textiles, and Stewart, in his naivety, thought, 'I was a hell of a fella, being asked to take this on—for about two days—and then I realized that it was in such a bad state that they'd said to themselves, "Well he can't make it any worse, and he might just conceivably do something to it, and he'll learn. He'll sink or swim."' Stewart once again emerged victorious, managing within twelve months to turn the company around. Stewart's descriptions illustrate how dangerous the period of mid-career is felt to be. The world he describes is polarized between survivors and failures (those who 'sink' or are got 'rid of').

While critical posts involving other managers are often represented in terms of a struggle staged for the benefit of influential older men, the fantasized audience in confrontations with manual workers is the shop-floor in general. Both kinds of battles involve stark contrasts between victory and humiliation. In the mythology of challenges from below, agitators plot to cut the boss down, while the manager aims to defeat them and so win popular support. Authority is secured by 'keeping your ear to the ground' for stirrers, and by a willingness to fight them. Working men 'can smell fear', Mr Wright explained. His time in the RAF had taught him that 'they will only respect someone who treats them firmly and who won't be pushed around.'

In recollections of this kind the subordinate presents a challenge, and dramatic action centres on how effectively the manager deals with it. For example, in the previous chapter we saw how the workers staged an elaborate initiation ceremony for Mr Grainger when he became production manager at Winwood. On their weekend trip he at first meekly endured 'the tricks they played', securing their admiration only when he beat the previous boss in a drinking match. Mr Wright's narrative of his experience as general manager of an Australian oil refinery exhibits similar features. He perceived that, in Australia, 'the philosophy is that "Jack's as good as his master"', and that consent to his authority would only follow once he had demonstrated 'how you shape up as a man'. Wright was careful to avoid the stereotype of the English gentleman, whose authority rests solely on his formal status. For example, he ordered that the sticker on his hard hat reading 'General Manager' was replaced by one which said simply 'Fred Wright'. Soon after arriving at the new job his manhood was put to test:

> You know you used to have what they call smokoes in Australia . . . concerts, you know, with beer and prawns and goodness knows what. And the blokes had one of those and I was invited. And, of course, it was really to have a look at the new boss and see what they can make of him. And during the course of the evening, the group sat around drinking beer, and the evening had gone on and the beer had gone on, and one of them started to belly-ache about Cowes refinery and how lousy it was to work there, so on and so forth, and said he'd previously worked for LCI at Botany Bay. And he ranted on, and everybody was watching me to see what the reaction was.
>
> And when he drew breath at one stage, I said to him, 'I know what I would do if I were you.' He said, 'What's that?' I said, 'I'd f—— off back to LCI.' That was the end of the conversation, and I didn't know until later on that that stood me in great stead because it had shown these blokes that I wasn't just going to sit back and be yelled at and belly-ached at by people like that. Two simple things. So yes, I loved it.

The narrative mode which Wright employs here is of the street fight. The stooge baits the outsider in the lead up, egged on by the pack. Wright realizes that it is a set-up but determines that he must roll up his sleeves and enter the fray. Demonstrating immaculate timing, he waits until his opponent 'drew breath' in between jabs, to land that one decisive blow. In the metaphor of the street fight there is perhaps also a trace of adolescent, dressing-room sadism. The new boy is taunted about his manhood as a way of getting him to prove himself. Wright obliges, stripping off so that the men could 'have a look at the new boss and see what they can make of him'; whether or not he did 'shape up as a man'. At the same time there is a covertly threatening element to their demands. Wright sees that he is in danger of a kind of violation. He refuses to 'sit back' and submit, ordering his assailant to 'f—— off'. His victory over the stirrer opened the way for a gentler affection to develop between Wright and the shop-floor workers. They gradually adopted first name terms and his potency was recognized without him having to 'underline it' with labels or heroic feats.

In the passage above, Wright expresses a commonly felt ambivalence about the critical posting. Initial fear of exposure gives way to satisfaction at surviving with enhanced manhood. Like the trysts in early career between older and younger men, virility is at stake in mid-career clashes with the shop-floor or rival managers. Cynthia

Cockburn has commented that, for male print workers, 'it matters crucially that their masculinity, as they have defined it themselves, is never in doubt. It is often felt to be challenged, and it is just as often reasserted.'[39] Exactly the same can be said of management. In the management culture typical of established industries, career success depends on the ability to survive these challenges to masculinity. The oppressiveness of this regime was revealed by those deemed to have failed their critical posting. They spent much of the interview coming to terms with that supposed failure. They puzzled over what they had done wrong, and tried to salvage a semblance of personal pride from occupations in which recognition had not been forthcoming. Underneath there was a nagging feeling that they possessed fundamental personal 'weaknesses'. Mr Dolan blamed his recent lack of promotion on the fact that he did not enjoy conflict. In order to reach board level a manager had to be 'prepared to make himself unpopular; throw his weight around'. Dolan realized the idiocy of a system which had elevated the refusal of co-operation into a managerial art. Yet he ultimately felt that his lack of mobility had been 'my fault'. A man must either 'impose' himself on colleagues or become invisible. There was no middle ground between survival and annihilation, masculinity and effeminacy.

Men who were pushed aside after their critical posting faced further threats to their masculinity. The usual correlations between age, gender, and managerial status were overturned. They might eventually find themselves being managed by younger staff, or assigned to staff jobs usually reserved for women or men in late career.[40] Mr Jones had been 'someone who might go places' at Swan Oil until he had a nervous breakdown in his mid-thirties. Instead of going on to a middle-management post in an oil refinery, he was given a post in personnel, where he stayed for the remainder of his career. When he first began in personnel, the contrast between his previous image as a bright young man and the aura surrounding the job had seemed particularly demoralizing. The industrial sociologist Joan Woodward has pointed out that, in the post-war period, the post of personnel officer was often considered a 'sinecure . . . for misfits who had been unable to hold down their jobs but who, for one reason or another, could neither be discharged nor demoted'.[41] Jones depicted the archetypal personnel officer in a similar light, as 'old-man-recruiting person who sort of drifted around interviewing people'. He was a young man consigned to an 'old, out-to-grass job'.

Even within personnel, the cult of toughness seemed to haunt Mr Jones, discouraging him from further career mobility despite the fact that he was seen as a 'fairly bright person'. While he felt confident in matters of staff and training, the sphere of industrial relations held out the only real promise for promotion. In the early 1960s he considered taking up a post as staff manager of Swan Oil, and becoming deputy to the personnel director:

> But in that whole situation I was conscious that I would never be comfortable in the real bang of industrial relations. In 1960 things were beginning to look unpleasant, and this sort of conflict stuff was going on. I never had any stomach for it at all. I think possibly I would have gone into his job even, if I'd been able to hold my own in the industrial relations area. And I knew I couldn't.
>
> It never actually arose. I was never actually interviewed as it were, for the job, I think it began to be felt that I was not going to be the person to take his job. So I was limited to the slightly calmer waters of staff deployment, staff management. There was a certain element of employee relations in it, of course. But not the real hard stuff, the union stuff.

Jones intimates that even jobs within one management function can be graded according to how 'hard' they are. In his mind's eye, personnel is split into the 'real bang' of confrontation between men and the 'calmer waters' of looking after staff. The divide between the two cannot easily be crossed. Jones shows yet again the scars which such divisions may inflict. He possesses an avid desire to escape from his present post—cosy as it is—yet the memory of sickness ('never had any stomach') prevents him. Ironically, Jones feels that his physical health is maintained at the expense of his masculinity. It is the 'hard stuff' that he lusts after; just being 'comfortable' is only a kind of half-existence.[42] Jones has conflicting feelings about the personnel function. On the one hand, he is a fervent supporter of it and claims for himself a part in shepherding it from its 'embryonic stages' in the 1950s to its role today as a fully fledged management function. Moreover, he applauds the subsiding grip of the 'hierarchical-minded, authoritarian manager' over the shop-floor, and his replacement by managers versed in the art of persuasion. On the other hand, he continues to wish that had he shown greater skill in the masculine art of confrontation. He has internalized the gender hierarchy which designated him as inferior.[43]

Mr Jones's story points to a contrary pull between the normative ideas about masculinity that are institutionalized in the management culture of manufacturing industries, and men's subjective identities. 'Losers' were caught between a continued desire to prove their masculinity through 'hard' work, and a realization that the cult itself was not actually productive. At the end of my interview with Mr Jones, he passed on a final comment which lingers in my memory as a testament to this conflict. He suggested that I would be an obvious candidate for a job in personnel, given my interview skills and training as an arts graduate. Jones advised that, if I chose this course, then I should steer clear of staff functions like recruitment or training, and pursue a career in industrial relations, for it was a field with far better prospects. I was struck by his selfless desire for me to succeed. His advice was a gift whose value lay in its admission of personal failure amidst the cult of toughness. Jones was counselling me to avoid the kind of career which he had been 'limited' to, and the model of manhood attached to it. Instead I must take on the rough and tumble of man-to-man confrontation, 'the hard stuff, the union stuff'.

The cult of toughness plays its role in the sex-typing of manufacturing as masculine, as does the mentoring system discussed in Chapter 3, and the process of technical innovation discussed in Chapter 5. The cult is part of the complex of mechanisms that help sustain men's pre-eminence in manufacturing. As Jones perceives above, the jobs which offer the greatest opportunities are frequently designated the most masculine. Aggression, ruthlessness, and an instrumental attitude are valued as the qualities most suitable for senior management. The cult of toughness extends across organizational hierarchies and individual men's gender identities. It is lived out, not only in fantasy, or in the heroic language with which men describe their careers, but also in their physical actions and decisions about matters like promotion.

While recognizing the sometimes unshakeable character of this alliance between the cult of toughness and the management culture in established industries, it is also important to reveal its contradictions. Organization men help perpetrate the cult of toughness, but it acts on them in ways that they cannot control. The life stories of the men of this generation reveal their ambivalence about the cult. They fought an inner battle to distance their work from anything considered soft or feminine, but were rarely successful. For a start, the management and gender hierarchies conflicted. Ex-working-class men revelled in the cult of toughness, but were not given the same opportunities as graduates. Middle-class men strove—even in their interviews with me—to demonstrate that they had got 'dirty hands'. Yet their very bravado illustrated the anxiety which they felt about whether or not they measured up. Thus a public-school man confessed that he had felt 'at a certain disadvantage' in the motor-vehicle industry, 'rubbing shoulders' with aggressive ex-engineers.

As Chapter 5 explains, the cult of toughness needs to be viewed in the context of generational change. Male managers of this generation, whatever their social background, today speak as one when stressing the significance of practical experience. This reflects the threat which they feel from the younger generation of formally trained managers. Organization men are still inclined to dismiss business-school graduates as mere 'long-haired intellectuals', who possess plenty of 'new-found techniques and tools', but lack the 'practical grasp' born of military service and a lifetime's industrial experience. The older manufacturing man may no longer have the upper hand in matters of company strategy, but he certainly prizes his superior toughness.

NOTES

1. Quoted in C. Baden-Fuller and C. Hampden-Turner, *Strategic Choice and the Management of Dilemma: Lessons from the Domestic Appliance Industry* (Centre for Business Strategy Working Paper, no. 51; May 1988, 17.
2. R. Crompton and K. Sanderson, *Gendered Jobs and Social Change* (London, 1990), 165.
3. Figures quoted by V. Beechey, 'Women and Employment in Contemporary Britain', in V. Beechey and E. Whitelegg (eds.), *Women in Britain Today* (Milton Keynes, 1986), 84.
4. P. Willis, 'Shop-Floor Culture, Masculinity and the Wage Form', in J. Clarke, C. Critcher, and R. Johnson (eds.), *Working-Class Culture: Studies in History and Theory* (London, 1979), 185–201. Similar ideas are taken up by D. L. Collinson (see 'Engineering Humour: Masculinity, Joking and Conflict in Shop-Floor Relations', *Organization Studies*, 9/2 (1988), 181–99).
5. Willis ultimately sees the 'masculine mystique' as a hindrance to effective collective action: the enemy remains the machine itself rather than the system which powers it. The element of heroism surrounding work sometimes prevents collective issues of safety and comfort, or control and ownership, being disputed. Instead, conflict with management is siphoned off into disputes about 'hard cash', part of a wider fetishizing of the wage packet ('Shop-Floor Culture', 196–7).
6. Ibid. 190.
7. C. Cockburn, *Brothers: Male Dominance and Technological Change* (London, 1983), esp. ch. 5, 'A Man among Men', 123–50.

8. Willis, 'Shop-Floor Culture', 193.
9. D. L. Collinson and M. Collinson, 'Sexuality in the Workplace: The Domination of Men's Sexuality', in J. Hearn, D. L. Sheppard, P. Tancred-Sheriff, and G. Burrell (eds.), *The Sexuality of Organization* (London, 1989), 97.
10. C. Cockburn, *Machinery of Dominance: Women, Men, and Technical Know-how* (London, 1985), 194.
11. L. Segal, *Slow Motion: Changing Men, Changing Masculinities* (London, 1990), 114.
12. See Ch. 7, where this issue is explored in the men's depictions of women managers.
13. R. W. Connell, *Gender and Power: Society, the Person and Sexual Politics* (Cambridge, 1987), 85.
14. Ibid. 85.
15. R. Scase and R. Goffee point out that this dilemma faces many entrepreneurs; like Johnson they are unwilling to relinquish control, which in turn limits possibilities for expansion (*The Real World of the Small Business Owner* (London, 1980), esp. 55–64).
16. T. Royle, *The Best Years of their Lives: The National Service Experience, 1945–63* (London, 1988), 35.
17. J. Fidler, *The British Business Élite: Its Attitudes to Class, Status and Power* (London, 1981), 98.
18. Ex-public-school boys were advantaged not simply because of their greater familiarity with military culture, but because (for the boarders at least) they were already inured to life away from home. As Mr Briar observed, having spent his youth in an all-male institution he was well prepared for the rough and tumble of the services:

    A lot of my fellows in the army had never left home for a night so they, poor things, felt pretty lost to start with. That aspect didn't worry me at all. I was used to living in a barrack room with fifty other people, some of whom were pleasant and some [of whom] had very unpleasant habits. Well that's sort of like a public school too.

19. See, e.g., D. Lodge's descriptions of weekend leave, where Jonathan Browne discovers that home no longer provides solace (*Ginger, You're Barmy* (Harmondsworth, 1982), 124). See also the account by David Morgan, who remarks that men from boarding schools had the edge over others because of their familiarity with the hardships of basic training; for men such as himself, however, national service marked the 'first prolonged period away from home' ('*It Will Make a Man of You': Notes on National Service, Masculinity and Autobiography* (*Studies in Sexual Politics*, 17; University of Manchester, Sociology Dept., 1987), 42).
20. Royle is profoundly ambivalent about the army's tactics of toughening men through 'dislocation'. He admits frequent cruelty by NCOs during basic training, but is unsympathetic to the plight of grammar-school boys who had led 'sheltered lives'. Royle thus mimics the cult of toughness:

    It was not uncommon for a hard-bitten lad, who had worked previously in a factory or on a building site, to be astonished by the sight of his

129

grammar-school educated neighbour weeping silently in his bed at night—a classic image of social collision between the stoicism of the working-class labourer and the inadequacy of the middle-class pen pusher. (*Best Years*, 47)

21. C. L. Williams, *Gender Differences at Work: Women and Men in Nontraditional Occupations* (Berkeley, Calif., 1989), 66–7.
22. See L. Segal, 'Look Back in Anger: Men in the 50s', in R. Chapman and J. Rutherford (eds.), *Male Order: Unwrapping Masculinity* (London, 1988), 76–80.
23. Morgan, *It Will Make a Man of You*, 50.
24. Other middle-class men recall a similar sense of shock at the habits of other men. In B. S. Johnson, *All Bull: The National Servicemen* (London, 1973), Jeff Nuttall recalls that his 'middle class fastidiousness' was 'shattered' by sharing barracks with working-class men (p. 24).
25. Royle, *Best Years*, 129.
26. Lodge depicts just this view. His novel ends with its protagonist, Jonathan Browne, becoming 'shackled' to a woman whom he does not love, but whom he has made pregnant; Browne's emotional life is reserved instead for his best mate (*Ginger, You're Barmy*, esp. 210).
27. In their 1971 study of directors, M. Young and P. Wilmott remark that a 'good war' often marked a turning-point in the career mobility of working-class men (*The Symmetrical Family: A Study of Work and Leisure in the London Region* (London, 1973), 239). Fidler also found that the ex-working- and lower-middle-class directors in his survey—particularly those who had been commissioned—emphasized the role of military service in leadership training (*British Business Élite*, 98).
28. Royle points this out (*Best Years*, 101–9), as does Lodge through his depiction of the grammar-school-educated officer, Gordon Kemp; Kemp lives in fear that 'I'll probably be thrown out of Mons', and is eventually pensioned out after taking an overdose of sleeping pills (*Ginger, You're Barmy*, 77–8, 172).
29. Similarly, Dowell explained proudly that 'I never heard a shot fired in anger'.
30. P. Fussell, *The Great War and Modern Memory* (Oxford, 1978), 75–113.
31. 'Management by Combat', *Director* (Sept. 1987), 110–11.
32. Baden-Fuller and Hampden-Turner, *Strategic Choice*, 17.
33. Mr Tinsley learnt the conventions of management in his late twenties, from a postgraduate course in Production Engineering and subsequently at the local branch of the Production Engineering Institute. There he met 'a lot of young chaps of my own age, with similar ambitions'. The procedures of the Institute replicated those of management: 'We had committee meetings once a month, we had lecture meetings once a month, we had works visits and all sorts of exciting things. You had to get up at meetings and propose votes of thanks. . . . You got given various jobs; I think I was publicity secretary and had to write a monthly newsletter.' Through activities like these Tinsley established networks with other working-class engineers, and together they rehearsed their management skills. Where he depicted himself in early career as a manual worker, his narrative of the late twenties centred on the task of learning to 'get up' and instruct men like this.
34. Grainger revealed his fondness for the production machinery at Winwood on

a guided tour where he explained the function, age, capabilities, and manufacturer of each piece of plant.

35. The Cook's tour is named after the nineteenth-century British travel agent Thomas Cook. Its function was to provide graduate trainees with a running knowledge of the company's products and its various divisions, so enabling them to pursue a career in the area which suited them best. Because life service was envisaged, it was extensive, lasting from a year to two years.

36. For example, the graduate Mr Bannerman began his career at United Steel in the tube mill as a member of a mill gang. Mr Jones and Mr Duncan both began as foremen, doing shift work at Swan Oil, while Mr Briar acted as charge hand in the family firm.

37. As with his period in the ranks during the war, the upper-class manager Mr Briar explained that one of the benefits of his Cook's tour was that it had placed him in close proximity to working-class men. There was a sense of amazement about this crossing of class boundaries, as Briar revealed in the comment that 'one had six weeks with . . . an actual living shift manager, following him around, and then took over'.

38. In their study of BIM members, N. Nicholson and M. West found that, among male senior managers (BIM Fellows), 21% were functional specialists while 79% were general managers; of the women 'Fellows', 44% were functional specialists and 55% were general managers (*Managerial Job Change: Men and Women in Transition* (Cambridge, 1988), 104, table 9.7).

39. Cockburn, *Brothers*, 137.

40. C. Sofer points out that older men managed by younger men find the situation 'embarrassing and discomfiting' (*Men in Mid-Career: A Study of British Managers and Technical Specialists* (Cambridge, 1970), 55).

41. J. Woodward, *Industrial Organisation: Theory and Practice*, 2nd edn. (Oxford, 1980), 22. Woodward claims that 10 of 59 firms in her sample had personnel departments which had originated in this fashion.

42. Mr Sorrell's story of his career in the motor-vehicle industry shows very similar features. Both men failed to cross the staff–line divide in their mid-career posting, with consequences which lasted until their retirement. Sorrell had been 'pushed out' from head office to an industrial-relations post in a manufacturing division, where 'they resented me . . . because I was a Turner man'. His failure was followed by a kind of 'demotion' to graduate recruitment. As Sorrell remarked wistfully of the incident, 'I plateaued out at that age.'

43. Voicing similar discontents, Mr Sorrell explained that the problem lay in the history of personnel itself, and the fact that it had become increasingly 'female dominated'. Instead of criticizing company cultures in which line and staff jobs are designed as 'masculine' and 'feminine', he blamed his marginality partly on women.

5

'Yesterday's Model': Product Fetishism and the Cult of the Producer

My son likes the same sorts of things. He likes the practical things. He likes to do things where you see the achievement at the end of the day. It's what I call jobs in the company. When you design something, it's got to have *man appeal* to the person who's going to install it. Because, if he enjoys doing it, he'll make a damn good job of it. Anybody will if they can say, 'God, I've done all that today.' They feel good about it, don't they?

Mr Baker, contracts director, Jennings Windows

In the early stages of this project I often emerged from interviews with organization men feeling slightly disappointed about the way the sessions had gone. I was interested in what their work memories told me about their present identities as men. Yet I sometimes ended up with a clearer picture of the technology surrounding managers than of the men themselves. I soon realized that the problem lay in my view of life history, and the kind of empathy necessary for a successful interview. I was looking for clues about the men's emotional relations with family or colleagues, and disregarding their enthusiastic descriptions of the physical objects which they dealt with in their work. They, however, did not distinguish clearly between things and emotions. They used products as prompts through which to convey their life histories. Rather than steering them away from stories about products, I began instead to explore why products assumed such

132

importance. By explaining the background and technical features of the goods under their control, organization men established confidence in me as an interviewer. The empathy between me and them was thus often based on objects—perhaps timing belts for car engines, landing gear for aircraft, welding equipment, or, in the case of production managers, process machinery. Reminiscences about products brought them to life, posing questions about the wider relationships between masculinity and things 'man-made'.[1]

Once I had begun to think of the interview as an event as well as a testimony, visual and aural, products became significant in two ways. They seemed to act as landmarks in memory, orientating managers in relation to their career history. Post-war boom, take-overs during the 1960s, and recession in the early 1980s, were recalled in the context of how they affected the technical characteristics and quality of products. Products—and the technology which gave shape to them— also anchored friendships between men. As Judy Wajcman asserts. 'It is evident that men identify with technology and through their identification with technology men form bonds with one another.'[2] Products were a major talking point in my interviews, and a focal point of relations between organization men. They were mediums of social as well as economic exchange.

This connection between the private and public functions of production has long been recognized. For example, the satisfaction of individual pleasures was central to Karl Marx's conception of production as 'human beings'.[3] An economy which allowed the free play of human production, he argued, would empower 'men' in two ways. Its products would enable them to realize 'the individual pleasure of knowing my personality to be objective, visible to the senses and hence a power beyond all doubt'. Furthermore, the knowledge of having provided a useful product would unite men. In such a world, Marx felt, 'our products would be so many mirrors in which we saw reflected our essential nature'.[4] Marx generally intended the word 'man' to cover both sexes, but at points in his writings it is clear that his image is of a male worker. Products were 'mirrors' which reflected most of all on *men's* 'essential nature'.[5] Elsewhere he refers directly to the way in which capitalist production undermines masculinity. Marx thinks of alienation—the separation of workers from the fruits of their production—as a state in which 'begetting' becomes 'emasculating'.[6]

This chapter explores the idea of products as the outcome of 'begetting' between organization men. It illustrates the connections between men's overall monopoly of the creative aspects of product design and manufacture, and the kinds of fantasies which they invest in that work. Feminist researchers have pointed to the ways in which, by eroticizing technology, male engineers and scientists seek to confirm their masculinity.[7] In his comments cited in the epigraph above, the organization man Mr Baker alludes to the fantasy life which products are endowed with. For him, as for many of my interviewees, good products lie at the very heart of industrial endeavour. He intimates a kind of romance in which the bond between father and son rests on their shared quest for a perfect product. As he goes on to say, not only relations between father and son, but 'jobs in the company' as a whole, revolve around the nurturing of beautiful products, from their design through to their installation and use. The organization man's language of industrial production thus shares many features with that of human reproduction.[8] What men like Baker enjoyed most about their position in the managerial order was the special freedom it gave them to create goods with 'man appeal'. Feeling 'good' depended on a man's ability to conceive an object and 'see the achievement at the end of the day'. The organization man's stories hint at a world of asexual reproduction, in which objects are conceived and reared in women's absence.

While this kind of psychic investment in products is a continuing dynamic of industrial management, its character differs between generations and sectors. It is important to recognize this, as some accounts of gender and technology, particularly the more psychologically orientated ones, take a rather too unitary view of masculinity. Men's passion for things technical is seen to derive from a universally experienced envy of women's reproductive abilities, or a compulsive need to separate masculinity from qualities considered feminine.[9] Moreover, such accounts jump too readily from men's fantasies about objects to their social control over the creative work of invention.[10] Far from signifying their dominance, the cult of products among British organization men reflected their loss of authority in the workplace. The power of producers was under threat from every side during the 1980s. Service industries rather than manufacturing were thought to hold the key to future national prosperity. Even within manufacturing firms, functions such as finance or marketing grew in importance as companies attempted to subordinate producer cultures to the task of meeting perceived consumer needs.[11] In

British industry, as Nicholas Abercrombie remarks, the emphasis during the 1980s 'shifted from the product to the means of selling'.[12] Organization men responded to these threats by clinging tenaciously to potentially anti-competitive habits, and continuing to focus their energies—physical and psychic—on the quality of products. These economic changes of course fed their way through to the telling of life history: our conversations were themselves evidence of the need to keep product fetishism alive. Interviewees harked back to the 'good old days' of their youth, when British technology reigned supreme and family firms had encouraged the acquisition of 'hands-on' knowledge about products. We saw in Chapter 2 how the shift to a corporate economy and the overall decline of manufacturing also had a generational dimension, as business-school graduates gradually overtook others on the promotion ladder. Organization men focused their anger at the decline of manufacturing on these younger men. Conflict between the generations centred on products, organization men feeling that their profit-conscious successors had tried to take away their toys.

Below I explore the psychic and historical foundations of product fetishism in more detail. The first section discusses the myth of products as the result of 'begetting' among men. From there I turn to the links between past and present, to look at how the organization man's stories about products reflect changes in the economy and capital structure of British industry. Finally, recent conflicts over business strategy are examined, for the debate over whether managerial authority should reside in product or profit fetishism not only illustrates generational differences, but also reveals competing versions of masculinity.

i. Product Fetishism in the Present

Product fetishism was often immediately apparent in a place of interview. Surrounding the boardroom walls of Ablex Brazing, for example, was a series of spectacular framed photographs of welds, in which tinted steel formed the backdrop for brilliantly coloured sparks and flame. The owner–manager Johnson held our interview in this room, and used these photographs to illustrate the way in which welding technology had changed during his career. As our interview proceeded it emerged that the pictures were set out in order of historical time. His account of early career consisted of explaining the skills necessary for arc-welding, spot-welding, and brazing. Later he moved on to TIG-welding, and concluded with a long description of the advantages of the latest plasma technology. The pictures which illustrated his story were decorations, but they also offered Mr Johnson a means of dovetailing his life history with that of the industry, and of conveying his fascination with the technology.

This interweaving of self and product was equally apparent with retired managers, who on leaving work often took objects of production with them. In such cases the original function of the article might become entirely subordinated to its aesthetic purpose. The image served as a memento of the company and expressed the organization man's continued loyalty to it. Mr Wright, a retired refinery manager with Swan Oil, provided the most startling example of this. A glance around his home revealed the company logo emblazoned like a coat of arms on lounge and dining-room furniture, and even on the bathroom soap holder, towel rail, and basin. Equally revealing were the retirement gifts which he showed me after the interview. Dominating the hallway was a grandfather clock, its face and cabinet engraved with the company logo. Wright explained that all the components, from the mechanism to the cabinet, had been handcrafted by 'his boys', the apprentices at Swan. Some two years before his retirement they had secretly begun work on this testament to their timekeeper, the 'grandfather' of the workshop. In the lounge was Mr Wright's favourite gift, a whisky dispenser presented to him by his fellow managers. The oak cabinet (Mr Wright's favourite wood) took up a whole coffee table and was surmounted by a large brass pipe and stopcock. Just like a refinery, it was designed to regulate the flow of liquid; an electric pump could dispense a single, double, or triple whisky. Like a refinery, it had built in fail-safe mechanisms, and would not operate unless a heavy-bottomed whisky tumbler was placed beneath the nozzle. Affixed to the side of the cabinet was a brass plaque, inscribed with a tribute to Mr Wright on it, along with the names of his colleagues.

The dispenser brought together the diverse elements which had constituted Wright's enjoyment of work. It commemorated his departure from that world, while bringing the machinery of production into his home. Wright had gained possession of his own little refinery. A working model of his career past, it also expressed the beauty which he saw in technology. From another perspective we might view the gift as a celebration of companionship between men.

The grandfather clock expressed vertical hierarchies based on class (apprentice–manager) and age ('boy'–'grandfather'), while the whisky dispenser represented the horizontal ties between managers. It combined the tasks of control over labour and process machinery into a symbol of virility. From the brass pipe, that magnificent shiny phallus, flowed whisky, the organization man's medium for socializing. The gift from his fellow managers offered the promise of continued potency, despite Mr Wright's retirement. To restate Marx, it made his masculinity 'visible to the senses and hence a power beyond all doubt'. So, too, it was a 'mirror' which reflected desires between men.[13]

I was struck in general by the number of models which adorned offices. Sometimes these were full scale, enabling visitors to view, *in situ*, components manufactured by the firm. For example, the lobby at Bridgend Motor Parts, the company run by the ex-boxer Reg. Johnson, featured a car engine which was painted vivid colours and cut away to reveal components manufactured by the firm. Managers also often displayed miniature models of products, blurring the distinction between toys and machines. Business commentators during the 1960s remarked on similar phenomena. Lord Stokes, the ex-engineer and managing director of British Leyland, had a collection of model buses and trucks on his desk.[14] Similarly, the desks of managers in my sample featured cars, trucks, and aeroplanes on stands.

In comparison to the way my attention was drawn to products, it is striking that I could scarcely remember what the men themselves looked like. Facial details were recalled easily enough, and I retained a general impression of size and height. While I registered that men invariably wore 'correct' attire—in other words a suit—I rarely left interviews with a clear image of their bodies.[15] Perhaps as a student I was simply insensitive to the nuances of middle-age male office dress. At the same time, however, there seemed here a kind of conspiracy to hide the male body, to neutralize and rob it of objectivity. As R. M. Kanter has observed, the suit and tie facilitate the sublimation of individual desires to bureaucratic loyalties.[16] On a visual level, the suit helped to deflect my attention away from the male manager and his personality towards the firm and its products. The neutrality of the suit exploits men's abilities to objectify others but keep their own sexuality out of view. There is a direct relationship between gender and dress here, since the ability to show off the body is regarded by this generation—particularly those in heavy industry—as a feminine privilege. The managing director of a Midlands automotive firm, Mr Dowell, revealed this in his comment that, while our interview had been interesting and enjoyable, I had 'overdressed'.[17] Throughout our session Dowell had praised the ingenuity of engineers like his father and grandfather, contrasting them to financiers, civil servants, or academics:

> I never discovered anybody from Oxford actually making, actually creating, any economic wealth. And I think in this country the people who are best regarded, get the benefit of the honours system—if that's a good thing anyway—socially are better regarded, are what I'd call consumers of wealth . . . You know, the army, the civil service, solicitors, educationalists . . . The guys who actually create it are not particularly well regarded.

Dowell's comment neatly sums up the cult of the producer and its gender implications. Engineers 'actually create' wealth, but service workers merely consume, and are lesser men by implication. As a non-worker (not even an 'educationalist'!), I fell completely outside the pale of masculinity. My attention to dress seemed to confirm to this gender hierarchy, for it made me into an object of aesthetic attention, and indicated that I was a consumer—both attributes signifying femininity in this man's mind.

Like many other managers, Dowell was surrounded by table-top models and photographs of his company's products. His views, personal appearance, and the work environment he had created reflect those of his brothers. While the business man's uniform of this generation desexualized the male body, products were 'dressed up'.[18] Products rather than men formed the visual focus of the office landscape. Making products desirable is, of course, essential in an economy based on the creation of demand, for goods must excite the consumer's passions if they are to sell. However, the manager's regard for the technical and aesthetic merits of products reflected real passion, not sales hype. Products occupy a special place in the organization man's psyche. They embody the elements of ownership and fruitful labour which distinguish the community of producers from the consuming 'other'. While the seeking of pleasure in products is, of course, not exclusive to post-war managers, or to men, it was accentuated by the economic changes which this generation witnessed during their careers.

The symbiosis between men and goods suffuses both the organization man's individual identity, and management cultures as a whole. Marx suggested this above in his perception that psychic as well as social identities are realized through relationships to products. Products may represent the organization man's own abilities, confirming his masculinity, but equally they may be objects of his pleasure, providing evidence of another's creativity. Products straddle the divide between fantasy life and the environment, the self and others. They sometimes represent the 'me', and at other times the 'not me'. In this respect they have the ambiguous but highly significant quality which D. W. Winnicott ascribes to the transitional objects of infancy.[19] Symbolizing the interdependence between a child and its other (for Winnicott, the mother), at the same time they engender a realization of separateness. Hence, as we saw in the case of Mr Wright, sometimes the product may be represented as phallic, and sometimes, as in the tradition of naming machinery 'she', it evokes femininity. The diversity of these illustrations reveals that products are polymorphous at a psychic level. They may represent women, fellow managers, or 'issue'. Sometimes they express potency and sometimes they are objects of desire.

This lack of distinction between subject and object is a hallmark of the organization man's images of products. In some accounts of gender and science—also based on object relations—the opposite point is made. Men's interests in technology are seen to result from their continuing struggle to disidentify themselves from mothers, and to demonstrate their mastery over the natural (feminine) world. It is the compulsive desire to separate object and subject that supposedly characterizes the male scientist.[20] In the case of organization men, there is not such a direct relationship between fantasy life and power in the workplace. Product fetishism does not only involve phallic images, or fantasies of mastery. The joy of production for this generation derived partly from the way it enabled them to appropriate 'feminine' qualities of reproduction. In the organization man's 'begetting', products could be dressed up as masculine or feminine. Placing goods at the centre of their emotional and work life, the postwar generation was able to rise above the strictures of biological sex to create a myth of male creation. At the same time, it was women's servicing labours in the home—keeping house, caring, and bearing children—or at work—codifying the organization man's thoughts through clerical work—which enabled male managers to indulge in full-time technical conception. As Dorothy Smith comments, women

6 'Lee Iacocca, The father of the Mustang'
This photograph depicts two organization men of equal status: the ex-vice presidents of Ford, Donald Frey and Lee Iacocca (shown on the right). Yet when Iacocca used the image in his best-selling autobiography, *Iacocca*, he entirely omitted Frey and the vehicle on the left. This re-working of the image makes the immensely successful Ford Mustang look like Iacocca's own personal creation. Paternity is clearly claimed in Iacocca's caption: 'the father of the Mustang'.   Lee Iacocca with William Novak. *Iacocca: An Autobiography* (London, 1988)

7 'Models on desks'
Sir David Plastow, ex-chairman of Vickers, makers of the Rolls-Royce. He sits with a model in the foreground, turned slightly towards it in a proud, perhaps protective stance. His body and the stylised lines of the Rolls-Royce seem to merge into one anther.
Graham Turner, Guardian, 9 April 1991

8 & 9 *'Objects of desire'*
In image 8 Gestetner promotes its product purely on the strength of its 'superb' looks. In 9 a secretary frames the duplicator, bringing an aspect of sexual glamour to the product and suggesting her role as an 'office wife', keeping house for the manager. Both images depict the product as an object of beauty; as the 'not me' rather than as an extentsion of the self.

The Manager, 8 Mar.1956 and 9 May 1956

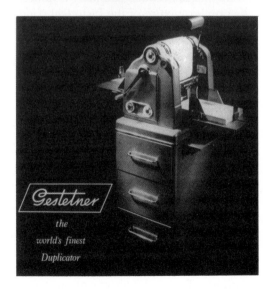

'do those things that give concrete form to the conceptual activities'.[21] Women's work freed organization men to play with objects, nurturing them to market, lavishing adoration on them, or showing them off as symbols of virility. Intimacy with products provided 'man appeal' of diverse kinds, allowing organization men to reap rich emotional and material rewards.

ii. Product Fetishism in Historical Time

Product fetishism reflects the organization man's energetic if ultimately illusory quest to find 'the self' in, as Winnicott puts it, 'what is made out of products of body or mind'.[22] However, a full account must consider its historical as well as its psychic context. Two interwoven themes shaped the men's stories about products. First was the relationship between economic and career cycles. Feelings of youth/empowerment and old age/decline were reinforced by the fact that interviewees began their careers during the post-war boom, and entered late career as manufacturing industry moved into recession. Nostalgia for youth sometimes took the form of regret at the decline of products. Secondly, the advent of a corporate economy, in particular the frequency of take-overs during the 1960s, forced a realignment of the nexus between company loyalties, masculinity, and products. A complex picture of the historical conditions surrounding product fetishism emerges from the accounts of the men I interviewed. Past merges with present, since, as we have seen, products acted as metaphors for the telling of life history. Products may be both the subject and the agent of career history.

We saw in Chapter 2 how, in the family firms which dominated Britain's economy until the 1960s, products were often treasured as embodiments of the founding father's wisdom. Associated with this was a disdain for formal management training, in favour of a lifetime's involvement in the business. As D. C. Coleman pointed out, the 'gentlemen amateur' tradition celebrated 'hands-on' invention and experience-based knowledge.[23] Skill was codified in products, which also represented the company and family pasts. This conception of the manager's role as a guarantor of products and company traditions grew out of family capitalism, but was adopted by career managers in public and family firms during the post-war period. Product-related knowledge provided them with a source of pride and authority, bridging their uncertain status between owners and workers. Such knowledge depended on life service, the expectation of which was fostered from the moment graduates began their careers. The Cook's tour played an important part in familiarising new recruits with the firm's product range.[24] It soldered ties between the firm, its wares, and its future managers.

The economic climate of the 1950s further buttressed these links. Boom conditions meant that companies were working to capacity and that new products and plant were constantly under development.[25] Expansion, youthful camaraderie, and the feeling of being in on something new, combined to generate a heady sense of the fulfilment that production could provide. The young graduate Mr Greenwood was part of a team at Swan Oil which had been sent in to rebuild a refinery after an explosion. The company 'crashed' resources on the plant:

> Because this was a crash programme, we were building without designs; they were designing behind us. It really was a major exercise. You were demolishing, building . . . You wanted to be back on stream, and we would break every rule that existed, but not doing it without thought. We had a whole, whole massive team of fellows we'd got there. Very very good fun.

In Greenwood's description we again see elements of product fetishism. He slips back and forth between memories of companionship and the joy of making things. The post-war boom seems to have intensified that connection, by providing unprecedented opportunities for creation. Even today, memories of the sheer, manic pace of production—the work of 'demolishing, building'—possess the power to heighten feelings of potency.

'Merger mania' during the 1960s hastened the shift towards a corporate economy, threatening this generation's investment of selfhood in products. There were on average 564 mergers per year in this decade, many of them in industries like textiles, electronics, and construction, which had previously been dominated by family firms.[26] The take-over boom was accompanied by the introduction of more stringent financial management, often resulting in a renewed drive to rationalize product lines. The general mood, as the management consultant John Tyzack remarked in the mid-1960s, was that 'once again . . . profit has not only become respectable but desirable'.[27] Courtaulds' chairman expressed the situation more bluntly in a 1964 directive to his board that 'we are desperately anxious to get more

143

profits everywhere . . . the emphasis being on profit, profit and then profit'.[28] The effect of take-overs and the general shift to stricter financial control on the men I interviewed had been equally far-reaching. It could generate considerable insecurity if a manager belonged to a firm being taken over, but equally created opportunities for those in acquisitive companies.[29] Either way, it placed the tenets of family capitalism, in particular life service and loyalty to products, under strain.

Because take-overs opened senior management up to talent, one might have expected career managers in family firms to view them as a liberating force. However, they often seem to have had the reverse effect, bringing owners and career managers together in an assertion of the firm's traditional values. Changes in ownership often reduced job security, but interviewees protested less about this than about the decline of product quality. They reacted to the decline of family management by becoming protective of 'their' products. This is illustrated by the cases of two career managers at the family firm of Jennings Windows. In 1965 Jennings had merged with another family enterprise, but, typical of such mergers, there was no overall restructuring and in some markets the two companies continued to compete. The merger had been a way of beating off hostile take-overs while maintaining a strong family presence in each firm. Then in 1968 the newly merged company was taken over by a 'corporate raider', who proceeded to sack staff and sell off parts of the business. Neither Baker nor Dolan was sacked; in fact Mr Baker recognized that he had benefited from the opening-up of management, and the generous pension schemes which the new owners had introduced. Moreover, the firm had gained in some ways from the introduction of modern accounting methods by the new management. But both men perceived the take-over as a threat to job security and the long-standing 'affinity' between family and employees. Profound attachment to the family culture went alongside recognition that the firm had been archaic in many respects. This affection and, more directly, the hostile character of the take-over are indicated by the sexual metaphors which they employed to describe them. While these are by no means consistent, there is an underlying conception of family capitalism as a union between employer parents. While the father represented ownership, productive capacity—the firm's capital assets—was associated with feminine qualities. Take-over represented a breaking-up of the family and the placing of the fruits of union—products—under threat.

The first merger in 1966 did not alter the partnership which had previously existed between the two sets of employer parents. Mr Dolan explained that it was a 'top merger. We didn't get into bed at all.' Mr Baker's explanation confirmed this state of faithfulness to the separate families: 'It was like a marriage and the couple never got into bed together, never consummated the marriage.' The point emphasized by both men is the absence of coitus. Whilst the two firms had embraced each other from the 'top', there had been no intercourse and no 'issue' in the form of new products. It was a marriage of convenience whose sole purpose was to assist the survival of separate productive and re-productive regimes.

Managers at Jennings described the second, hostile take-over in precisely the opposite terms to those generally employed by business historians. Instead of dragging a backward looking, paternalist firm into the age of corporate capitalism, the take-over was retrograde. 'Cruel' young men were called in to reorganize Jennings, which they did by metaphorically murdering the 'father' and violating his 'assets'. Mr Baker explained that the 'marauder' had

> married this rich widow, and it was like going back to feudal property rights; that the wife had no rights at all. And so he married this rich widow and stripped her of all her assets, and said, 'Well, I've done the best for you my dear, you're on your own now.' Which is what happened. He creamed it, didn't he?

The memory provoked a more angry reaction from Mr Dolan: 'They raped Jennings and then chucked them out into the cold again, eventually after raping them, taking all their assets. Yes, it was a classical asset-stripping exercise.' Metaphors of rape and despoilment appear often in their stories. Concern focused on the stripping of 'assets'— that is, the violation of creative capacity. The removal of capital in turn discouraged product development. Under the new regime 'products suffered badly, there's no doubt about that'. Asset-stripping struck at the very roots of creativity among men:

> One of the hardest things in my career has been to adapt from a man who makes good windows to a man who is selling profitably. And they're two different things. I mean Jennings were proud of the fact that they managed to make good windows. The fact that they managed to make damn good profits as well was . . . I suppose it was good management but it was [also] good luck in a way I suppose. They thought of themselves first of all as makers of good windows, not as makers of money. They did make money.

One's whole upbringing was that Jennings made a good window. Anyone could make a window cheaper than us if they wanted to, but we sold a good one at a good price. It's been a hard lesson to learn that you're not in business to make a beautiful product, you're in business to make money for your shareholders. [Pause.] I find it rather hard to reconcile myself to the Mammon aspect of it. I'd far rather be making a good window. [Pause.] I'm not so naïve as not to realize that you've got to make a decent profit on your product, but I'd still be happier making a good window than making a lot of money.

It is tempting to interpret this passage as yet another example of the necessary trauma involved in dragging the British economy into the age of corporate capitalism. Martin Wiener would doubtless see in Dolan's statement a further confirmation of the 'English disease': implicit distaste for making money and a preference for aesthetic considerations.[30] But to adopt such a stance ignores, first, the deep-seated connection between masculinity and technical creativity among career managers of this generation, and, secondly, the extent of the emotional scars inflicted by their successors.

A desire to produce beautiful windows pushed career managers at Jennings to new heights of technical endeavour. The traditional management culture successfully exploited the relationship between masculinity and delight in things mechanical. 'One's whole upbringing' in the firm taught managers the value of in-house knowledge about how to make and appreciate a 'beautiful product'. Take-overs helped push to the fore a new generation of managers who attempted to undermine the ethos of family capitalism by subjecting technical pursuits to more rigorous financial control. The older generation narrates this story in terms of fantasies about being dominated. Accountants and economists were described as 'hatchet men', who had metaphorically castrated the older generation by denying them the pleasures of invention. Lacking the capital to influence the course of change, and coerced into 'making a lot of money for other people', the post-war generation lost a source of beauty and well-being. Its predicament threatened a state of alienation, where, as Marx put it, 'begetting becomes emasculating'.[31]

Far from shaking the older generation's faith in products, financial uncertainties in the 1960s sometimes intensified it. Managers like Baker and Dolan subverted the new order by perpetuating pre-take-over traditions of pride in the product. Dolan has reacted to the take-over by manœuvring himself into a position where he can once again exercise aesthetic control. While the actual standard of goods might be beyond his grasp, he can at least safeguard the company's traditions:

> I regard myself also now as the keeper of the company's external image; its guardian, making sure that its livery looks right, that any output from the company is in keeping with our standards. You can't catch it all, but you try and make sure. Without ever making much fuss about it, I've managed to grasp most of that to myself now, so that I can see that the company's logo is used properly, and is used where it should be, and the company's products are described by their right names and not by some fancy code name. All those things where it is important that the company is seen to be expressing itself and is visible in the right way.

Dolan has carried forward the family 'livery', its traditions of quality workmanship, and, in a finance-dominated, consumer-driven climate, he has transformed them into marketable assets. By appropriating *images* of the product, he has succeeded in reconciling the 'Mammon aspect' of capitalism with creative satisfaction. Trading on icons and traditions, Dolan liberates himself from the whims of ownership while restoring the cult of the producer to its rightful place.

We have seen that management cultures which celebrated technical excellence were also often those in which life service was expected. The cult of the perfect product not only survived increases in job mobility during the 1960s, but influenced the choices of managers who chose or were forced into changing their employers. Mr Gidley is a good example. He wanted to stay in the firm where he began his career in 1961, but after it was taken over in 1967 he became increasingly disaffected with the management. In 1974 he moved to Plastex, a newly established injection-moulding firm. He was offered only a slight salary increase, but, even although he and his wife had that year incurred the added financial burden of a second child, Gidley took the job. He was, he explained, simply drawn in by the 'technical merits' of the product.[32]

Where Mr Dolan depicted the product as a vulnerable child in need of protection, Mr Gidley viewed it as a kind of temptress. It seemed to beckon him over, banishing the bread-winner's responsibilities from his mind:

> I was fascinated by the technology. Every salesman dreams of having a product which is unique. Nobody else has it, or if they do they can't

compete technically. It gives no pleasure to a salesman to sell anything on price. That's not real selling in my book, particularly if you're selling a technical, semi-technical product. So the challenge was to sell on technical merits. And by doing so, of course, to achieve a much higher profit margin. So that was the fascination . . .[33]

Gidley here voices the sentiments of his generation in his preference for products over profit margins. Making money is not the aim of managerial work, it is simply the outcome of enjoyment in technical wizardry. Such accounts seemingly confirm Weiner's comment that British business men remain disdainful of salesmanship.[34] More than mere snobbery is intimated in this passage, however. We also see an echo of Marx's comments about the satisfaction of psychic drives through production. Gidley draws constantly on a language of romance. He 'dreams' of the perfect product, just like Mr Baker and his son. Their quest is for 'satisfaction', 'challenge', 'fascination', and 'pleasure'. Gidley's comments reveal the ways in which personal well-being is sought through the possession of an attractive product. In an obvious sense this is because a 'unique' product enables its seller to dominate the market. However, such an interpretation does not explain the psychically charged language of the passage. Gidley points out that '*every* salesman dreams' about a unique product. In these dreams the salesman himself might become an object of admiration, as the holder of an object—at once masculine (technically advanced) and feminine (an object of desire)—which other men lack. Accounts such as this convey an image of business as a competition between men for the possession of beauty. Perhaps they also allude to a homoerotic economy in which men's desires for each other are projected on to external, 'safe' objects.[35]

The organization man's scope for technical play was further reduced during the 1970s and early 1980s by the accelerated onset of industrial decline, and the accountants' drive for profitability. Managers of this generation sometimes responded by continuing to pursue the 'unique product', even as companies fell victim to the vicissitudes of the market. After three years with the plastics-moulding division of Plastex, for example, Mr Gidley was forced to accept a promotion to a division which was not selling 'a prestige product quite the same way that I had been before'. He was unhappy there and soon afterwards decided to leave. His next job was also chosen on the basis of technical merit. The attractions of the product led him to ignore the financial problems which his new firm was facing:

It was the Rolls Royce of plastic packaging. [Pause.] It commanded the cream of the market but the market could no longer afford such packaging. It came from an expensive raw material, imported largely from the States. [Pause.] The upshot of that was that the company went into receivership only a year after I'd joined. And very shortly before that I was made redundant. That was in 1980 and at that time it was practically impossible to find a job.

Sixteen per cent of the men in my sample were made redundant in the early 1980s.[36] They could not easily separate their memories of the recession from an abiding sense of personal depression. Injury at being cast aside—'put out to grass' as one called it—was expressed in protests about Britain's failure to maintain its technological lead. They had become old men, unable to conceive new products or even to defend yesterday's models. With decline of the product went decline of the Nation, a particularly poignant fact for this generation because of the inroads which foreign producers, especially those whom they defeated in the war, had made into British markets. Their advances placed those conscious of technical merit in a paradoxical situation. They resented the dominance of foreign goods but admired the quality of design and construction. One man admitted that the quality of Japanese electronic components was consistently better than that attained by his own firm. The managing director of a truck distributorship who had remained loyal to British firms was angry about their tardiness in keeping up with overseas advances. After the war, he explained, British manufacturers

> didn't change much. Gave them a heater in the cab and such luxuries as that, and said to the driver, 'Think yourself lucky.' Out came the Scandinavian vehicles with sprung seats, heated mirrors, *comfort*, tilted cabs, all manner of things. And industry in this country looked at it and literally pooh-poohed it.[37]

Today the post-war entrants retain their keen sensitivity to technical aesthetics. It has survived declining competitiveness, the vagaries of company ownership, and even redundancy. This struck me most forcibly in the case of Mr Gidley. After a traumatic eight years involving two redundancies, it appeared that he was about to be made redundant yet again. The division of the British company for which he worked had been sold to an American firm, and it was probable that the head office would be relocated there. Gidley resented having put so much into the company without any promise of job security, yet continued to work inordinately long hours. An entire wall of his office was lined from floor to ceiling with tins of paint, all neatly stacked with the labels facing forward. I puzzled over this until Gidley explained proudly that the logo had been his own design. In the face of yet another corporate betrayal of his old-fashioned loyalty, it had been important to demonstrate intimacy with the product. Mr Gidley seemed to view the logo as a kind of signature, a personal claim inscribed on the product.

Whilst managers such as Gidley continue to hold the product close to their hearts, the epoch of the technical man is undoubtedly over. The product provides small solace in an era where older managers are sometimes forced to play second fiddle to younger, formally trained managers. The rising generation is blamed for severing the ties between national pride, company loyalty, and products. Traditional morality combined patriotism with paternalistic traditions such as life service, and expressed them through shared affection for products. Goods formed the basis for a community of men. Motivated by private gain alone, today's managers are seen to prostitute themselves. They are loyal to neither nation nor 'governor'. Worse still, they feign their fathers' passion for the product:

Reps . . . they've got no allegiance to a company or a product. If you were a rep. and came to me and said, 'I'd like to sell Seddon Atkinson trucks', and I said, 'Alright. I'll give you 5,000 a year, Michael, and I'll train you to sell Seddon Atkinson trucks', you'd say, 'Yep, Seddon Atkinson's the best thing since sliced bread'. Out you go, and six months later you come in and say, 'Sorry governor, I'm going off to sell Volvos.' 'Why is that?', I'd say. 'Well, they're going to pay me 6,000 a year' . . . And I say to myself, 'How the hell can that man go in to a customer and say "Seddon Atkinson's the best thing since sliced bread"?' Six months later he says, 'Seddon Atkinsons, terrible. Volvos are the greatest.' Six months after he's back in there again, 'Volvos, Seddons, terrible things. Scanias, great!'

How can a man do that? There's no *faith* in the man that's buying the truck, in the guy that's selling it to him! Don't like that. I feel that the man who sells a Seddon Atkinson truck, he's a die hard Seddon man. He'll sell Seddons till the cows come home.

The erosion of product loyalty threatened the roots of the organization man's creativity. The young wimps of my age gain no inherent pleasure from objects, but instead adopt a feminine stance, offering up body and soul for money. They model themselves instead of dressing up the product. At least their fathers refused to be bought and sold, and so will go out like men, will 'die hard', dreaming of the perfect product.

iii. From Product to Profit Fetishism?

Among those who entered industry in the 1950s, masculinity is today represented in images of 'hands-on' experience which take a physical form as products. The members of this emergent generation of professional managers adhered to the traditions of family capitalism, in which invention hinged on a partnership between 'practical men' and 'gentlemen amateurs'. Interposed between owners and workers, they borrowed guises from both. They prided themselves on their practical knowledge, but, in common with inheritors, they enjoyed their privileged access to the fruits of production. This alliance between managers and products has faced threats from many sides over the past quarter century. On the one hand, the transition to a corporate economy was associated in the organization man's mind with a move away from product-led management to financial control. On the other hand, the increasing complexity of technology meant that production became a more closed art, particularly as mechanical components were gradually replaced by micro-chips. It was no longer enough simply to have practical knowledge of the plant and an appreciation of engineering excellence.

If in these ways the organization man's masculinity has been shaped by wider changes in capital, the opposite is also true. Management has also been shaped by conflicts about the kinds of qualities which a successful man and manager should possess. In her 1959 analysis of British industry, *The Theory of the Growth of the Firm*, the economist Edith Penrose noted that there were two principal types of manager. There were 'product-minded' ones, who favoured internal growth over growth by acquisition. They took 'pride in their company', and expressed this by directing their interests 'towards the improvement of the quality of their products; the development of better technology'.[38] Penrose contrasted this kind of manager to the 'Empire-builder', who regarded business as a matter of 'financial manipulations', and would buy and sell firms with regard only to 'quick profits'. Such men, she commented, 'must have initiative and be aggressive and clever in the strategy required to bargain with and successfully outmanœuvre other business men'.[39]

These two images of the manager represent contrasting forms of masculinity. While the strategist's authority rests upon his mental agility, the production man feels that his technical competence makes him the superior man.[40] We have seen above how, in the post-war period, there were clear tensions within manufacturing firms between the representatives of these two masculine archetypes. At stake is the right to claim primary responsibility as the nation's bread-winner. Accusations fly back and forth between the two camps, the financiers accusing product men of having lost their competitive edge, while product men accuse general managers of being 'prima donnas', as one interviewee put it.

Penrose's ideal types speak volumes about the post-war history of British business. Historians now record that the 'product-minded' organization men lost out during the 1980s to financiers, marketing managers, and strategists.[41] Yet these years also saw increasing concern at the dominance of narrow financial management.[42] In the early 1990s the national mood in business seems to be shifting away from a perceived 'short-termism', and towards policies which facilitate the rebuilding of Britain's manufacturing base. Still, however, calls to restore the power of producers are conveyed through the heroic language of the technical man. This tendency is particularly pronounced in the work of two prominent American business commentators, Robert Hayes and William Abernathy. In the early 1980s they published a polemical piece in the *Harvard Business Review*, republished in a British collection on technology strategy, aimed at overturning what they called the 'new management orthodoxy'. They criticized the creed that innovation should be controlled by profit centres; that firms must be market driven above all else; and that they must be organized by 'a remote group of dispassionate experts primarily concerned with finance and control and lacking hands-on experience'.[43] Here we see direct echoes with the post-war organization man, in the idea that passionate devotion to products is the secret to competitive success.

What really stung Hayes and Abernathy was the fact that 'over-analytical' managers had limited the exercise of creative spirit by production men. The financial community had given all the macho kudos to strategy-makers; as they remarked provocatively, 'being called a "gunslinger", "white-knight" or "raider" can quicken anyone's blood'.[44] Hayes and Abernathy sought to counter this heroism of the financier by repossessing the language of masculinity on the product man's behalf, and attributing feminine features to their adversaries. The 'passive' attitude of the strategy-maker, the 'cowardice' of financiers in matters of investment, were to blame for the United States' loss of 'technological vigour'. Economic health could be restored only by removing these 'less technologically aggressive' men.[45] Distinctions must be reinstated between consumers and the masculine activity of production:

Inventors, scientists, engineers and academics, in the normal pursuit of scientific knowledge, gave the world in recent times the laser, xerography, instant photography and the transistor. In contrast, worshippers of the marketing concept have bestowed upon mankind such products as new-fangled potato chips, feminine hygiene deodorant, and the pet rock.[46]

Hayes and Abernathy here compare the gifts given to the world by technical men and marketing managers. Domestic and feminine images are used to belittle the creations dreamt up by marketing people. While production men make great technical strides, marketing men pander to the needs of children (pet rocks or potato chips) or women. 'Feminine hygiene deodorant' conveys the trivial personal obsessions of women, but also a sense of revulsion. Hayes's and Abernathy's cult of the producer is strikingly similar to that of British organization men. It is a cult which constantly seeks to align the masculine with the truly creative. It rises above human bodies, and their pleasures or discomforts, and fixes instead on the perfection of 'hard' technology. It identifies a consumer-led economy with a feminized one in which function is subordinated to presentation. Appearance is everything; Marx's 'mirrors' reflect only on the self. 'Begetting' has indeed become 'emasculating'.

It is important to reposition the post-war history of business in terms of these battles for supremacy between two generations of managers and two dominant representations of masculinity. We might then begin to understand the nature of the acrimony between the two camps. The deep social rifts which we observe in business between the advocates of production and of marketing or finance is replicated among business men as at a psychic level. Far more than industrial policy is at stake in these battles between managers; so too are their gender identities. Martin Wiener's decline of the industrial spirit cannot be remedied simply by a restoration of the producer. It is also necessary to recognize the cult of the producer for what it is: a fantasy of masculine supremacy.

Men's hold over technology has proved extremely tenacious, despite dramatic changes in the kinds of skills necessary to manage it. For example, Cynthia Cockburn has observed how the decline of cold composition in the print industry during the early 1980s resulted in a sense of disempowerment among male printers, and in efforts to prevent women's access to the new machinery in order that they might re-establish their monopoly over 'skilled' work.[47] At the managerial level a similar pattern emerges: control over the creation of products provided organization men with a treasured source of pleasure, which they attempted to preserve from women, from the onslaughts of technical change, and from a generation of financial 'whiz-kids'. Ultimately the joys of production are beyond gender. Like the organization men in this study, the women I interviewed also expressed pleasure at being close to production. Mrs Handley-James recalled that 'I loved factories. I did find them quite fascinating, and I thoroughly enjoyed the process, and there was quite a range of products . . .' At the same time, in early career she experienced all kinds of exclusion: prohibited from the directors' dining-rooms, and sent to guest houses at night while organization men stayed in the local pub. Like so many other women of this generation in manufacturing, Handley-James spent her later career at head office in a staff function. We need to know more about the many different ways in which exclusion like this operates. This chapter has suggested a starting-point, by exploring the historical links between the organization man's monopoly over the interesting work in production, and the fantasies which they lived out through products. As long as the interplay between masculinity and technical endeavour remains unexplored, calls for 'long termism' only risk reviving the exclusionary practices of the past.

Notes

1. During the field-work I kept a journal which I filled in immediately after each session. It was particularly useful for recording the visual aspects of interviews.
2. J. Wajcman, *Feminism Confronts Technology* (Cambridge, 1991), 22, 141.
3. K. Marx, 'Comments on James Mill: Éléments d'économie politique', in *Collected Works*, iii (London, 1975), 227.
4. Ibid. 227.
5. When describing the relationship between masculinity and technology, C. Cockburn paraphrases Marx; she explains that one of the pleasures which engineers found in team-work was that 'one sees oneself reflected in the

admired eyes of other men' (*Machinery of Dominance: Women, Men and Technical Know-How* (London, 1985), 172).

6. K. Marx, 'Economic and Philosophic Manuscripts of 1844', *Collected Works*, iii. 277.

7. See Cockburn, *Machinery of Dominance*, 171–6; S. L. Hacker, 'The Eye of the Beholder: An Essay on Technology and Eroticism', in S. L. Hacker, *'Doing It the Hard Way': Investigations of Gender and Technology*, ed. D. E. Smith and S. M. Turner (London, 1990), 205–23; R. Pringle, *Secretaries Talk: Sexuality, Power and Work* (Sydney, 1988), 'Technology and Power', esp. 174–84; and Wajcman, *Feminism Confronts Technology*, 137–40. B. Easlea illustrates in macabre detail the sexual metaphors used by nuclear scientists to describe the development of the first atomic bomb: Edward Teller apparently thought of the H-bomb as his 'phallic triumph' (Easlea, 'Patriarchy, Scientists, and Nuclear Warriors', in M. Kaufman (ed.), *Beyond Patriarchy: Essays by Men on Pleasure, Power, and Change* (Toronto, 1987), 207).

8. It has been argued that men seek immortality through technology; production compensates for their inability to reproduce. See L. Sargent, (ed.), *Women and Revolution: A Discussion of the Unhappy Marriage of Marxism and Feminism: A Debate on Class and Patriarchy* (London, 1981), 170–82. See also Easlea, 'Patriarchy, Scientists', 205–6; Wajcman, *Feminism Confronts Technology*, 137–41.

9. See, e.g., Easlea, 'Patriarchy, Scientists', 211, or L. Hudson and B. Jacot, *The Way Men Think: Intellect, Intimacy and the Erotic Imagination* (London, 1991). Hudson and Jacot argue that the technical enthusiasms often displayed by men provide a means of 'executing primitively psychological manœuvres' (p. 99). Unable to sustain intimacy, men compensate by the passionate pursuit of enterprises in the inanimate world (pp. 81–97).

10. This is something which Hacker, with her rather categorical view of masculinity, tends to do (see, e.g., 'The Culture of Engineering: Women, Workplace and Machine', in Smith and Turner (eds.), *Doing It the Hard Way*, 111–26).

11. N. Abercrombie, 'The Privilege of the Producer', in R. Keat and N. Abercrombie, *Enterprise Culture* (London, 1991), 177.

12. Ibid. 175.

13. Marx, 'Comments on James Mill', 227.

14. According to Anthony Sampson, Stokes exhibited his 'passion' for cars via the models (*The New Anatomy of Britain* (London, 1971), 606).

15. This was not the case in interviews with women, or with men when they were interviewed in casual clothes at home.

16. R. M. Kanter, *Men and Women of the Corporation* (New York, 1977), 48.

17. I had tried to indicate conformity by wearing a plain tie, faintly striped white shirt, sports jacket, and wool trousers, but it seems that my efforts only rendered me visible!

18. At the time of my interviews, there was something of a revolution in dress taking place among the younger generation of men in the financial sector. 'City fashion', embodied by the Next look in particular, accompanied 'big bang' and the stock market boom during 1987. Wide and colourful ties, braces and vests soon became the stock-in-trade of high-street men's fashion (see F. Mort, 'Boys Own? Masculinity, Style and Popular Culture', in R. Chapman

and J. Rutherford (eds.), *Male Order: Unwrapping Masculinity* (London, 1988), 204). Self-conscious play with dress codes by the younger generation of financiers was captured in Hollywood films of this period, notably *Wall Street* and *Working Girl.*

19. D. W. Winnicott, *Playing and Reality* (London, 1988). See, esp., ch. 1, 'Transitional Objects and Transitional Phenomena'; ch. 4, 'Playing: The Search for the Self'; ch. 5, 'Creativity and its Origins'.

20. Wajcman, *Feminism Confronts Technology*, 7. Her comments summarize Elizabeth Fox Keller's biography, *A Feeling For the Organism: The Life and Work of Barbara McClintock* (San Francisco, 1983).

21. D. E. Smith, *The Everyday World as Problematic: A Feminist Sociology* (Milton Keynes, 1988), 83.

22. Winnicott, *Playing and Reality*, 64.

23. D. C. Coleman, 'Gentlemen and Players', *Economic History Review*, 2nd ser., 36/1 (1973), esp. 92–103.

24. Having decided to join Jennings windows, for example, Mr Dolan went 'round to all the departments . . . learning the various products and how the company handled them and how it did its business, straight from the estimating and pricing, costing of windows, right through to the design, the ordering of them, the manufacture of them in the shops, and the fixing of them on site'. For a full description of the Cook's tour, see Ch. 4.

25. An example of diversification in product range and markets is Mr Dowell's company, Hill Components, which extended its operations during this period to South Africa, Australia, and France, and branched out from the supply of brakes and clutches to cover steering and suspension, rubber pressings, hydraulics, and aircraft parts.

26. L. Hannah, *The Rise of the Corporate Economy*, 2nd edn. (London, 1983), 94; S. Pollard, *The Development of the British Economy, 1914–1980*, 3rd edn. (London, 1983), 302–5.

27. Quoted in A. Sampson, *The Anatomy of Britain Today* (London, 1965), 511.

28. D. C. Coleman, *Courtaulds: An Economic and Social History*, iii. *Crisis and Change* (Oxford, 1980), 318. Courtaulds had fought off an attempted bid by ICI in 1961, its directors only maintaining their independence by a promise of increased profitability.

29. Of the thirty managers in the sample, half mentioned that mergers or take-overs during the 1960s were a decisive factor in career moves. Four (all employed in predator firms) felt that mergers had been beneficial, while a further seven felt their careers had been disrupted by mergers. In four cases a take-over had led directly to a change of employer.

30. M. J. Wiener, *English Culture and the Decline of the Industrial Spirit, 1850–1980* (Harmondsworth, 1985), 3.

31. Marx, 'Economic and Philosophic Manuscripts', 227.

32. Writing in 1970, C. Sofer noted that 'the general area of plastics has glamour' among technical specialists (*Men in Mid-Career: A Study of British Managers and Technical Specialists* (Cambridge, 1970), 297). Another example of the same general phenomenon is Mr Summers. His first career move, from a large public company to a small family firm which manufactured electronic components, was partially based on admiration for their product line. The owner

'kept his ear to the ground' for technical developments in Germany, and had 'a very good eye' for new and exciting products.

33. A further aspect of Mr Gidley's fascination was the way the firm reintegrated the production process:

> They did a complete turn key operation. They produced the raw material, they produced the machinery to process the raw material, they sold the technology to go with it. And they also took customers' metal articles and coated them themselves. So they did the whole process, which of course gave the company a unique experience.

In his new firm the whole of the production process was visible. Confirming Marx's observations about the division of labour, involvement in this kind of operation was empowering.

34. Wiener, *English Culture*, 141.

35. The boldest statement of this idea is L. Irigaray's notion of a homosexual economy between men which is masked by their exchanges of women (see 'Women on the Market', in *This Sex Which Is Not One*, trans. C. Porter with C. Burke (New York, 1985)). Irigaray argues that 'The use of and traffic in women subtend and uphold the reign of masculine hom(m)o-sexuality, even while they maintain that hom(m)o-sexuality in speculations, mirror games, identifications, and more or less rivalrous appropriations, which defer its real practice' (p. 172). The organization man's quest for a perfect product, while seeming rivalrous, in fact suggests a homosexual economy. For a particularly insightful reading of Irigaray's work in relation to secretaries and bosses, see A. Game, 'Secretaries and Bosses', *Journal of Pragmatics*, 13 (1989), 343–61.

36. The majority had an engineering background.

37. Mr Lloyd's loyalty to the local truck industry did not extend to his personal transport, however, an area in which he allowed his product fetishism free reign. He had bought a French vehicle because the combination of features he desired—automatic transmission and a turbocharged diesel engine—was not available in British vehicles.

38. E. Penrose, *The Theory of the Growth of the Firm* (Oxford, 1959), 39.

39. Ibid. 40.

40. These contradictions are well illustrated by Wajcman, *Feminism Confronts Technology*, 142–50.

41. See. H. Perkin, *The Rise of Professional Society: England since 1980* (London, 1989), 504.

42. The reaction against 'paper entrepreneurialism' gained momentum in Britain from the late 1980s, as recession began to affect the service sector as severely as it had hit manufacturing at the start of the decade.

43. R. Hayes and W. Abernathy, 'Managing our Way to Economic Decline', in E. Rhodes and D. Wield (eds.), *Implementing New Technologies: Choice, Decision and Change in Manufacturing* (Oxford, 1985), 164. Originally *Harvard Business Review* (July–Aug. 1980). Their sentiments are echoed by T. Peters and R. H. Waterman in the 1980s management best seller, *In Search of Excellence: Lessons from America's Best-Run Companies* (New York, 1982). See, esp., ch. 2, 'The Rational Model'.

44. Hayes and Abernathy, 'Managing our Way', 164, 172.

45. Ibid. 162, 175.
46. Ibid. 165.
47. C. Cockburn, *Brothers: Male Dominance and Technological Change* (London, 1983), chs. 5, 6.

Part Three

Women and Men

Part Three

6

Images of Wives and Secretaries

....

> From Betty I gained not only the first rags of self-confidence that had
> so constantly eluded me, but also the beginnings of an understanding
> of how much women had to offer and the strengths they possess—
> which so often compensate for male weaknesses and prejudices.[1]
>
> Sir John Harvey-Jones, ex-chairman of ICI, 1991

In the passage above the British industrialist, Sir John Harvey-Jones, pays tribute to his wife's skills in the emotional arts. It was she, he tells us, who nurtured his self-confidence, thus enabling him to become one of Britain's best-known and admired business leaders. Harvey-Jones here illustrates a central contradiction in the lives of organization men, between their social dominance in the workplace and family, and their emotional needs. The role of wife or secretary was clearly a subordinate one, yet the men believed that women were the more powerful sex.

The organization man's social power over women manifested itself in a number of ways. Their wives were, almost without exception, full-time home-makers. As 'company wives' they were incorporated in various ways into their husband's work. The wife's life conformed to his and the company's demands in terms of where couples lived, when they spent time together, and when she was required to provide corporate hospitality. As Janet Finch points out, his career structured her life, setting 'limits upon what is possible for her'.[2] Inequalities were equally apparent in the divisions of labour between men and their wives. It was the work of wives in keeping house and taking the main responsibility for child-rearing that enabled men to devote themselves whole-heartedly to career. Similarly, as C. W. Mills noted, the organization man expected his secretary to do 'the housework of his business', leaving him free to immerse himself in the creative work of management.[3] The secondary nature of the tasks done by wives and secretaries, and their limited control over when and where that work was done, reflect their lack of social power.

However, this picture of inequality defined in terms of the different tasks that women and men perform does not tell the whole story. It ignores the 'emotional work' done by secretaries and women like Sir John Harvey-Jones's wife. The social subordination of such women is linked to the emotional character of their relations with men. In a study of flight attendants called *The Managed Heart*, Arlie Hochschild defines emotional labour as the manipulation of one's own and others' emotions in order to create an atmosphere of contentment. It 'requires one to induce or suppress feeling in order to sustain the outward countenance that produces the proper state of mind in others—in this case, the sense of being cared for in a convivial and safe place'.[4] In the service work done by women such as secretaries or wives, personal charm, empathy, and other 'relational skills' were fostered, while anger was suppressed. Wives offered emotional support to men in exchange for 'secondary gains' such as material comfort, while secretaries performed similar duties in return for a wage.[5]

The men I interviewed relied upon women to manage their feelings: to empathize with their anxieties about work problems, to encourage their ambitions, or to dissipate their anger at colleagues.[6] They viewed wives and secretaries as the mediators of their 'softer' emotions. Rosemary Pringle has argued that bosses tend to define secretaries in negative terms as representing everything that they are not.[7] Curiously enough, at a psychic level the reverse was also true. Wives and secretaries could stand for the men's own more emotional, largely unacknowledged parts of themselves. Facing an occupational culture where rationality was the hallmark of masculinity and fitness for management, men expressed their 'other half'—their feelings of insecurity or fear—through women. This is what Harvey-Jones describes in the above tribute to his wife, Betty. She stands for his caring and sensitive self, qualities which make possible the masculine façade of self-confidence. Harvey-Jones reverses the power relations between women and men in his account. Where men are characterized by their 'weaknesses' in the emotional realm, wives have 'strengths'. Like his peers, Harvey-Jones notes the sacrifices his wife made in moving house continually or enduring his long absences, but not her powerlessness. He does not see that her skills in the emotional arts are a function of her dependence on him as the bread-winner.[8]

An even more extreme division of emotional labour is depicted in one of the best-selling business autobiographies of the 1980s, *Iacocca*, written by the ex-chief executive of Ford. Lee Iacocca's account shows women loving or languishing on men's behalf. The principal theme of the book is Iacocca's sacking in 1978 at the hands of his former mentor Henry Ford II, and his successful come-back in the face of this blow. Henry Ford II alone gets forty-seven entries in the book's index, while Iacocca's wife is mentioned only seventeen times. Nevertheless, women play a crucial narrative role in the book, as the dedication testifies. They convey Iacocca's own feelings of tenderness and anguish, feelings which he—unlike Harvey-Jones—rarely owns for himself. Iacocca recalls the tears of his secretary at the indignity of his sacking, and believes that the 'trauma' of this event resulted in the eventual death of his wife.[9] The women in Iacocca's autobiography act out his pain for him. In common with many other organization men, he projects his 'feminine' feelings on to women.

This chapter is based on the British organization man's depictions of wives and secretaries, and explores the nature of their emotional relations with women. It looks at the psychic consequences for the men of the post-war cultural divisions between bread-winners and home-makers. Hochschild's work has shown us how the emotional labour of enhancing others' status and well-being reinforces the subordination of middle-class wives and service workers.[10] But we lack an equivalent understanding of what it was like for the men who relied on women's relational skills for their emotional well-being. Life history's focus on self-disclosure, on the fashioning of identity in interviews, reveals how male managers are empowered by the emotional labours performed by women. Equally, it indicates the men's emotional dependence upon women. Like Harvey-Jones and Iacocca, the men I interviewed channelled their emotional wants through women, as if the women were extensions of themselves.

Parallel with this dependence there existed elaborate psychic defences against intimacy with women. We saw in previous chapters how products or the institution of mentoring, for example, might act as mediums for the expression of intimacies between men. The rigidity of the post-war division in gender roles between feminine sensitivity on the one side and career ambition on the other, and the belief that women alone possessed the power to bridge that rift, placed a tremendous burden on relations between women and men. In the men's case, it led to a split vision of women. They were either wholly loving figures, like the 'good mother' described by Melanie Klein, or persecuting and manipulative. Women who had remained loyal became objects of excessive idealization, as we see, for example, in Harvey-Jones's homage to his wife Betty. Those who did not conform to the domestic ideal were regarded with hostility. Lurking behind the figure of a secretary or wife there was often a domineering female figure, outwardly caring but secretly desirous of taking men's place. The splitting of wives and secretaries into good and bad mothers reveals the men's difficulties in separating themselves in psychic terms from the women around them. It was their own anger or love that was projected on to women. Wives and secretaries thus gained social status vicariously through the position of their husbands, while organization men gained emotional satisfaction vicariously through women. This trade-off between emotional and material security, and the anxieties which it aroused, is at the very heart of boss–female secretary and man–wife relations.

Below I explore the men's fantasies about secretaries and wives. Beginning with the portrayal of wives, I trace the boundaries which men drew between work and home, and how these were worked out in marriage. From marriage the chapter moves to depictions of wives at work, exploring the contradictions between women's 'incorporation' and men's attempts to limit their influence. Such tensions were most apparent when domestic life was on display at dinner parties or company functions. Repugnance towards so-called 'masculine women', the telling of dirty jokes or the use of wives to regulate each other's behaviour, were characteristic of such occasions. The final section turns to the parallels between the images of wives and of secretaries, particularly the maternal aspects which characterized both relationships. The watchful eye cast over women at work, and the harsh way in which non-conformists were treated, reveal the men's anxieties that they had passed the control of their gentler emotions to women.

i. Organization Men and Marriage

From my interviews with the men I did not gain much sense of the kinds of women they had married. They conjured vivid descriptions of the men who had influenced their careers for better or worse, but were strangely unforthcoming about the personalities of their wives. One of the symptoms of this thin characterization was the tendency not to use their partner's first name. Only one man of the twenty-five ever called by his wife by her first name. Partners were generally called 'my wife', or, less frequently (as they recalled the early years of their union), 'the girl I married'.[11] Sometimes the woman's identity was subsumed within the term 'family', when it was actually a wife who was being referred to. At other times her identity was subsumed within the institution of marriage. In five interviews the sole allusion to a spouse was via recall of a date of marriage. Even this mention tells us more about work than women, for, as we saw in Chapter 3, marriage symbolized the organization man's passage from novice to company bread-winner.

What are we to make of namelessness? In his work on the novels of the German *Freikorps* soldiers, Klaus Theweleit observes a similar habit of leaving wives nameless. The *Freikorps* soldiers' psychic world was split between the morally chaste 'white women' who supported them in the cause of fascism, and the 'terrifying sexual potency' of Communist women.[12] 'Red' women always had first names, but never family names. Giving a first name to the Communist woman served to deny her family ties. By contrast, the nameless *Freikorps* wives and lovers remained unarmed, pure, and under men's control. 'Leaving one's own wife nameless', Theweleit concludes, 'is a powerful piece of magic.'[13] The men I interviewed also represented the women they approved of in terms of their family ties. So, too, they drew stark contrasts between worthy and unworthy women. Unlike the *Freikorps* soldiers, however, this generation of male managers looked to wives to nurture their affections. They idealized women's emotional skills and talked of how important it was to have a retreat from the hurly-burly of work. As Mr Grainger put it, explaining the frustrations of a managerial career: 'She's always been so supportive and put up with it . . . You could never do it if you didn't have the backing of the right sort of woman.' Wives did not often appear in their own right, independent of the institutions of marriage or family. Namelessness points to the submerging of women's identities in the emotional work they did for men.

In contrast, I learnt a great deal about the character and idiosyncrasies of husbands in my interviews with women managers. There was a similar tendency to highlight the institutional connection;

165

women managers did not usually refer to husbands by name. But men were mentioned in connection with the division of labour in the home, whether they cooked, washed dishes, cleaned, or shopped. Women also discussed the problems which husbands had experienced in being married to a successful business woman—often more successful than they in career terms. The question of whose career should come first had frequently been a source of tension. Reversal of the usual divisions of status and emotional labour meant that women talked at length about their relations with husbands.

Inhibited emotional expression seems more characteristic of the organization man's relations with women than with other men. As we observed in Chapter 3, men were comparatively open in their expressions of affection towards other men. Despite the homophobic culture of management, it cultivated emotional attachments between men. Consider these two excerpts, spoken one after the other:

> The man in charge of our section, the chief development engineer, a man called T. E. Grantham, he again was a qualified engineer and there was a group of about a dozen or so engineers in their twenties, and we had to do economic studies in the steelworks; investigating new methods of manufacture, evaluating them, costing them . . . So he was a man I remember with great respect. [Pause.] He was a very challenging person, but he always made you feel that, no matter how difficult the task was that he threw at you, he made you feel that he believed you could work it out. And if you were unsure about anything you could always go to him. [Pause.] It wasn't a soft option. In fact, I think the essence of developing people is to stretch them, stretch them to their limits sometimes, because that's the only way you ever grow . . .
>
> I didn't marry until I was 34 years of age. Which meant that all the way through my twenties I could do exactly as I liked in terms of career development. I'd got no responsibilities of keeping a family. It was more by accident than design I suppose. I had a lot of girlfriends but none of them ever got me up the aisle, fortunately, and I'm still married to the girl that I fell in love with. In fact, we're just coming up to our twenty-fifth wedding anniversary.

In the first passage Tinsley recalls one of the many father/bosses, or 'idols' as he calls them, who assisted him on his career. Grantham performs emotional labours akin to a wife or mother, helping the young recruit to believe that he is capable of great feats. Like a mother providing unconditional love, 'You could always go to him.' Yet Tinsley is quick to add that, despite this caring, there was nothing 'soft' about their relationship. He stresses Grantham's toughness, being 'stretched' by the older man, and having tasks continually 'thrown' at you. This is the quality that separates his caring from that of women. Contrast this with the description of Tinsley's wife. Here the affection is more subdued. Women (his wife apart) are described as wanting to manipulate men into marriage, restricting their freedom to enjoy the company of fellow engineers. Tinsley is proud of the resilience of his marriage, and of 'the girl that I fell in love with', but he provides few clues about what attracted him to her. Marriage is recalled primarily in the context of the 'responsibilities of keeping a family'. Tinsley celebrates a landmark in their tie, the wedding anniversary, but does not evoke his wife's character as a mature woman. She appears as a romanticized figure from his youth, a 'girl'.

The post-war generation of managers revelled in male companionship. We have seen this reflected in the mentoring role, and the mixture of resentment and admiration which surrounded relations between younger and older men. While the domestic ideal promoted women as the principal object of men's affections, in fact considerable emotional uncertainty attended the relations between husbands and wives. Many commentators on post-war Britain have remarked on this tension. Lynne Segal notes that, while sociologists in the 1950s concluded that relationships between middle-class men and women were becoming more symmetrical, in fact men were 'rarely at home, were ill at ease with their emotions, and attuned only to the mysterious demands of "work"'.[14] The bread-winner ethos excluded men mentally if not physically from the emotional life of the household. Its counterpart, the idealization of motherhood, played an equally strong role in fostering ambivalence towards women. As the historian John Gillis observes, the enshrinement of femininity as motherhood deprived men of a language appropriate to adult relationships with women.[15] J. M. and R. E. Pahl have shown that relationships between male managers and wives of this generation involved a contractual separation of responsibilities into homemaking and provision, in which the woman's role as mother was uppermost.[16] This perception was often voiced by men in my sample. If they did not actually mention marriage, it was sometimes difficult to ascertain whether they even had a partner. 'Home' and 'family' could be shorthand for either mothers or wives, depending on which stage in his past a manager was referring to. As the accounts analysed below suggest, the men's idealization of motherhood had the effect

167

of desexualizing women. In the post-war domestic ideal, women's identities were defined principally in terms of motherhood, and men's in terms of bread-winning.

Mr Tinsley suggests above that marriage signalled the men's introduction to bread-winning 'responsibilities'. Similarly, Mr Duncan recalled the anxiety of his generation, their youth prolonged by military service and university, to marry and become bread-winners: 'The pressures on us were enormous because we all wanted to get married and set up families.' Becoming a husband might involve increased work 'pressures' rather than more time at home, as men sought to maximize their income and social standing for the family. Marriage often brought with it an awakening of career ambition, as Mr North recalled. In 1960 he had 'married, and started to have a family, and gradually, really, waiting for dead men's shoes in the accounts department . . . so that I could move on'.[17] The significance of marriage lay as much in provision as in companionship.

Sexual intimacy was recalled in the context of family-making, desire being channelled into procreation. As Tinsley again indicates:

> By this time I was 39ish. I was married now, and I'd got a small son who then would be 6 years of age. Also we were expecting a second child . . .
> I can't remember whether we were expecting a second child or trying very hard for one! But we were determined we were going to get one, which we did. So the domestic ties were stronger than they'd been for many a long year.

Tinsley's image of 'ties' is very significant. He imagines himself as an autonomous figure who becomes gradually drawn into domestic relations because of children. His reflection on the absence of family connections 'for many a long year' suggests an image of the life cycle in which bonds with women are loosened during youth, and retied in adulthood through marriage. On one level he is romanticizing the domestic ideal, but 'ties' also hints at the possible constrictions imposed by life as a family man. Being with any woman, mother, or lover involves men in a delicate balancing act between freedom and domesticity. If the association of femininity with motherhood conditions the character of sexual relationships, so too does the collapsing of masculinity with fatherhood. Even sex is described in terms of responsibility, pleasure being taken from the effort of begetting ('trying very hard'). The men I interviewed established their 'ties' to the domestic domain through children, just as they established their ties to the workplace through their care of products.

The men's tendency to depict freedom and family life as mutually exclusive had its precedent for many in the experiences of youth and early career. Many men of this generation had been compulsorily removed from 'domestic ties'. Separation from mothers was considered essential for the fostering of independence among middle-class boys at public schools.[18] Military service performed a similar role among lower-middle- and middle-class men, once again enforcing a period away from the domestic sphere in a hierarchically organized, all-male, 'total institution'. Military service placed similar constraints on relationships with wives and girlfriends. Weekends together were few and far between, and, as David Lodge recalls in *Ginger, You're Barmy*, men on leave found it difficult adjusting to the absence of male comrades.[19] Future husbands were often absent prior to marriage, which tended to set a precedent for men's absences after marriage. One man had little contact with his wife-to-be for most of his six years' war service, but married immediately on returning to England. Two others married whilst completing their military service, but saw little of their wives, since they were serving overseas.

At other times it was the demands of travel in early career which necessitated separation. A typical case was Mr Dolan, who got engaged before leaving England for Karachi, and after nine months sent for his wife 'saying, "Come on, Let's get married out here."' Duncan became engaged the day he graduated, but took a post in Trinidad for twelve months before marrying; Briar went on a one-year holiday to the West Indies before marrying and starting work; and Gidley worked in Switzerland and the Middle East before returning to the United Kingdom to marry. Mr Baker got engaged and then went to Singapore at the start of his career. After three years he returned, fearing that he might be 'forgotten': 'Then I came home and got married. The trouble was, if you stayed out in those places you tended to get forgotten. You just got into that narrow field of export; very nice job, but . . .' Baker may well have returned to Britain partly because he feared being forgotten by his fiancée, but speaking in his role as an organization man he explains that he had purely instrumental motives. He presents himself as anxious above all to secure a position within the company 'home'. Marriage followed once his future as a bread-winner was secure.

Men who were not physically separated from wives or lovers might nevertheless attempt to place limits on their emotional ties with women. Tinsley felt that he had been fortunate in marrying a woman who accepted that they would have limited time together. His wife-to-be 'knew what she was in for because I was already in Draytons', he explained, as if this commitment was unavoidably to the detriment of their relationship. Absences prior to marriage thus set a precedent for the kind of contribution which future husbands would make in domestic activities. Marriage was an interlude in the male worlds of work or war. Although the men sometimes expressed regret that their home lives had 'suffered' because of work pressures, in another way they kept women at a distance. Adhering to the breadwinner ethic, they channelled their energies into production, seeking the single man's 'freedom' as Tinsley put it, and nurturing men's company in much the same way that they had in their youth.

This pattern of intimacy and absence is apparent in the descriptions of marriage as well as courtship. Honeymoons signified a temporary abandonment to women, after which the responsibilities of work once again took precedence. As Briar explains, the tension between a wife's needs and men's work rhythms was apparent from the very first moments of their 'normal' married life:

> After we got back from our honeymoon I went on night shift. Left my wretched wife to get used to shift work, which she didn't enjoy. The first week I went on to night shift, and I always remember I went off on Sunday night, which is a painful business anyway, came back Monday morning at 8 o'clock in the morning and went to bed, then got up at 7 o'clock in the evening, had a meal and went off to work again. So she didn't think that was much of a day!

Briar's memories of the honeymoon are eclipsed by recollections about the limits of his availability. Mrs Briar must 'get used to' his work patterns, learn to provide the food and not to become too emotionally dependent. He recalls with some pride the minutiae of his efforts—the fact that he managed to work all night, sleep, eat, and then repeat the cycle. What remains absent from the passage is Briar's own regret at leaving his wife, which he projects upon her instead. Leaving is 'painful' to him in the sense that he feels guilty. In contrast his wife is 'wretched', reflecting his sympathy but also a certain unease at her expression of need for him. Briar experiences his 'softer' emotions—the loss of intimacy and increased stresses involved in returning to work—through his wife. Lacking the ability to articulate these qualities himself, he is in fact highly dependent. The discomfort surrounding this complex pattern of dependence and withdrawal is clear in Briar's recollection of escaping back to work. 'So she didn't think that was much of a day,' he muses. Once again he makes her the barometer of his feelings, portraying himself as a man with few emotional needs or limits to his physical endurance.

Others expressed a similar ambivalence between attraction to a wife and a desire to preserve a degree of personal independence. It seemed as easy for Mr Grainger to sustain love for his wife in her absence as with her. He married at the beginning of his national service, and for two years saw his wife only at weekends and leave breaks. Being married and living apart put restrictions on their time together, easing them more gently into marriage:

> The big problem was being married. That was difficult. She was working at the time [as a secretary]. Looking back I think it was a good start to a marriage. I know that sounds funny, but every weekend was like a honeymoon. It set us up very well, and I've had a good marriage and I'm happy now. Looking back we always say it was pretty tough at the time but it really kept us pretty fresh for the first two years.
>
> The problem is, in those days the money was terrible. I was always about four hours away from home where I was stationed, and always trying to get home weekends, so she was more or less supporting me to get back weekends. But there were a hell of a lot of people in the same boat in those days.

Voicing an often-aired complaint, Grainger claims that his enjoyment of national service was marred by the fact that his meagre income did not allow him to pay his own way home. Instead his visits were sponsored by his wife. In common with the other married men in the army, Grainger's wife was 'more or less supporting me'. Being married was a 'problem' for national servicemen because they could not carry out the bread-winner role adequately. The men's absence was not a problem; on the contrary, this made in some ways for a more satisfactory union, keeping them 'pretty fresh for the first two years'. In Grainger's statement we see confusion between a belief that men should be the sole earners, and a certain feeling of enjoyment associated with a different division of labour. His memory of the relationship feeling 'fresh' stems partly from the limited time they had together, but partly from their position of mutual independence. Like his fellow managers, Grainger has used the demands of managerial work to perpetuate the delicate balance between intimacy and independence, presence and absence. He has satisfied his 'wanderlust' by working in Wales, Essex, Liverpool, London, Peterborough, Brazil,

South Africa, and Japan. Absences continue to make his heart grow fonder. Grainger explained that 'it is lovely coming home', but equally refreshing to travel alone. Physical separation from women freed men to fantasize about romantic harmony, but this was perhaps more difficult to sustain in their presence.

Underlying the men's narratives is a profound ambivalence about intimacy with wives. It is preferable to express affection within fixed bounds like the weekend 'home' or the honeymoon, rather than risk being swept away by a wife's sexual and emotional demands. Distancing mechanisms like these are based on paradoxical images of women. While men wanted their wives to be always at the ready, 'fresh' for their husbands, at the same time this suggested an active female sexuality which men could not control. In the passage above Grainger is equivocal about the fact that his wife displayed her yearnings for him by helping pay for their time together. This uncertainty about intimacy is functional for the business world, which demands whole-hearted loyalty to work, imposing demands that militate against closeness. The missing element in the men's accounts is their own yearnings. Like Lee Iacocca above, they depended on the women in their lives to express these for them.

ii. Wives and Work

In his description of shift work Mr Briar refers to the 'wretched' feelings of his wife after their honeymoon as he resumed his work, and she began her life as a full-time housewife. In financial terms, a wife's position after marriage was most often one of dependence. Over three-quarters of the wives in this study did not work after marriage.[20] Moreover, as Leonore Davidoff and Catherine Hall have argued for the nineteenth century, it seems that men generally deferred marriage until they had consolidated their career position and could support a family.[21] Among the ex-working-class managers particularly, it was a mark of pride that their wife had never worked, as this indicated their success in bread-winning. As Tinsley put it:

MSR. Did your wife work after you were married?
TINSLEY: No. She finished work three months before we were married, and got the home ready. Bearing in mind I was away, you see. She hasn't had paid employment since . . . She's done a lot of voluntary work over the years, but . . .

woman at work

Lady attached to those legs knows how to use people. People like us. People prepared to give themselves a hard time to make life less hard for *her*, in as many ways as we know how. Like putting deep and accommodating Dunlopillo cushioning in her armchairs and mattresses; dirt-and-wear-resisting Dunlop Vynolay on her floors; the bliss of a Dunlop hot water bottle in her bed; protective Dunlop housegloves on her hands – and a whole lot of other antidotes to human wear and tear she probably doesn't even know come from Dunlop. But we're quite happy to stay out of the picture if it helps her to put her feet up now and then – in Dunlop slippers of course.

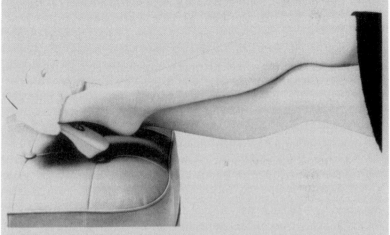

DID YOU KNOW THAT
Dunlop domestic products include: DUNLOPILLO mattresses, pillows, divans, bunk beds, furniture upholstery materials · carpet underlay · VYNOLAY vinyl flooring, D-I-Y floor tiles · housegloves, hot water bottles · FORTIFLEX dustbins, fuel hods, buckets · slippers and weatherproof footwear.

 THE DUNLOP COMPANY LIMITED

10 'Woman at work'
This advertisement plays on the incongruity of a working woman. It rather clumsily combines two versions of femininity: the faithful wife and playgirl. Women's sexuality—the text and the image of the legs suggest—gives them the power to 'use' others. Men thus work at supplying life's luxuries to women in exchange for domestic and sexual services.
The Director, Aug. 1969

There were many instances where the men's financial circumstances at marriage had not enabled them to support their wives full time at home. Working wives jeopardized the masculine status of bread-winner. We saw above how ambivalent Grainger felt about his wife's ability to pay for their weekends together. Although this arrangement kept them 'fresh', it had been a 'problem' that Grainger was unable to provide adequately. Other managers expressed a stronger sense of discomfort about financially independent wives. When Mr Greenwood decided to undertake a chemical engineering diploma in 1954, for example, he was supported in part by his fiancée, who worked as a nurse. They postponed marriage until he had obtained a managerial job, at which stage she gave up work. Mr Wright's wife also worked while he studied for an honours degree in chemical engineering. She had been a bank clerk but was dismissed when they married, whereupon she decided to become a teacher. Wright explained that through teaching she merely 'earned a few bob', as if her income had been pin-money, when in fact she had supported them both. Her work was depicted as a way of enabling them to enhance *his* career prospects rather than as a career in its own right. He had 'a good wife who backed me up'. Infant teachers 'were desperately short in those days'. Wright was, then, reluctant to acknowledge financial dependence on his wife. He regarded his wife's work as emotional labour—work carried out for the well-being of her husband and the socially dependent.

Difficulties were sometimes recalled in situations where husbands and wives had worked in the same industry or firm. Ambivalence about the wife's financial independence was in these cases compounded by a feeling that she was intruding on her husband's territory. This was true of Mr Duncan, who married his wife in Saudi Arabia in 1952 after a year's absence, during which she completed her medical degree. Despite her superior qualifications and earning power they had agreed at marriage that she should follow him 'where the work was'. Shortly after her arrival, however, one of the company doctors was taken ill and she was the obvious person to replace him. Duncan's account illustrates yet again the tendency to portray a wife's employment as charity, undertaken because of pressing social rather than personal needs. Duncan today jokes about their time in Saudi Arabia and his inferiority complex: 'Of course the doctors had a very much higher status than an ordinary chemist did, so when the general alarm went [at the refinery], I used more or less to have to get on my bicycle and cycle, or get my old battered car out and drive to the refinery, but a chauffeur driven car came out to collect my wife.' Duncan's light-hearted comments hide a moment of tension between his wife and himself. After the interview Mrs Duncan explained that she had overheard us talking about Saudi Arabia. She went on to put her side of the story. She had enjoyed her time there immensely and had found her subsequent employment in England— part time in an Infant Welfare Centre—unstimulating by comparison. She hinted that the decision to leave Trinidad was partly due to her husband's discomfort at the disparity in their occupational status. His own subsequent narrative confirms this. 'I decided that we were coming home', he explained, on the curious grounds that he wanted his then 1-year-old daughter to have an 'uninterrupted education'. He therefore took a post at Swan Oil Research Centre in 1955. Although it was 'in some ways . . . a demotion', the job involved working with new technology in a group of research chemists. In his new job, wife firmly ensconced in the home or Infant Welfare Centre, Duncan was 'very much one of the lads again'.

Examples like these reveal that career decisions were sometimes motivated by the wish to preserve work as a masculine sphere. Given the discomfort which men expressed about working wives, it was not surprising that company functions, in which wives played informal but crucial roles as host and companion, were often mentioned as a source of tension. Company anniversaries, recruitment, and buying and selling were all activities which might necessitate the presence of a wife. Wives were most fully 'incorporated' in their husband's work during such occasions.[22] In recruitment, for example—as has occurred within the personnel function itself—women's supposedly superior abilities in character judgment were called upon.[23] Not only did wives vet prospective male managers, they also scrutinized each other.

For example, even though his wife was often unable to explain to him 'why she formed the opinion she did', the chairman of Hill Components, Mr Dowell, had learned to 'trust her judgement of people'. He usually set up interviews for senior managers so that, at some stage in the proceedings, he, the prospective employee, and their wives could meet and vet each other. However, Dowell was also anxious not to overemphasize the part which a wife should play in such meetings. He would never refuse to appoint a man simply because his wife 'said she didn't like him or something. [Pause.]

That's misuse of a wife.' Dowell's wife had always done her best to socialize with other wives in the automotive industry, because this could assist sales:

> People who've been in the industry a long time tend to have made friends across the industry and consequently their wives meet, and, whilst I don't think it does any measurable good, it's one of those things. If the guy happens to know the managing director or chairman of this company and their wives get on, chances are they'll opt for you [rather] than the other guy he doesn't know. So that [pause] wives are important.

There is a tension here between needing the assistance of a good wife and wanting to underplay her influence. Dowell attributes his wife's astuteness in judging character to intuition rather than to formal management skills, thus underplaying the significance of her contributions. It was simply that 'she's got a bit of an ability to *tap* people who are genuine or phoney'. He provides a good example of how blurred the boundaries are between the domestic and quasi-managerial work of wives. This seems to make him ambivalent about the influence which wives have. While he finds his own wife's skills 'a great help', at the same time he fears that too often wives influence men's careers 'merely on the basis of a personal dislike'. What Dowell finds disturbing is the fact that women might actually be deciding men's business. Hence, while he admits the critical role that wives play in business, he prides himself on his ability not to be unduly swayed by them. His concern about the 'misuse' of wives in recruitment arises from a belief that wives should not possess the power of deciding a man's career, rather than from any recognition of the burden which that task imposes on the woman herself. Paying tribute to his wife for remaining 'tolerant' of his work, Dowell seemed to be indicating relief that she had only ever used her relational skills to help him. He referred to fellow managers whose 'unstable' home lives had impaired 'their ability to perform well'. One man in particular had become entangled in a divorce action which 'really destroyed his ability for about a year'.

Sociologists looking at this generation of managers have pointed out the common belief that career success depends on a wife's emotional support. Pahl and Pahl assert that 'much company folklore is attached to the ways in which a wife can help or hinder her manager husband'.[24] Although they see some truth in this, they claim that the

176

role of the manager's wife is much less clearly defined in Britain than in the United States, from whence the folklore derives.[25] Yet the myths which Pahl and Pahl single out—excessive ambition for a husband, the propensity to drink to excess or to dress 'outlandishly'— were narrated so frequently in interviews that we need to ask what function they serve. In *Married to the Job*, Janet Finch points out that, the more senior the man, the more likely it is that his spouse will be required to act as a 'helpmeet'.[26] Like emotional work, helpmeet functions are usually invisible, only becoming an issue when women refuse to carry them out.[27] Finch asserts that the fear of harming her husband's career is 'part of the process through which wives' contributions are elicited'.[28] What lies behind these pressures to conform, and how is the myth of the harmful wife constructed? Men in this sample focused their concern about wives on issues of drinking, joke-telling, and aggressiveness. Such behaviour invited sanctions against both the woman and her husband. A drunken wife risked opprobrium from other women and could jeopardize her husband's career. As one manager recalled, nothing could endanger career mobility more than if 'somebody's wife had a drink problem or was a bit awkward with the other women'. His division had compiled a 'black list' of men with wives considered unsuitable, and would not promote them. There is thus more to the issue of non-conforming wives than the shame of the husband/manager. An aggressive or joke-telling wife has the potential to undermine the company as a whole, not just her spouse. Drunken or joke-telling wives were assumed either to want to deprive men of their power, or to be ridiculing them.

Female drunkenness not only threatens men by reversing the gender stereotypes; it also arouses fantasies of sexual availability. There is a fundamental confusion in the men's narratives between desire and retribution, the drunk or aggressive woman being suggestive of a whore and a castrator. Consider Mr Dowell's story about a manager in his company:

DOWELL. I've known people in this company who I thought were extremely competent, but, you know, gave themselves an impossible handicap to work under because of the way they lived their lives. And sad to say in one case, his wife was unbelievable. And everyone was saying, you know, 'He's a super bloke but how can we put him on the board? He'd bring his wife, and god, what would happen if she met some of our customers?'

MSR. What was the problem as far as his wife was [Dowell cuts in].

DOWELL. The problem was that his wife was extremely aggressive; given to drink . . . She wasn't a drunk but she drank more than she should, which meant she got more aggressive and was inclined to tell dodgy jokes to people that she didn't know too well. And the motor industry—certainly the wives of the motor industry—could be said to be somewhat conservative. And the net result was that the wives of some of our customers—important people—were quite likely to say 'don't ever bring him and his wife again'. And if he's a managing director and he's a big customer, you've got a big problem.

Dowell's fantasies emerge strongly in this narrative. The wife he describes is 'unbelievable'—more dangerous in the fears she sets in motion than her actual acts (telling risqué jokes) suggest. Dowell senses this tension between fantasy and reality, moderating his criticism by admitting that the wife was not actually alcoholic. She probably drinks no more than her male counterparts, but for a woman that is 'more than she should'. Dowell's comments are striking because of his refusal to acknowledge the personal unease which the joke-telling woman causes him. In his account, women carry out the 'emotional work' of expressing his disquiet. They police the company community on men's behalf, expelling the bad wife. What is it about the drunken wife that Dowell finds disturbing here? First, she is a sexual figure, who employs innuendo with 'people that she didn't know too well'. Moreover, she usurps the masculine prerogatives of drinking and dirty-joke telling, behaviour which is often directed by men against women.

At a psychic level, we might argue that the drunk wife renders men impotent by appropriating their weapons. Neutered by his wife, one 'case' (he no longer has a name) suffers an 'impossible handicap'. Dowell's nightmare is a woman who not only castrates but entirely engulfs the men to whom she is close, thus assuming a masculine exterior. The man in his story literally does 'bring his wife' into the boardroom, inside his damaged male body. Dowell's concern stems from this image of women controlling men from within. That is why the 'sad . . . case' Dowell describes cannot be admitted to the board. The reverse side of fantasies about masculine potency are fears about women who stand in the wings, waiting to cut off the 'big customer'. Like Theweleit's Communist women, disobedient wives were depicted as full of subversive sexual energy which they direct against men.[29] This justifies the weight of managerial authority being used against them, which, in Dowell's case, involves sacking the husband.

Florence. Tea-maker Extraordinary.

11 *'Office wife'*

In this image new technologies enable the secretary to carry out her role as 'office wife' more effectively. Its message is that automation can increase efficiency whilst at the same time preserving the personal services which bosses enjoy. *Management Today*, October 1971

As he explains, partially admitting defeat at the hands of the 'problem' woman, 'in the end enough was enough and we couldn't handle it any longer'.

Observers of company culture have correctly emphasized the part which women play in policing each other's behaviour at company gatherings.[30] The 'incorporated' wives in this study upheld both men's social authority as managers and their emotional well-being. Men's anxieties about their masculinity were revealed in particularly condensed forms at the points where usually clear divisions between home and work threatened to merge. At such moments fantasy life took over, dividing good from bad, pure from sexually active women. Women who refused conformity were experienced as trying to 'handicap' or metaphorically to castrate their menfolk. Their antithesis was found in the good wives, Theweleit's 'white women', who helped sustain men's virility. They were, as Dowell puts it, 'conservative' in the sense that they sought to maintain men's emotional stability and career pursuits.

iii. Secretaries

In *Secretaries Talk*, a study of boss–secretary relations in Australia, Rosemary Pringle identifies three discourses traditionally associated with the occupation of secretary. From the inter-war period through to the 1960s, secretaries were most often represented as 'office wives'. Images of the secretary in training handbooks and advertisements stressed her deferential, ladylike qualities. As in a marriage, the office wife was expected to 'love, honour and obey'.[31] During the 1960s and 1970s this image was challenged by the 'sexy secretary', a discourse in which the ideal secretary was defined by her sexual attractiveness. The 'sexy secretary' has increasingly given way during the 1980s to representations of the secretary as career woman. This professional discourse 'emphasises skill and experience, resists the familial and sexual definitions, and plays down the "special relationship" between boss and secretary in favour of being an autonomous part of the management *team*'.[32] Elements of all these discourses can be seen in British representatives of the secretary, sometimes even co-existing within the one image.[33] In the life stories of British organization men, however—reflecting their age cohort perhaps—the image of the secretary as office wife was dominant. It was the familial, and in particular the maternal, qualities of secretaries that they promoted. Replaying their tendency to think of wives as mothers first and foremost, they looked to secretaries for intuition, sensitivity to their whims and moods, and a capacity to nurse.[34] Elements of the 'sexy secretary' or 'career woman' were also present, but were subordinate to the presumption that a secretary's main task was to undertake the servicing of men's emotional needs.

Despite the language of subservience which men employed when describing the work of secretaries, secretarial work calls for a very wide range of competencies. It demands a combination of technical skill (word processing or dictation), organizational ability (creating and maintaining company records, or channelling verbal and written communications), and emotional labour (playing hostess or acting as a 'gatekeeper' for managers). The all-round character of an office secretary's skills makes it not unlike that of a general manager.[35] Indeed, R. M. Kanter has argued that it is the office secretary's potential ability to *replace* her boss which necessitates the functional separation between managerial and secretarial streams.[36] Despite these obvious overlaps between the content of secretarial and managerial work, organization men preferred to stress the amateur nature of a secretary's skills. Where Dowell, in a passage cited earlier in this chapter, spoke of his wife's strictly advisory role in matters of recruitment, so managers stressed the secondary nature of secretarial work. Behind the men's attitudes to secretaries lies the same reluctance to recognize women's abilities as we observed in the case of wives. Like wives, secretaries could use their skills in the emotional realm to undermine men as well as to support them. The representation of women as mothers, and the paradox between wishing women's incorporation at one level, but feeling unease on another, characterized men's perceptions of both relationships. In the section which follows I shall illuminate some of these parallels.

The symmetry between wives and secretaries was evident from the first moments of the interview. Sessions at home usually began with a wife answering the door and ushering me in to meet her husband. There would follow an initial exchange of pleasantries between the three of us over tea, after which the wife generally left the room (often the house itself). Then the 'business' of recording life history would commence. If our interview was held at work, I was usually met at reception by a secretary who would make me feel 'at home' by asking questions about my trip down or where I was studying perhaps, as we worked our way to the office itself. After ushering me in she would ask whether I wanted coffee or tea and withdraw after serving it. Women in both these cases acted as facilitators of the real, productive work between men, leaving once it was clear that we were comfortable. The only difference between wives and secretaries was the wife's greater prominence in conversations prior to recording.

These surface similarities between the roles of wife and secretary were further demonstrated by the blurring of domestic and secretarial responsibilities in the men's narratives. Managers spoke of the importance of 'personal services' performed by secretaries. These usually involved interventions in family life of one kind or another. For example, secretaries might make travel arrangements for wives, remind managers of family events like birthdays, or chauffeur them around. Duties like these could bring secretaries into close personal contact with the family. Mr Dowell's secretary acted as a go-between for his children as well as his wife and colleagues in the company. He was often inaccessible during the (long) work hours, but 'the children, if they can't raise me they know they can get on to her'. Dowell's secretary was a 'family confidante', by which he meant that she was close to his wife. Both women were Welsh and sometimes went out shopping or for a meal together. Their friendship had vaguely disturbing undertones; as Dowell explained, 'My wife and she often go out [pause] and kind of talk about me behind my back.'

Similarities between the emotional labours carried out by wives and secretaries were also apparent in the men's tendency to cast secretaries as nurses in the workplace. This might actually involve women attending to medicinal needs. One man recalled how, on the Monday after the firm's annual weekend drinking binge, the managing director's secretary would tactfully lay aspirin pills out on a shelf in her office. By the end of the day, he recalled, all the pills would have disappeared. Others imagined their secretaries rather as healers of emotional wounds—women who helped alleviate the pressures of work. It was the secretary's job to make me and clients feel 'at home' in a strange office, and most of all to provide a safe haven for the managers themselves. A good secretary should 'protect you to some extent', explained one man, by putting off difficult clients or colleagues. Or she might 'take some of the load off you' by doing minor managerial tasks, perhaps composing letters as well as typing them. A competent secretary could read her boss's emotional state, shielding him from the demands of other managers or relieving him at times of stress. Alternatively a secretary might provide these services for other men. Mr Dowell did not feel that he had any use for the healing balm of a secretary himself, but he greatly prized his secretary's ability to console the victims of his wrath. His secretary represented Dowell's caring side to male colleagues: 'She's extremely tactful with people. If I get cross with them (she knows I'll shout at 'em!), she'll speak to them softly.' Dowell's 'other half' at work was his secretary. She played the nurturer to his tyrant. The emotional divisions of labour in marriage and at work mirrored each other, good women being highly attuned to, and acting out, men's more tender feelings.

Men's fear of subversion encourages contradictory attitudes to secretaries. On the one hand, managers were dismissive of their work. I was repeatedly told that it was 'trivial stuff' which 'didn't really need a great deal of thought'. On the other hand, the shortage of skilled secretarial staff was a commonly voiced problem.[37] Among the qualities which they wished for were 'obviously good shorthand/typing', and someone 'who knew how to compose a decent letter' and was 'competent on the telephone, knowing when to put a call through and when to stop one'. Further skills might be the ability to construct logical filing systems, drive a car, or perhaps do odd research tasks such as consulting the company archives. Secretaries rarely possessed the full range of abilities demanded by men. Mr Nash's usual secretary was a good typist but an under-confident driver, whilst his current temp. was a 'shocking' speller but was happy to act as chauffeur. So, while, on the one hand, men regarded the work as semiskilled at best, on the other, they actually required secretaries to perform an extraordinary range of tasks. Even the 'cannon-fodder' audio-typists needed wide-ranging skills:

> Even here it's helpful to have a girl that doesn't immediately throw her hands in the air and run screaming through the office if you use a Latin expression. It would be nice to have a girl who wouldn't faint or get hot flushes if you said something like that on the tape. If in fact she had enough wit to look up the legal dictionary on the shelves behind her and try to work out what it was that the dictator was saying.

Nash's comments point to the tension between an often unconscious preference for secretaries who have limited technical abilities, and the professional manager's call for better trained, more intelligent staff. In the quotation he professes concern about the poor performance of most audio-typists, but this is eclipsed by the delight he takes in projecting images of feminine weakness upon women. The hot flushes and fainting remind us of adolescent sexuality (perhaps the swooning pop-fan). Nash is making a joke to me here, a fellow man, about women's tendency to become hysterical. Such passages reveal a paradox between the wish to increase efficiency in the workplace, and the security provided by women who were clearly of inferior intellect.

Women whose competence was beyond question posed great difficulties for the men I interviewed. I was initially rather taken aback by one manager's abuse of a secretary who often stayed back as late as he (8 or 9 o'clock) to complete her work. Whilst he had no qualms about her competence, he claimed that the only reason she worked late was because 'she has no family life'. Gidley shared a widely held perception that, since women's first priority was family, women who enjoyed work must have failed in the domestic sphere. He resented the number of hours his secretary worked, since this deflected attention from his own—extremely arduous—labours. Nash's relationship with his 'very very good' secretary revealed a different kind of discomfort. She reminded him of his personal inadequacies:

> MSR. So what qualities would you see as being important in your situation for a secretary?
> NASH. I happen to be lucky. [Pause.] My secretary is actually quite reasonably well educated. She's got several O levels and I think she probably went to a grammar school. She didn't go on to university. You wouldn't expect to find a university educated secretary. That's very rare. In other words, she's bright. That has its down side as well, because, being bright, she gets frustrated because she thinks she ought to be able to progress higher. So she occasionally has her moments of moodiness and so on . . .
> Anyway, she's bright, and she's also just slightly older than I am. So therefore there is a certain amount of rapport. I mean, she's not sort of coming in and thinking only of boys and discos and so on. She's a mature woman. She's intelligent, and had children of her own, and brought up her own family. So there is a certain rapport. And although we do have enormous communication problems [pause]. That's one of my personal problems, communicating, you wouldn't believe it. [Pause.] I don't pick up vibes, people's vibes, very easily.

Nash displays considerable uncertainty in this testament to his secretary. He is at pains to stress her intellectual abilities, and to sympathize with her frustration in career terms. Whilst the similarity between them in age and intelligence brings a certain 'rapport', the relationship is clearly not without its difficulties. Nash begins by explaining that they communicate well, but is soon reminded of the secretary's accusation—perhaps echoing the words of his wife—that he is emotionally insensitive. Nash speaks here of equality, but is also anxious to defend his independence. He points out, for example, that his secretary is only 'slightly older than me', and elsewhere that he is in no way 'dependent' on her. Like Lee Iacocca and Sir John Harvey-Jones, Nash relies on women to awaken his expressive self. At the same time, their very abilities in this area are threatening. Nash feels intellectually secure but, in emotional terms, very much the boy.

The anxieties provoked by skilled secretaries bring to mind men's concern about the 'misuse' òf wives in company affairs. The line which divides support for a man and possession of power in its own right is a thin one. Nash's difficulty in comprehending his secretary's emotional life must be set in the wider context of managers' relationships with wives. His dilemma centres on the encroachment of domestic conflicts into work. Perhaps the secretary's comments echo a wife's demands for greater emotional sensitivity. Mr Nash's discomfort arises from the ghostly presence of his *own* need for affection in an environment where so much has been done to exclude 'emotional vibes', projecting them instead on to women in domestic roles.

Previous research on relationships between male managers and their wives has pointed to the contradiction between women's incorporation in the enterprise at one level, and their exclusion on another. These accounts have tended to underemphasize the fantasy life of men and women, yet it is partly through this that the social inequalities faced by secretaries or full-time wives are structured. Women occupied a paradoxical position for this generation of male managers. They were the sole public guardians of men's emotional needs, acting as mothers but in the formal mould of a wife or secretary. Men looked to women for the merest 'rags of self-confidence', as Harvey-Jones puts it. At the same time they were unable to admit the extent of this dependence on 'mothering' women. Pringle observes that 'men would agree that "office wife" was an appropriate way to describe their secretaries, while the secretary would insist that "mother" was more accurate'.[38] Organization men played down the vicarious power which wives and secretaries possessed by virtue of their emotional labours. In their view, secretaries were either not skilled enough to carry out the job efficiently or the job itself was 'incidental tittle-tattle', as one man put it. Struggling against their own needs, as Pringle comments, they would 'insist that she was replaceable'.[39] Contradictions like these point to psychic tensions which we must explore if we are better to comprehend the relationship between women's marginality in the workplace and men's attempts to limit their social power. Such a project requires that we try to understand more about the emotional life of women and men at work, as well as the 'externalities' of gender stereotypes or exclusionary mechanisms.

NOTES

1. J. Harvey-Jones, *Getting it Together: Memoirs of a Troubleshooter* (London, 1991), 207.
2. J. Finch, *Married to the Job: Wives' Incorporation in Men's Work* (London, 1983), 2–3.
3. C. W. Mills, *White Collar: The American Middle Classes* (New York, 1951), 203.
4. A. R. Hochschild, *The Managed Heart: Commercialization of Human Feeling* (Berkeley, Calif., 1983), 7.
5. Ibid. 163–4.
6. As D. H. J. Morgan puts it, 'if male identity is based upon work and employment, men often need women to confirm and reinforce this sense of identity and selfhood' (*Discovering Men* (London, 1992), 78).
7. R. Pringle, *Secretaries Talk: Sexuality, Power and Work* (Sydney, 1988), 1.
8. At the same time, Harvey-Jones is very aware of the personal costs borne by his upper-middle-class background: an emotionally distant father and a harshly regimented public school education. For him, 'Getting it together' has involved cultivating a 'balance' between the masculine and feminine parts of himself. Whilst he had experienced 'too much feminine and too little masculine influence in my early years', in later life the responsibilities of business had kept him away from home and family. Only in retirement does he begin to combine what he calls the 'soft' side of his nature with his public persona. Indeed one might regard the act of writing his autobiography, baring his soul to a public audience, as a means of healing the rift in his psyche between his feeling self and his actions as a public man (*Getting it Together*, 60, 303–5).
9. He explains that 'on each of these occasions when her health failed her, it was following a period of great stress at Ford or Chrysler' (L. Iacocca with W. Novak, *Iacocca: An Autobiography* (London, 1988), 301).
10. Hochschild, *Managed Heart*, 182–3.
11. Sixteen men referred solely to 'my wife', a further three to a 'girl'.
12. K. Theweleit, *Male Fantasies: Women, Floods, Bodies, History* (Cambridge, 1987), 75.
13. The name 'itself has a sexual and an aggressive quality . . . it functions, then, as a penis-attribute' (ibid. 75).

14. L. Segal, 'Look Back in Anger: Men in the 50s', in R. Chapman and J. Rutherford (eds.), *Male Order: Unwrapping Masculinity* (London, 1988), 76–7.

15. John Gillis quotes Robert Robertson, who wrote in *The Classic Slum* that, in sexual relationships among the working class, the woman often denied sexual knowledge, and the man, 'if he talked on the pillow at all, was permitted only euphemisms—private, infantile and dialectical. And that was how he wanted it, for the wife he so often called "mother" was a "good" woman' (J. Gillis, *For Better, for Worse: British Marriages, 1600 to the Present* (New York, 1985), 276).

16. J. M. and R. E. Pahl, *Managers and their Wives: A Study of Career and Family Relationships in the Middle Class* (London, 1971); see, esp., ch. 5, 'The Wife's World'.

17. Pahl and Pahl point out that men often attribute career ambitions to their wives (*Managers and their Wives*, 60).

18. For an account of the psychic scars which this separation wrought, see P. Lewis, 'Mummy, Matron and the Maids: Feminine Presence and Absence in Male Institutions, 1934–63', in M. Roper and J. Tosh (eds.), *Manful Assertions: Masculinities in Britain since 1800* (London, 1991), 168–83.

19. See, e.g., D. Lodge's depiction of Jonathon Browne's release from national service. Browne's much-longed-for holiday with Pauline turns sour as he becomes more and more obsessed about the fate of his comrades (*Ginger, You're Barmy* (Harmondsworth, 1982), 207–11).

20. In their study, Pahl and Pahl found that an equally low percentage of wives (13 out of 86) had employment outside the home; only three worked full time (*Managers and their Wives*, 126).

21. L. Davidoff and C. Hall argue that the comparatively late average age of marriage amongst middle-class men in business was 'associated with building up a business position' (*Family Fortunes: Men and Women of the English Middle Class, 1780–1850* (London, 1987), 222).

22. S. Tremayne, 'Shell Wives in Limbo, in H. Callan and S. Ardener (eds.), *The Incorporated Wife* (London, 1984), 130; Pahl and Pahl, *Managers and their Wives*, 184; R. Kanter, *Men and Women of the Corporation* (New York, 1977), 119.

23. For a good account of the stereotyping of personnel functions as 'feminine', see K. Legge, 'Women in Personnel Management: Uphill Climb or Downhill Slide?', in A. Spencer and D. Podmore (eds.), *In a Man's World: Essays on Women in Male Dominated Professions* (London, 1987), 33–61.

24. Pahl and Pahl, *Managers and their Wives*, 176.

25. Pahl and Pahl argue that such myths gained credence through American soap operas (ibid. 177–83).

26. Finch, *Married to the Job*, 85–6.

27. In her article on Shell wives, for example, Tremayne argues that 'only when a wife overseas acts in a way that puts the company's interest and reputation at risk is her presence and negative effect acknowledged' ('Shell Wives in Limbo', 123). See also Pahl and Pahl, *Managers and their Wives*, 180-3; Finch, *Married to the Job*, 85.

28. Finch, *Married to the Job*, 93, 110–11.

29. Theweleit, *Male Fantasies*, 72–5.

30. Tremayne, 'Shell Wives in Limbo', 125.
31. Pringle, *Secretaries Talk*, 6–12.
32. Ibid. 16.
33. Ibid. 8. See, e.g., Figs. 11–12.
34. F. McNally also comments on the parallels between the work of wives and secretaries (*Women for Hire: A Study of the Female Office Worker* (Surrey, 1979), 55, 59).
35. Ibid. 64.
36. Kanter comments that 'she would have a potent set of weapons to use in the struggle for the position' (*Men and Women*, 82).
37. Older women secretaries were thought to be of a higher calibre. Ironically, the reason they gave for this was the lack of opportunities for women of their generation. The present shortage of skilled secretaries was attributed to the fact that 'intelligent' women are today more likely to take A levels and enter management themselves.
38. Pringle, *Secretaries Talk*, 55.
39. Ibid. 54–5.

7

Images of the 'Lady Manager'

MSR. Have there been many women managers in Chemtex?
STEWART. No, not enough. It's a thing that bothers me, because, although I don't think there's any anti-female thread in the company, I think subconsciously there must be, because we just don't have that many senior women. We've never had a woman on the board...
    I think the real reason [pause]. There must be a subconscious sort of selectivity, but I think the real reason is that, in a company like this, which is still heavily based on manufacturing, it's quite difficult for a woman to get the continuity of experience. If she's going to get married and if she's going to have kids, it's quite difficult for her to do what I did. You know, it's difficult for her to push off to Russia for long periods, or run a factory. That break in experience is quite real. I mean, in what I would call staff jobs, it's immaterial. A woman can go off and do her family bit and then re-enter without any discontinuity.

                Mr Stewart, deputy-chairman, Chemtex

Gender segregation in employment is usually considered either as a function of women's domestic responsibilities, or as the result of direct discrimination by men. Whereas the first approach concentrates on women's role in reproduction, the second focuses on production, and how men as workers exclude women.[1] In the culture of post-war management these aspects of segregation were woven together. Organization men explained the dominance of men in senior management as the result of women's domestic role. A vision of motherhood as the proper fulfilment of femininity provided them with a powerful rationalization of exclusion. This vision was one which women managers of this generation shared to some extent. They talked at length about the obstacles to promotion which they had faced, ranging from the disapproval of husbands or male colleagues to the divisions in management between 'male' spheres such as production, and functions like personnel. Yet most had settled for jobs which did not make full use of their abilities, on the grounds that women of their generation could not expect to pursue a bread-winner's career. This chapter analyses women's and men's accounts of gender segregation in management. Comparing the men's images of women with the ways in which women managers spoke about their work, it illustrates how the domestic and organizational dimensions of inequality mesh together.

One of the difficulties in interpreting the men's accounts is that, while they expressed concern about inequalities in management, they were reluctant to think about their practices as husbands and managers. They pointed to factors supposedly beyond their control: in the tradition of continuous service, or in women's choice to opt for family above career. Inequality was thus transformed from a problem brought about by systematic exclusion to one resulting from women's preferences. In the epigraph above, Mr Stewart clearly illustrates this pattern of recognizing the existence of discrimination while disclaiming a personal part in it. As he ponders the reason for the lack of senior women at Chemtex, he is drawn towards the thought that discrimination must be operating 'subconsciously'. Yet that idea makes him uncomfortable. Instead of pursuing his insight about the subconscious, he searches for alternative ('real') reasons why a woman could not have had a career like his. He points to the example of production jobs, as if there was something intrinsic to the work itself which necessitated continuity. In claiming that women's own decisions hamper their progress, Stewart reveals his own 'subconscious selectivity'. By the end of the passage he is affirming the existing gender regime[2] at Chemtex. Women are back in their rightful place as managers in service functions, or rearing children, acting out the maternal roles appropriate to their sex.

There was often an 'anti-female thread' in the subconscious thoughts of my interviewees about career women. The hostility which they sometimes expressed towards wives and secretaries was even more pronounced in their depictions of women managers. Women managers in competition with men were thought to have forfeited their femininity, and, like the husband with his tipsy wife that

Mr Dowell described in the previous chapter, risked the loss of senior-management support. At the same time, even the most misogynist of men I interviewed claimed support for equality in management. Women managers were just as contradictory. Some vented their anger at men who had blocked their promotion by depicting them as effeminate, so promoting the discourse of hard masculinity. Others found pride in 'mothering' skills—cooling the tempers of organization men or providing emotional support.[3] Relations between women and men in management reproduced the gender relations of family life.

Much of the literature on women in management has ignored these connections between the gender regimes of family and workplace. It has tended to focus on the practical strategies for assisting women, while leaving what Judi Marshall calls the 'deep structure' of gender inequality beyond question.[4] Strategies are offered for combating the stresses which being a 'token' woman might cause. Women are encouraged to be more assertive, to learn relaxation techniques, and to network with other women so as to help overcome men's resistance.[5] Rather than assuming that responsibility for change lies principally with women, we also need to consider the systematic nature of exclusion by male managers. In her study of women and men managers, Deborah Sheppard remarks on the tendency for both groups to focus on 'femaleness' as an issue. She comments that 'Maleness remains embedded in the organizational cultural context and as such is not experienced as problematic.' All the pressures work the other way around, forcing women managers who desire success to recast their gender identities rather than 'challenging the prevailing organizational norms and structure'.[6] By putting the spotlight on men's images of women managers, we avoid reinforcing the tendency to pass off equality as a woman's issue.

Below I explore the various ways in which organization men rationalized gender segregation, thus deflecting attention from their own discriminatory practices and those of their employing firms. Section i compares the men's explanations for gender segregation with the explanations given by women. Section ii looks in more detail at the issue of career breaks. While full-time motherhood was seen as a woman's choice, in fact the men *expected* women managers to take prolonged career breaks, and extended their moral approval to such women. In addition, as Section iii explains, they tended to view relations with women managers in family terms, imagining themselves as bread-winners providing assistance to their dependants, or looking to women for emotional support in the way that they might with a wife. The support which they gave often had the effect of confirming the women's subordination. Some argued that women had an increasingly important role in management because of their 'people-handling' skills. However, as Arlie Hochschild argues in the case of airline attendants, emotional labours like this simply reinforce gender segregation since they involve women caring for people's immediate needs in the workplace as well as the home.[7] The image of women as home-makers, either mothers-to-be or professional healers at work—an image shared by both sexes—had the effect of limiting women's career progress. They were exalted if they conformed to the norms of domestic femininity, but disliked if they preferred open competition with men.

i. Gender Segregation and 'Subconscious Selectivity'

The emphasis which this generation placed on mothering needs to be seen in the context of the early 1950s, when they began their careers.[8] Military service provided men with a model of manhood and a direct route into management. By contrast, the five women in this sample reached working age either during or just after the war, when political efforts were directed towards restoring 'men's work' to ex-servicemen, and the domestic ideal was at its zenith. Writing about this period, Denise Riley argues persuasively that we should be wary of attributing the wave of post-war pronatalism solely to the popularizers of psychological theory such as John Bowlby or D. W. Winnicott.[9] Bowlby's writing 'cannot in itself be held accountable for the phenomenon of "Bowlbyism"'.[10] Furthermore, the concern with adequate mothering as a guarantor of social stability was not simply a post-war phenomenon engineered by government officials during demobilization, but had formed a continuing preoccupation during the war.[11] Riley reminds us that subjective beliefs about gender rules are not a simple mirror of public prescriptions. At the same time, we can dispute neither the post-war pressures on women, nor their own wishes, not to take mens' jobs but to become full-time home-makers. 'Bowlbyism', which Riley defines as the 'intense concentration on the married mother permanently in the home with the child as the unique and adequate guarantee of the child's psychic health', was believed in by women and men alike.[12]

Manifestations of the home-maker creed are evident in the women's memories of their schooling and early careers through the 1940s and 1950s. They were not encouraged in the belief that they had a working life ahead of them, unlike the men, who increasingly at public and grammar schools were receiving vocational training.[13] Education for girls remained, as one put it, 'totally inadequate as far as advice on careers was concerned'. The women viewed their careers as an interlude before marriage. Finch recalled that 'the attitude in those days was "here you are. One day you'll be married with a family, so you've got to do something until you reach that point." Nobody ever suggested that you would make a career out of the job that you went on to.' Marriage brought with it a change in the women's commitment to career. Finch decided not to pursue a post as director of a small insurance company; Handley-James stopped work completely; and the trainee architect Gould took her husband's advice to 'give your career up, go back to shorthand typing where you can sort of leave'. Baraclough remained in the family firm, but was nevertheless 'doing my best to be a dutiful wife, and that meant curtailing my personal development in the business sense'. Only one woman of the five felt that marriage had made no difference to her career commitments.[14]

The women's stories of early career illustrate the tensions which they continue to experience between the desire to compete with male colleagues, and the need to be a 'dutiful wife'. Facing resistance from men, they oscillated between a combative, 'masculine' stance, and an emphasis on their femininity. Handley-James's story shows how men might seek to frustrate women's progress by manipulating the home-maker creed. But it also shows the enjoyment that was to be had in beating men at their own game. In her first job at Chemtex, Handley-James was refused permanency by her immediate boss, who, she claimed, disliked her because she had a first-class degree whilst he had never been to university. He expressed his worries by mentally marrying her off:

Particularly in the early days, it was difficult. I think my first boss, this rather neurotic gentleman, really didn't like me, and he was hoping that I would go. I mean, he prevented me from being invited to join the pension fund for six months, which was not often done to people. And his excuse when I asked him about that was that he'd seen me lunching with some man or other and thought I was going to get married. Which meant that he wanted me to leave and get married. Somehow he didn't like the competition that finally came.

Handley-James's story illustrates the men's use of ideologies promoting marriage and motherhood to minimize competition with women. At the same time, Handley-James had little doubt as to who the superior manager was: her boss was simply not equal to 'the competition that finally came'. His weakness is depicted in gendered terms, manifesting itself in the 'female malady' of neurosis.[15] In the passage above Handley-James represents herself as the better man. Yet, when I questioned her about whether she had felt threats to her own competence as a manager, she responded by explaining that there were advantages to be had by emphasizing her femininity:

> MSR. Did you ever feel a sense of threat, perhaps the way that you were a threat to this chap early on who left?
> HANDLEY-JAMES. He resolved it himself early on, by being pushed. Because he took a silly risk and put a silly ultimatum . . . As soon as he told me he'd done it, I thought, 'Did you do this as a considered thing?' That was his weakness. I think in the end it was quite obvious to everyone that I was a woman, and not without certain attractions, and that I was a warm personality, and I found it, if anything . . . People used to tease me and think that I could twist everybody around my little finger. Which was quite untrue.

Handley-James here shows that men's hostility to women managers was responded to in similarly gendered ways. Women competed for promotion on the terms established by men. Sometimes they played upon feminine arts, presenting a warm and vivacious persona to men, while at other times they might adopt a more combative, masculine posture.

Other women recalled using similar strategies for coping with animosity from men. Mrs Gould provides a particularly good example of the tendency to alternate between promoting a more masculine stance and emphasizing women's special qualities. Gould was in many ways a pioneer. She had worked for Reed Shipping, was the first woman company secretary in the industry, and the first woman member of its professional association. She and her husband had gone against the pronatalist trend in deciding that they would not have children. Yet their decision also reflects the pervasiveness of the post-war belief that, to be 'good enough', mothering must be full time. She explained that, 'It's something I've not regretted. I'm not maternally minded. If I'd had children, I think I'd have been a mother first and a career woman second.'

Gould felt frustrated that she had been unable to realize her career ambitions at Reed. She had begun there as a secretary, but over the years had taken on the responsibility for the Operations function, encouraged by her immediate boss who had become ill and needed a good assistant. His successor, however, felt uncomfortable about Gould's skills:

MSR. Me I'm just wondering whether he [the previous boss] would have seen you as a successor to his job . . .

GOULD. I didn't even expect to be a successor to his job at the time, but I did think that the man who came would allow me to carry on in the way I had been. But he was one of those paranoic people. It wasn't just me. Anybody that sort of seemed to be able to use their initiative just got the push because [long pause]. He really was one of those people who worked intrigue, who told tales. To give him his due, he was very clever, very conscientious, he did his job perfectly, no doubt about that, but he couldn't accept anybody coming anywhere near his domain. And unfortunately the boss didn't back me up. But I stayed. I was married, it really didn't matter. So I was channelled off into handling the stores and spares . . . I didn't like it as much as Operations, but it was very responsible. This man channelled me off, because, to put it frankly, I was too much of a threat to him. At least he thought I was a threat. I wasn't looking for his job, because one just didn't expect to have that sort of job.

Gould was deeply fatalistic about this loss of the Operations job, which she was qualified to do and had found immensely exciting. Throughout the interview she kept puzzling over why she had stayed on where a man would have changed firms. She had internalized the image of womanhood as defined primarily by marriage. The fact that she was married seemed reason enough to limit her ambitions, even though she and her husband had agreed that she should put her career first. Her feeling of resignation ('it really didn't matter') was accompanied by profound anger at the man who had 'channelled me off'. Gould spent much of our interview venting her 'hatred' for him. Like Handley-James above, she undermined his authority by stressing his irrationality. Underneath the 'very clever, very conscientious' façade, he was 'paranoic'. He told tales and spread rumours, rather more like a housewife than an organization man. Later in the interview Gould again cast aspersions on the operation manager's manhood, metaphorically castrating him with the remark that 'he had to be cock of the walk'. Gould achieved belated revenge on the Operations director by ridiculing his efforts to become the perfect organization man.

Gould's account illustrates the ways in which subjective images of masculinity and femininity find expression in exclusionary practices. Her career had been blocked by the company's owners, who refused to promote her, despite her superior experience in the job. In criticizing the possessiveness of the Operations manager, Gould revealed her own desire to possess the job. Yet she expressed her frustration in contradictory ways. On the one hand, she claimed that it did not matter because, after all, career ambition was a male prerogative and she was a wife first and foremost. On the other hand, she subverted the masculinity of the man who had taken her job.[16]

The post-war generation of women managers in many ways shared the anti-feminism of their male contemporaries. Locke explained that, 'I'm not one of these women who believes in full equalization. I shall never be burning my bra, I need it.' Some provided graphic illustrations of discrimination, but responded negatively to my direct question of 'did you feel disadvantaged in any way being a woman in management?'[17] Instead they explained how they had put their feminine skills to advantage. Gould had sometimes been able to speed up orders for crucial supplies by being charming: 'You perhaps get a rapport which is more than a man would get, with some of the heavy industry people, anyway. Well, if you are nice to them they might just do a little bit extra.' Baraclough felt a certain sense of freedom in being a woman: it was 'an advantage in that there are so few women in industry that men are unaccustomed, and therefore don't have a stereotype in mind of business women'.

Emphasizing their femininity had sometimes proven to be a useful tactic for getting what they wanted from men, enabling them to manoeuvre around resistance from husbands and male managers. The women had become skilled at working within the masculine culture of management. Gould reacted to her marginalization by mastering the cult of toughness, her 'stand-up battles' with the Operations director giving her authority in the office. At the same time, she felt unsure about whether it was right to act in this 'masculine' way. Speaking as the good wife, she remarked that 'fighting was perhaps not the best way to go about it. I should have been more subtle.' Baraclough's way of dealing with aggression revealed similar tensions. She prided herself on having developed a consensual management style. To a certain degree this involved manipulation, wheedling concessions from men rather than gaining them through the 'unreasoning and unreasonable' aggression of her entrepreneur father. Yet she explained her gentler tactics in the phallic terms favoured by men: 'I think it's sensible to adopt a certain amount of camouflage so that men are reassured. You know, not kick open the traces unless it's really necessary. Bit of strategy to be acceptable on most fronts, and concentrate one's fire where it really is important.' Here Baraclough explains her management style of remaining quiet in order to lull men into a sense of security. Beneath this 'camouflage' of demure femininity, however, there lies a formidable weaponry of authority. She feels in some ways *more* potent than the men, more able to 'concentrate one's fire'. The women's daily struggle to fashion an identity as a career woman in the face of hostility from men meant that they were highly attuned to the gender regimes which operated in management. At the same time, they could not alter the terms of those regimes. The cultural expectation that they should be wives and mothers before managers was deeply engrained. It hampered their career progress, but also provided a stance from which to obtain certain concessions from male managers.

Confusion about the kind of image they should project as a manager and a woman was thus one of the main themes to emerge from my interviews with women. The men conspired in this focus on 'femaleness' as the problem. Discrimination, they claimed, was principally a woman's issue. They professed support for women, but explained that, since they were men, they could never be properly aware of inequalities. Moreover, while women spent the interview exploring the many dimensions of exclusion, the men often talked as if companies had already entered the age of equality. The association between masculinity and organizational norms discouraged them from critical examination. Mr Nash could not imagine himself outside his sex. Instead he relied on women to make the issue of sex discrimination more visible:

MSR. Do you think it is a fairly male atmosphere to work in?

NASH. I'm not sure what you mean by that. What's a 'male atmosphere'? ...

MSR. Well, I wonder, do you think there are reasons as to why the structure works that way, that has to do with [Nash cuts in].

NASH. I don't think there's anything special about the structure that causes it at all. No. One's not very sensitive to this. A woman could answer that question better than I can. [Pause.] Talk to any woman, in the same way almost that you would talk to any coloured person, and they would perceive hurdles and difficulties that you just didn't realize were difficult.[18] But, having said that, I don't think the system in any way consciously inhibits the progress of women, and I don't think individual managers consciously inhibit the progress of women. The reason why it's largely a male society is historical and social and [pause]. There's nothing peculiar about where I work.

Nash follows a very similar line of thinking to that shown by Stewart in the epigraph to this chapter. He recognizes and then represses the thought that there might be something systematic about exclusion. He admits the existence of inequality but is unable to see that he might have some personal part in it. A feeling of protectiveness towards the company and his male colleagues makes him reluctant to explore further what the 'hurdles' might be. He becomes a little defensive, claiming the very normality of a masculine working environment as a justification for his inability to appreciate the problem. Nash leaves within his unconscious, unseen and therefore unchanged, a host of psychic barriers to equality. He senses the immense importance of this opposition within men's minds, but then quickly retreats to the safe territory of explanations beyond his control, 'historical and social' explanations.

Other men displayed a similar hesitance to think about their attitudes. Two personnel officers from Swan Oil talked about the 'anti-woman thing' in the past tense. Their company had been 'very early in on "be nice to women"', so that competent secretaries were able to make the passage into personnel by the end of the 1960s. This advance had opened the way for women graduates in personnel. Jones felt that, if anything, the company had been too nice, and had 'over-promoted' women in personnel. The Swan Oil men believed that the presence of women in personnel indicated the firm's success in implementing equal opportunities. Yet their accounts contradict the overall trend in personnel during the 1960s, which saw its increasing domination by men as industrial relations became a critical strategic issue. This was a period in which women were being excluded from personnel rather than the reverse.[19] Duncan and Jones recognized this at one level. Jones had tried for a job in industrial relations during the late 1960s, but failed on the grounds that he was not considered tough enough to be a negotiator.[20] He himself had been the victim of a labour division in personnel which favoured masculine qualities for the top jobs. At the same time he felt that the company had pursued what amounted to a policy of positive discrimination towards women in personnel, and that this had perhaps been mistaken. Jones was engaged in a refashioning of the historical record, replacing the gradual exclusion of women from personnel with a portrayal of female domination.

Not all managers denied institutional prejudice or sexism on the part of colleagues. Yet even those who confessed its existence seemed at a loss to pin-point how it might operate. A manager who had worked in the construction industry explained that 'it's traditionally not a feminine industry . . . not through prejudice, but it just traditionally isn't'. On further reflection he reviewed that statement, deciding that perhaps he could think of colleagues in the firm who 'would be horrified at the thought of women being in senior positions here, secretly'. More significant than personal prejudice, however, was a natural division of labour between men and women. Building was an activity involving contact with tough men such as builders. This explained 'why women are strange objects in the construction industry . . . regarded as freaks'.

The men's views about discrimination seem to follow a pattern. They begin by admitting the possibility that men might be excluding, or might once have excluded, women. This thought leads them to the role of the 'subconscious'; what men think 'secretly'. But the implications for personal practice are not followed through, and, as a result, the men end up reiterating discriminatory beliefs. Hence Mr Baker and Mr Nash argued that women managers were not common in their industries because the work was men's work. Certain managerial tasks were naturally masculine in character. The supposedly fixed character of the gender order served as a reason for leaving resistance to women managers within the unconscious, unseen and therefore unchallenged.

ii. Career Breaks and the Cult of Motherhood

The reluctance of the men I interviewed to think about their part in perpetuating discrimination finds its most elaborate defence in the belief that women's own desire for motherhood prevents their further advancement. The men argued that, because women often left work to bring up families, they would inevitably pursue more limited careers than men. The concentration of women and men in different management functions was also traced to this division of domestic responsibilities. Production management was thought to require continuity because of its critical importance in the firm's commercial success. Staff jobs like personnel, involving supposedly intuitive faculties like sociability, could be more easily left and resumed.[21]

The accounts of women managers in the sample alert us to the problems which they faced when attempting to re-enter management after a career break, even in staff functions. Particularly if a woman had only held a managerial post by virtue of in-house experience, it could take a long period as a secretary, perhaps, before a managerial post was once again within reach.[22] The negative effects of the career break should be seen in the context of the men's belief that unbroken service was essential for advancement in core management functions. The idea that promotion depended on continuity was a kind of exclusion mechanism. It prevented women returners from competing with men for the more powerful management jobs.

Mobility through 'stepping into dead men's shoes', as one put it, was a basic tenet of the post-war management culture.[23] Organization men measured their progress against a fantasized sequence of career steps: each job should lead to that job, in a perpetual upward spiral. Yet, while men cherished the ethos of continuous upward mobility, for most it had not been a reality. The older ones had left civilian careers for up to six years in order to serve in the war. Others had moved sideways, perhaps from jobs where they were unhappy, or to gain wider experience. Increased mobility was often forced upon career managers by the mergers of the 1960s and again by the sharp contraction of the economy in the early 1980s, as we saw in Chapter 5. All these factors belied the opportunity for continuous advancement, either within or between firms. While the ideal of unbroken service remains pervasive, it does not actually explain men's greater career success. Each career move involved men starting afresh to a certain extent, just as it did for women returners.

It is, therefore, not clear in terms of career patterns why organization men maintained that career breaks explained women's absence from more senior management jobs. Despite its limited applicability to their own lives, men maintained their belief in continuous service as a guarantee of mobility. Mr Nash expressed it thus:

> In the nature of things it's just biological. This is one of women's perpetual problems. They want to do other things in life. There are not

many women now in the 40–50 bracket who have been prepared throughout their working lives to stay at work and work their way up organizations. Virtually all the senior managers and directors who are male, they may happen to be male, but they're also between 40 and 60. And they've been working their way up some company structure for twenty, thirty, forty years. In other words, I don't think the fact that there are very few women there has anything to do with sex, except incidentally.

This statement reveals the subtle ways in which gender images structure beliefs about promotion. It is remarkable in its mixture of essentialist and voluntarist beliefs. On the one hand, women are seen as having completely free choice about whether they become full-time parents. On the other, the problem of the career break is thought to stem from predetermined, 'biological' differences between women and men. Men possess the qualities of persistence needed for career success, while women's desire to 'do other things' makes them less reliable. Most remarkable of all, after arguing that men's domination of management can be explained as the result of biological differences, Nash dismisses 'sex' as a relevant factor. This generation did not consider the possibility that the responsibility for child-rearing might be culturally determined, seeing motherhood instead as the ultimate expression of women's role.

Women managers who made motherhood a high priority, taking time out to bring up children, were strongly supported. Men assumed that such women would not compete with them for senior jobs. At work they would play the role asked of wives and secretaries—that of the nurturing and protected woman. Even men who claimed to be advocates of sex equality naturalized the image of the mother manager. Mr Bannerman was a management consultant who had discovered that there was a 'niche market' in restoring women to managerial posts after their career break. This is how he described his 'cases':

MSR. Do you think there are other differences—apart from the career break which you have mentioned—between the experiences of men and women in industry?

BANNERMAN. If I can just deal with the break problem first of all. What we found was that women tended then to aim low. They had maybe been managers, but they thought, 'Here am I, a woman of 45. I am out of date, I'm out of touch, all I'm good for is a clerical job.' So that's quite wrong. Very often they've done a kind of managerial job for a long time. And more often than not if one could actually string together the things that they've done—the sort of woman that wants to get back managerially has probably run the local WI—then by the time you add up all those sorts of activities then they can actually get back in.

Having got back in I think that women certainly do have a problem, in that some of it is self-inflicted: I think they feel that they have to do just that much better than men. And I think that sometimes they lose a bit of their femininity in the process. But it's very variable. In local government, for example, the woman is coming through quite rapidly. And you will see quite a few chief officers who are women. Women are at quite senior levels. I don't personally think that there is that much prejudice now. The fact that you don't have as many women at the top as men is simply because, biologically, a lot of women still do in fact opt to have a break in their career.

Like their fellow managers, Bannerman and Nash conflate women's function as child-bearers with issues concerning the social responsibility for parenting. This determinism persists alongside an insistence that women today face no obstacles to promotion. The gains made by some women managers are offered as evidence that motherhood is no longer the sole option open to them. Thus Bannerman speaks of women who 'opt to have a break in their career', and Nash of women who 'want to do other things in life'. Yet again we observe a tendency to speak of equal opportunities as a historical phenomenon. In the new climate of equality, any woman who chooses to rear children full time demonstrates a (whole-heartedly endorsed) preference for motherhood. There is a contradiction between the men's perception that women in today's society have free choice, and their inner world in which mothers alone are favoured. Yet men of this generation sees no connection between their ideals of family life, their socially dominant position in management, and the possibilities open to women.

Furthermore, the lack of success which women frequently experience in trying to get back into managerial posts after a career break was viewed as a woman's problem. According to Bannerman, women managers are either too dominant or too submissive. On the one hand, their lack of success in returning to work was due to an inferiority complex which meant that they 'tend . . . to aim low'. On the other hand, as the management literature has often pointed out, women who aimed too high would not succeed either.[24] While

Bannerman empathized with under-confident women, he disliked those who were openly competitive.

Underlying the men's comments about the career break is the process of splitting between good and bad mothers which we observed in the case of secretaries. Either women at work are depicted as an unrivalled source of comfort and care, in which case they deserve the support of men, or they are experienced as destructive megalomaniacs. The men's positive feelings were projected on to women who seemed to fill the role of loving mothers. They defended this image of the good mother by idealizing those women who had struggled to re-enter management after the career break. In contrast, women who threatened to frustrate their own career ambitions became objects of the men's destructive impulses. As Klein remarks of the bad mother, ambitious women were experienced as 'dangerous and persecuting'.[25]

The men's explanations of exclusion thus accord with Klein's concept of splitting. Such theories are often criticized for the tendency to assume that psychic processes are universal.[26] However, the fantasies of my male interviewees about women managers were grounded in a highly specific cultural context. For example, they made good use of contemporary discussions about feminism to protect their idealizations of the good mother. When Bannerman mentioned women's tendency to 'aim low', he was taking up a strand of liberal feminism and weaving it into the material of fantasy. Advocates of women in management had, in their attempts to foster confidence among women, argued that role conditioning led them to be 'their own worst enemies'.[27] Bannerman now fixed on the public discourses about women's lack of assertiveness to extend his assistance to such women. In romanticizing the good mother, Bannerman also presented himself as a pro-feminist man.

iii. Good and Bad Mothers

The final section of this chapter turns from the post-war generation's explanations for gender segregation to explore the men's descriptions of women managers they had worked with during their careers. My account so far has focused on the inconsistencies and psychic dilemmas which surfaced in explanations of phenomena such as the career break. The men's tendency to over-determine women's identities as mothers emerges clearly in their images of women managers.

Anxieties about their own fitness for management were awakened in particularly strong form by women who showed competence. That anxiety was in turn projected on to able women, who might take the form of persecutors attempting to undermine men. Women managers who accepted the division in management between feminine-support and masculine-production functions were more likely to become objects of excessive idealization. By seeming to fit the men's image of a good mother, such women enabled the men to take on the identity of a providing father. Just as the post-war gender order defined men's family status in terms of bread-winning, so their work status was enhanced by providing assistance to women.

In her study of the 'sexual regime' in a high-street retailing firm, Cynthia Cockburn identified similar tendencies among an older cohort of male managers. At times they were outwardly courteous to women managers, at others they believed that women were 'fitted only for kitchen and nursery'. Cockburn concludes that, 'These men were puzzled by the ambitious and successful new women at work.'[28] Men in this study, like the older men in high-street retail, wavered between protective concern towards women managers and outright hostility. Their support extended mainly to those 'lady managers' who had taken motherhood seriously. The post-war generation thus greeted the increasing numbers of women managers with a revival of attitudes which David Collinson, David Knights, and Margaret Collinson aptly describe as 'highly paternal, protective, and gentlemanly'.[29] This paternalism manifested itself in attempts to relegate women to 'domestic'-type tasks within management and in their exclusion from the 'manly' confrontations which so often resulted in promotion. They could not easily pursue career ambitions without offending men's desires for them to remain dependent.

Women who had requested help in starting a career in management were recalled with affection by men. In such cases the clearly subordinate status of the women concerned made it easy to be generous. Like Bannerman's 'cases', perhaps they were attempting to re-enter management after a career break, or to cross the secretarial–managerial divide.[30] In the passage quoted above, for example, Bannerman supports women who have taken motherhood seriously: who have stayed with their children until they entered adolescence and who now wish to re-enter management at a junior level. Such women do the right thing by coming to their male superiors and asking for guidance. Men in turn gained immense satisfaction from demonstrating the improvements achieved by their counselling.[31] In the account above Mr Bannerman emphasizes how his marketing skill enabled women 'actually to get back in'. The woman's own talents become submerged beneath Bannerman's fantasies about his power as a provider of management posts. Mr Briar showed a similar lack of ability to recognize independent managerial ability in women:

> I had a very good secretary . . . After [she had been in the company] about a year, a vacancy appeared in personnel in head office, and the chap in charge of administration counselled this girl who was interested not to take this job, to stay as a secretary. And I encouraged her the opposite: 'Have a go; you can do it.' She's now a personnel director of a well-known public company! It's one of the occasions where one's advice works, and it's very satisfying when it does and you've made somebody's career.

By way of contrast, this is how Mr Briar described his first mentor at the Briar and Peacock Food Works: 'I sat at [his] . . . feet . . . and watched him in action, because he was immensely capable. Highly accomplished technically: got a knighthood for technical work on fuel-saving during the war, a first-class sugar refiner and author of the textbook on it. And a formidable manager. The morale of the place was sky high . . .'

Such passages reveal the different emotional complexes that operate in depictions of women managers, and of other men. Briar's admiration for the older man knows no bounds. As he explained later, he felt completely 'overshadowed' by his mentor. Expertise is the mark of the older man—in 'hands-on' and formal knowledge of the industry, and in management as well. Yet, in Briar's description of his ex-secretary, he emphasizes only her fitness for the job. A woman manager may be 'very competent' or 'good at her job'; the emphasis tends to be on whether or not she possesses sufficient competence. Women are very rarely seen as brilliant in the all-round, technical, and managerial way that men are. This difference in representations reflects the men's inability to move beyond the position of protector. They found it difficult to separate women's achievements from their own. Men told me mostly about themselves and their acts of kindness towards women, which had the effect of depriving women of agency. The men's stories were about how they had 'made somebody's career', not about 'masterful' women.

Stories about the helping hand they had occasionally extended towards woman managers were offered by male interviewees as proof of their freedom from prejudice. Yet that very protectiveness could be an obstacle to women. Assistance was contingent on them remaining 'lady managers', and in particular on rejecting aggression as a mode of control. In Chapters 3 and 4 we saw how deep-seated the cult of toughness is in manufacturing industry. The post-war generation adhered to a promotion system based on the subjection of younger managers to the authority of older men. While senior managers instructed their juniors through regular 'bawlings-out', they were 'protective' towards women. Thus Mr Grainger remarked that 'things happen on the shop-floor and you come up here in a hell of a temper and you know that you'd have it out with a fella straight level, but with the girls you find you let them off'. Lenience marked them as gallant, but the more perceptive among them could also see that, in culture which prizes toughness so greatly, the shielding of women from confrontation 'does . . . limit their effectiveness to a certain extent'. The cult of toughness gave women little choice between accepting an accessory role or adopting character traits thought more appropriate to men.

The men perceived no middle ground between the good mothers they had assisted and those who had deserted the ideals of true womanhood. As Mr Bannerman put it in the quotation above, women lost their charms when they attempted to do 'just that much better than men'. Such comments were couched in terms of concern for women, but exhibited men's fears for the security of the gender order. They did not just fear that ambitious career women would 'lose a bit of their femininity', but that the men whose paths they crossed might lose a bit of their masculinity.[32] Metaphors of battle are common in the men's descriptions of how they dealt with openly ambitious women managers—just as they are in the women's accounts of how they dealt with men who opposed them. As we saw in Chapter 4, images of combat could convey a range of meanings. Violence or 'rough play' between men sometimes had a comradely edge to it. In contrast, men's battles with over-ambitious women had a decidedly bitter edge.

Two final examples of 'battles' with women managers illustrate the depth of men's ambivalence towards women who did not hold traditional notions of femininity. They point to a continuing theme of anxiety mixed with hostility in men's depictions of powerful women, whether wives, secretaries, or managers. Such attitudes were not only held by more blatantly 'traditionalist' engineering men such as the Chairman of Hill Components, Mr Dowell, but also by men like Bannerman who claimed professional knowledge of the difficulties facing women, and commitment to their alleviation. Dowell's account points to the similarity in mens' fantasies between the figures of wife, secretary, and lady manager. In his view, women have a more central part to play in servicing spheres such as personnel or finance than in the wealth-creating work of production or the strategy-making role of general management. Dowell is comfortable with the existing divisions of labour at Hill:

MSR. Are there any women in management at Hill?

DOWELL. Ahm. I don't think we do have any at the moment. [Pause.] We have had them. [Pause.] Depends what you mean. We've certainly got women chief accountants in the divisions. I suppose you'd say women in purchase, yes, personnel certainly. Women in engineering or managing division, no. [Pause.]

We had a woman engineer who was in charge of all our computer operations who was extremely good, but eventually she became unemployable because [pause]. She was an absolutely first-class engineer, very competent, but she was so determined to make this female [pause]. You know, she became more male than, than the males in her job. She was so aggressive and so difficult that in the end you couldn't hold a balanced, reasoned argument with her, because if you said anything that implied criticism of her because she was a woman, you got the woman bit. [Pause.] So that in the end [chuckle] we had to call it a day.

Dowell's depiction of the woman engineer is similar to his description of the drunk wife which I analysed in the previous chapter.[33] The tension between fantasy and reality threatens to break to the surface in both passages, leading to an elaborate process of rationalization. In his role as chairman Dowell stresses his capacity for even-handedness. In order to demonstrate that he is not sexist, he mentions the woman engineer's competence and later he explains that he thinks women are generally more efficient than men. Yet it is precisely her ability that disturbs Dowell. The woman's expertise lies not in marginal functions like personnel ('depends what you mean' by management) but in the computer technology which controls the very heartbeat of production. She was 'in charge', and 'first class' in that capacity. Instead of encouraging her obvious talents, Dowell sees her aggression as a threat to the gender regime at Hill. The woman engi-

neer's confrontational nature—a quality so admirable in a man—
makes her 'eventually . . . unemployable'. She simply refuses to
become a 'lady manager'.

Dowell tries to resolve his conflicting feelings about the woman
engineer by constructing a 'balanced' justification of her dismissal.
Yet the irrational fears motivating his action are clearly apparent. We
observe this in the movement of the passage. A memory of the
woman's competence leads Dowell to reflect that she became 'more
male than' a man. He then symbolically castrates her with the remark
that she was hysterical. She raves uncontrollably about the 'woman
bit', refusing to pay heed to the masculine voice of 'reasoned argument'.

Women who successfully compete with men in occupations like
engineering have often faced animosity from men.[34] However, so too
might women in traditionally more acceptable spheres like personnel, particularly if they were in positions of seniority over men. Faced
with a woman boss, men might attempt to cancel out their subordinate status through exaggerated shows of masculinity. Bannerman
illustrates the anxiety which could be provoked by powerful women,
and the tendency to react by aggression. He had been called in for an
initial interview with the controlling board of a large public utility.
Bannerman responded to the unease he felt by identifying a 'bad
mother' whom he could attack:

> The chairwoman was the acting director of personnel. And she opened
> the bowling and said something like, 'Well before we go into detail, Mr
> Bannerman, I'd like to tell you a little bit about the job that you've
> applied for.' And I stopped her there and said, 'I'm sorry, but I haven't
> applied for the job. I've been asked if I'm interested.' For some reason
> she was slightly flustered at that, because perhaps she hadn't realized
> that it was a head-hunt job, or perhaps she just wasn't used to it . . .
> Well anyway, she said, 'Are you interested?' And I said, 'Yes, that's
> why I'm here. It sounds a very interesting job.' But in a sense it subtly
> shifted the balance of the interview.

This passage illustrates how a consciousness of 'good practice'
towards women managers could coexist with continued hostility
towards them. Bannerman is keen to demonstrate his familiarity with
the language of equal opportunities. Whereas his peers always
referred to the chair as masculine, the phrase 'chairwoman' slips naturally off his tongue. This reference built on his earlier depiction of
himself as the friend of women returners. However, the dominant

tone of this passage is its belligerence towards the woman personnel director. Understandably nervous as he begins the interview, Bannerman vents his persecutory feelings on her. Through his victory over the woman personnel director, he gains the self-confidence to tackle questions from the real competitors—the men on the interview panel. Like Dowell with his 'male' woman engineer, Bannerman feels a certain pleasure in stripping away the personnel director's façade of power. He makes a point of telling me that she was, after all, only 'acting' in the capacity of director. In order to achieve his victory Bannerman draws on the techniques learnt from his consultancy sessions with women. He provokes the very signs of feminine under-confidence in the personnel director which he earlier claimed to have done so much to overcome in his clients. 'She just wasn't used to it,' he concludes, the gentlemanly metaphor of the cricket match, suddenly suggestive of more violent contests.

Bannerman's job application climaxes in an interview with the managing director in which the men are left alone to fight it out. Here his narrative is full of the joy of manly confrontation. Its comradely bent contrasts with the sniping hostility he directed towards the woman personnel director. Where women competitors provoke fantasies of castration, the rough play between men enhances potency:

I went ahead and met Hanover again at 5 o'clock on a Friday evening. And we had we had two hours of very fast moving, hard hitting, open-ended discussion really. It wasn't an interview, it was just a kind of debate almost. Which I very much enjoyed and I think he enjoyed. And I thought, 'I can actually work for this bloke.' And that was what swung it. If he'd been anyone else, I wouldn't have come. But I thought 'yes'.

Bannerman's story exemplifies the organization man's contradictory attitudes towards women. Despite his professed sympathy for women managers, Bannerman still sought to marginalize them from the 'hard-hitting', really productive jobs. This generation of men have responded to the pressure to cede power by extending the post-war divisions between bread-winners and home-makers. They see themselves as family men providing assistance to mothers in the shape of aspiring women managers. Yet, while men's domination of senior management means that they have a considerable influence over the careers of women, at a psychic level these power relations are reversed. The idealization of 'feminine' managers and the persecutory feelings aroused by more aggressive women reflect the men's emotional dependence upon women. It would be easy to dismiss the imaginings of men like Dowell or Bannerman as harmless, were it not for the fact that they are projected upon real women. Sackings, refusals of permanence, small humiliations, or the 'channelling-off' of women into peripheral management functions are real forms of retribution, despite their fantastic origins.

Business commentators, men and women alike, have sometimes assumed that, although the gains made by women so far have mainly been in the lower reaches of management, the future will see their increasing presence at senior levels. Pushed by the impending skills shortage, women in business are seen as leading the way to a new, more equal gender order.[35] This is a variant of the organization man's 'bread-winner' ethic, which holds that a combination of hard slog and the march of time will guarantee promotion. Now that women are on the managerial ladder, the argument goes, with the boost of professional training, gender segregation will eventually be reduced. Men's resistance to change is largely ignored in this way of thinking. Equal-opportunities policies are sometimes based on a similarly optimistic notion that the shortest route to equality lies in making gatekeeping practices such as recruitment and promotion more 'professional'.[36] While such initiatives at least recognize the existence of exclusion by men, they still leave untouched the psychic dynamics that motivate it, and the ways in which the gender regimes of family and workplace lock together. This chapter has shown that the very definitions of what it means to be a woman or man are brought into question in discussions about practices like the career break. Yet, because the struggle for equality in management has generally been seen as a woman's issue, the links between men's fantasies and their actions as managers have remained largely unexplored. The women in management literature have shown how the 'typecasting' of women as nurturers means that they are often rewarded for service rather than for independent action.[37] In this study I have tried to illustrate how deep-seated this typecasting is. In their dealings with women managers, organization men resorted to a psychic baggage deriving from family relations. Their stories reveal how difficult it was for them to recognize women—wives, secretaries, or managers—as autonomous actors rather than as the providers of material and emotional services. Organization men judged women managers in terms of the emotional comforts they did or did not provide, and offered them gifts of advice or promotion in ways which bolstered their own position as company bread-winners. While the men's portrayals of women are creations of the mind, they do have real consequences in terms of gender inequalities in management.

NOTES

1. This observation is made by J. Lewis, *Women in Britain since 1945: Women, Family, Work and the State in the Post-War Years* (Oxford, 1992), 69, 82.
2. The term 'gender regime' is used by R. W. Connell to describe the state of play of gender relations in particular institutions such as the workplace or family (*Gender and Power: Society, the Person and Sexual Politics* (Cambridge, 1987), 120.
3. R. M. Kanter comments that men's tendency to view women managers as mothers at work has a number of consequences. The 'mother' is rewarded mainly 'for service and not for independent action'; and the role of emotional specialist reinforces men's stereotypes of women as less rational (*Men and Women of the Corporation* (New York, 1977), 233–4). See also C. L. Cooper and M. J. Davidson, who comment that this was a stereotype which women felt they must avoid if they were to be taken seriously as managers (*High Pressure: Working Lives of Women Managers* (Glasgow, 1982), 70).
4. J. Marshall, 'Issues of Identity for Women Managers', in D. Clutterbuck and M. Devine (eds.), *Businesswoman: Past and Future* (London, 1987), 20. See, e.g., Cooper and Davidson, *High Pressure*, and M. J. Davidson, and C. L. Cooper, *Shattering the Glass Ceiling: The Woman Manager* (London, 1992). These books consider the structural and social context of inequalities, but much of the emphasis is placed on coping strategies for women.
5. Cooper and Davidson, *High Pressure*, 202–25.
6. D. L. Sheppard, 'Organizations, Power and Sexuality: The Image and Self-Image of Women Managers', in J. Hearn, D. L. Sheppard, P. Tancred-Sheriff, and G. Burrell (eds.), *The Sexuality of Organization* (London, 1989), 144.
7. A. R. Hochschild, *The Managed Heart: Commercialization of Human Feeling* (Berkeley, Calif., 1983), ch. 8. See also H. Wainwright, 'Women and the Division of Labour', in P. Abrams and R. Baker (eds.), *UK Society: Work, Urbanism and Inequality* (London, 1984), 198–212.
8. A good general account of the period is in Lewis, *Women in Britain since 1945*, esp. 16–26.
9. D. Riley, *War in the Nursery: Theories of the Child and Mother* (London, 1983).
10. Ibid. 109.
11. Ibid.
12. Ibid.
13. C. Heward, *Making a Man of him: Parents and their Sons' Education at an English Public School, 1929–1950* (London, 1988), 39–47.
14. Locke had married in her early thirties, a good ten years later than the other women in the sample.
15. The term is taken from Elaine Showalter, *The Female Malady: Women, Madness and English Culture* (London, 1987).
16. In Kleinian terms, the Operations manager was Gould's 'envied object'; she

211

showed her aggression by symbolically depriving him of his 'cock' (M. Klein, 'A Study of Envy and Gratitude', in J. Mitchell (ed.), *The Selected Melanie Klein* (London, 1986), 218–20).

17. Judi Marshall observed a similar contradiction in her survey of women managers; women often explained that they did not feel disadvantaged, but would then go on to illustrate the armoury of tactics they used to combat men's hostility; ('Issues of Identity for Women Managers', 16).

18. A similar view was voiced by Mr North, a board member at Chemtex. North was 'conscious of the fact' that for most of his working life Chemtex had been 'a man's world'. At the same time he found it 'surprising' that women still experienced difficulty in 'getting through' to senior management.

19. In 1950 almost half the members of the Institute of Personnel Management were women, but by 1970 the figure was just below 20% (see K. Legge, 'Women in Personnel Management: Uphill Climb or Downhill Slide?', in A. Spencer and D. Podmore (eds.), *In a Man's World: Essays on Women in Male Dominated Professions* (London, 1987), 38–46).

20. See Ch.4, sect. iv.

21. See D. L. Collinson, D. Knights, and M. Collinson, *Managing to Discriminate* (London, 1990), for a discussion of this 'bread-winner' ethic; the authors describe how line managers presented themselves as 'producers of profit and wealth' for the firm, so enhancing their power over functions like personnel (p. 86).

22. Two of the five women managers I interviewed had re-entered work as secretaries after career breaks.

23. R. Scase and R. Goffee, *Reluctant Managers: Their Work and Lifestyle* (London, 1989), 7.

24. Collinson, Knights, and Collinson provide an excellent example of this contradiction; they report that line managers tended to prefer married male staff because they were more 'stable', but criticized married women who opted to remain at work on the grounds that they were too 'aggressive' (*Managing to Discriminate*, 97).

25. M. Klein, 'The Origins of Transference', in Mitchell (ed.), *The Selected Melanie Klein*, 202.

26. See Introduction.

27. Cooper and Davidson talk about the 'low expectation trap' in which many women are caught (*High Pressure*, 158).

28. C. Cockburn, 'Equal Opportunities: The Short and Long Agendas', *Industrial Relations Journal*, 20/3 (1989), 222.

29. Collinson, Knights, and Collinson, *Managing to Discriminate*, 150.

30. Two of my women interviewees recalled the critical role played by men in transferring from clerical to managerial work. Gould's boss had 'allowed' her to undertake some of his tasks, and her success at these prompted her to take the shipping insurance examinations. Finch's first managerial post was in a small insurance brokers, six years after she had begun her career with the firm as a secretary. She was trained and appointed by the director himself, who apparently preferred women managers because they were less confrontational (this is an interesting inversion of the mentor relationships between

men discussed in Ch. 3, which often pivot on confrontation). Typically, Finch's skills were not recognized by her subsequent employers, necessitating further training and a temporary return to secretarial work.

31. Bannerman talked at length about a case he had taken on for a career woman's magazine. It involved a divorcee who had once been director of a small travel company. He had been given three months 'to try and get her back in at the same level as she left'. Due to his extensive network of contacts he succeeded just within the stipulated deadline. The articles 'created an enormous response from . . . literally hundreds of women . . . trying either to get back in to work or in many cases trying to change', and resulted in Bannerman being able to take on a partner in his firm.

32. As Cockburn comments of the older male managers in high-street retail, organization men 'put down and marginalized those they could and were resentful of those they could not' ('Equal Opportunities', 83).

33. See Ch. 6, sect. ii.

34. See, e.g., P. Newton, 'Who Becomes an Engineer? Social Psychological Antecedents of a Non-Traditional Career Choice', in Spencer and Podmore, *In a Man's World*, 198.

35. 'In Business', Radio 4, 4 Apr. 1988. The programme featured a panel of four, including two male management consultants and two women entrepreneurs. There was agreement around the table when one of the women explained that

> If you're looking at women in senior business today, then you have to look at the age factor, and you're looking in traditional companies at older women, because it takes time to progress up the career tree. And I think women have changed a lot; the education and their expectations have changed dramatically in more recent times. And you're likely to see this having a knock-on effect, and many more women in senior positions in the nineties.

36. The problems with this approach are highlighted in Janette Webb's study of psychometric testing ('The Gender Relations of Assessment', in J. Firth-Cozens and M. A. West (eds.), *Women at Work: Psychological and Organizational Perspectives* (Milton Keynes, 1991), 13–24).

37. Kanter, *Men and Women*, 234.

CONCLUSION

The Fall of the Organization Man?

....

The past two decades have seen a rise in the proportion of women in management. Between 1971 and 1981 the number of women employers, managers, and professional workers rose by 45 per cent, over double that of men.[1] However, these changes have been concentrated at lower- and middle-management levels. Less than 1 per cent of Britain's chief executives are women.[2] As the Hansard Society has commented, women executive directors are 'scarcely visible'.[3] The existing literature on women in management is strong on recommendations for change, but provides few clues about why the pace of change at this level has been so slow. It tends to move directly from describing the barriers which women face, to prescriptions for change.[4] Aimed at women and at a managerial audience, it recognizes men's resistance to change as a problem, but concentrates on legislative programmes or 'coping mechanisms' for individual women. Researchers have pointed out that, as a result of men's near monopoly over senior management, women are often forced into a position of choosing between becoming an 'honorary man', or emphasizing their femininity.[5] But there has been a dearth of work on what it is about men and bureaucracies that places women in this 'no-win' position. This study suggests that, after two decades of action on equal opportunities, the attitudes and practices of male managers in manufacturing industry are little changed.

The preceding chapters have thus tried to broaden the agenda by putting business men rather than women under scrutiny. In one sense, of course, men's visibility in business is the whole problem. But connections have not often been drawn between the actions and the gender of business men. Masculinity is evident across a range of domains in management: as part of the collective discourses about business, as an aspect of particular business regimes, and, most important for this study, as a part of the self-image of male managers. We saw in Chapter 1 how representations of masculinity are often visible in discussions about the economy, or in public commentaries on the rise and fall of individual business people. Indeed one might even characterize the 1980s debates about Britain's industrial future in terms of male hysteria, given the tendency among both politicians and academics to interpret industrial decline as a form of national impotence. The economic sectors and institutions which compose particular business regimes also exhibit gendered features. In Chapter 4 we saw how industries such as motor vehicles or machine tools are frequently contrasted to 'soft' sectors such as financial services. Similar distinctions operate within firms, in the differentiation between functions such as the 'caring' sphere of personnel, and the wealth-generating task of production.

In this study, however, I have focused on the subjective identities of one generation and one industrial sector: the post-war entrants to manufacturing industry, many of whom held senior posts. My aim was to explore through life history how their sense of themselves as men was conveyed in the stories they told me about management. Rather than looking only at the points where they excluded women, I wanted to go back a stage and understand how organization men dramatized the pleasures and discontents of masculinity in their work. What emerges is the necessity to look beyond gate-keeping practices such as recruitment, training, and promotion. An understanding of the ways in which domestic and organizational regimes are linked is the key to a more nuanced picture of how gender inequalities operate in management. The post-war generation reproduced the cultural separation of spheres between home and work *within* management. David Collinson, David Knights, and Margaret Collinson signal these connections with their concept of the 'bread-winner ideology'.[6] Organization men not only saw themselves as bread-winners for wives and children, but for the nation as well. They contrasted their manly productive work with the effete city gentlemen who consumed the wealth they had created. When describing the divisions of labour in their companies, they belittled the emotional labours performed by secretaries and valorized work metaphorically 'at the coal face'.

If in these ways the gender regimes of business are more

deep-seated than we have often realized, at the same time, they are not intractable. The gender regimes created by organization men were tenuous in two respects. First, there was a basic contradiction between the *position* of middle and senior managers in non-manual jobs, and the heroic language through which they depicted that work. Thus, while the senior managers in this study occupied jobs at headquarters, they looked back wistfully on their early days 'outdoors' in company divisions, or described strategy-making in a combative language. Images of toughness pervaded their stories about take-overs or their internal equivalents, those 'palace revolutions' in which younger generations seized power. Yet, despite all the bravado, there was no escaping the fact that their labours were sedentary.[7] Moreover, organization men rarely felt equal to the cult of toughness which they so ardently promoted. Acting the hard man was just as often born of the fear of being oppressed themselves as from a conscious desire to dominate women and other men.

Secondly, the organization man's sense of himself as a man was undermined by the changing fortunes of British business. The postwar generation presented an image of hard masculinity based on its practical expertise in mechanical engineering, but microchip technologies threatened to render this kind of skill obsolete. Furthermore, the period after 1945 saw the gradual decline of Britain as an international manufacturer, and a parallel decline in the national stature of manufacturing men. While organization men imagined themselves as heroic bread-winners for the nation, this was in the face of a steady *loss* of economic influence. Shifts like this should also make us wary of viewing the connections between managerial power and masculinity in a too categorical way.

The internal contradictions and social forces which shape masculinity demonstrate that, despite the outward appearance, men's monopoly over the senior posts in management is not rock solid. This book thus has a twofold message about the nature of men's power in organizations. I have argued that we need to look beyond the barriers facing women managers. Understanding why the passage of equal opportunities has been slow entails turning our attention to men and the emotional economy of leadership. Yet this study reveals that organization men were equally empowered and inhibited by the gender regimes which they helped to fashion. Career success as a public man often went with an abiding feeling of personal failure. As the ex-head of ICI Sir John Harvey-Jones reflected in his autobiography, even in late career 'I had not yet succeeded in "getting it together" in a personal sense'.[8] By way of conclusion I want to explore these tensions in more detail. First, how does a focus on masculinity help us to understand the ascendancy of organization men over the most senior, most fulfilling jobs in management? Secondly, what are the social and psychic forces which make their power contingent? Finally, where next? What does the recent profusion of discourses about gender in business, from the 'decline' debates to the soul-searching of men like Lee Iacocca or Sir John Harvey-Jones, suggest about the future? Will gender inequality fade away with the organization man?

The prescriptive literature on women in management approaches the relationship between masculinity and men's power in organizations in three principal ways.[9] One strand focuses on the structural obstacles to equality, another provides a catalogue of personal 'coping strategies' which women managers can learn to minimize the problems of being a 'token woman' in a male environment, and a third celebrates sexual difference. The mainstream over the past decade has been occupied by those who, following the lead set by R. M. Kanter in *Men and Women of the Corporation*, seek to overcome gender inequality through the further professionalization of management. Kanter began her book with the observation that authority structures within management were dominated by 'masculine principles'.[10] Yet she did not follow this insight through. Instead, she argued that the problems facing women workers stem from the fact that they are either 'tokens' at the top of organizations, or concentrated at the bottom. Change was ultimately a matter of numbers rather than gender. What followed from this was a programme which stressed the need to alter the structure of bureaucracies in order to get more women to the top. Kanter called for flatter hierarchies, for bridges to be built between clerical and managerial job ladders, for job design to be broadened, and for more 'flexitime'. She also called for rigorous recruitment and performance appraisal systems, and for the formalization of mentoring.[11] As Joan Acker comments, Kanter 'implicitly posits gender as being outside structure'.[12] Much equal-opportunities work since the passing of the Sex Discrimination Act in 1975 has been motivated by a similar presumption that structure rather than gender is the key to the barriers faced by women managers. Efforts have been directed towards 'professionalizing' recruitment and promotion.[13] Subjective and therefore discriminatory attitudes, it was hoped, would gradually be squeezed out of existence by formal practices. What emerges from my study is the extent to which the masculinity of organization men was shaped according to the kind of company in which they worked. We have seen how they projected gender differences on to the distinction between finance and production, head office and divisions, staff and line. The organization man's emotional investment in the existing gender regime ran deep. For him, the kind of career path a man had pursued was an indication of his masculinity. So, while the post-war generation oversaw the rise of professional management, it belied the myth that the personal could be separated from the public practices of the bureaucracy.

A second approach to gender discrimination also calls for changes in entry and promotion practices, but directs its attention mainly to women managers. The emphasis here is on the personal costs of working in a male-dominated environment. For example, Marilyn Davidson and Cary Cooper have claimed in numerous studies that the pressure to *act* masculine, to be confident and aggressive, is a major cause of stress in the lives of women managers.[14] They provide ample illustration of the ways in which women may be hampered by the masculine values of management—either dismissed from serious attention but approved by men if they play the 'earth mother' role, or seen as objects of hostility if they compete as a man would. Despite these observations, such approaches ultimately leave the nature of men and masculinity off the agenda. When the appeal is directed towards the incumbent managers, it is principally to ask for their assistance in formalizing gate-keeping mechanisms.[15]

A third strand of the women-in-management literature steers around men's resistance to equality by celebrating the special strengths which women have to offer. This approach begins by recognizing the implicit gender bias of many organizational cultures, but tries to capture the support of managers by emphasizing the utility of women's more consensual management style. Such approaches may derive from a radical feminist or conservative politics. In her study of British women managers, Judi Marshall perceptively points out that, when women adopt impersonal, competitive management styles, they are in fact colluding with 'male power structures'.[16] She counsels the need for women to develop different strengths, recovering their 'connectedness'.[17] Approaches which emphasize sexual difference beg as many questions as those which try to legislate it out of existence. They, too, leave masculinity hidden in the 'normal' competitive and supposedly rational endeavours of management. At worst such approaches provide a positive encouragement for existing gender regimes. For example, in the prestigious *Harvard Business Review*, Judy B. Rosener revives the distinction between masculine or 'transactional' management styles, and women's more 'transformational' approach. She argues for a change in corporate culture so as to take advantage of women's mothering skills. Where organizations usually adopt a masculine, 'command and control' mode, Rosener promotes a more vicarious style of leadership, in which managers use their power to energize and enhance the self-worth of others.[18] The emotional labours traditionally performed by women are here elevated to a managerial creed.

Despite their differences, these strands of thought have similar limitations. Existing change strategies either disregard or exploit the gender divisions which pervade management. Rather than recommending an alternative between exalted mother-managers or commanding men, we need to know more about the particular contexts in which distinctions between masculinity and femininity are constructed. How are men's gender identities confirmed by the process of management succession or the social relations surrounding production, for example? As Cynthia Cockburn argues, the agenda for change needs to be broadened from its current focus on removing the barriers to free competition for managerial labour, to an admittedly more diffuse project of identifying the means whereby men's power in organizations is reproduced. This would include, among other things, understanding how gender may be implicated in company strategies, labour market policies, changes in status between management functions, the split between domestic and career responsibilities, and the particular gender regimes of firms.[19]

Family relations and the symbolism surrounding them emerge as key elements in the reproduction of men's power. In Chapter 1 I stressed that a full understanding of gender segregation requires that we look not only at how women are disadvantaged, but at how men advantage each other. A focus on the family imagery through which management is represented reveals the connections between inclusion and exclusion. As we saw in Chapters 3, 4, and 5, the splits between feminine and supportive work on the one hand, and the truly masculine endeavours of production on the other, were also sustained *within* 'men's work'. The organization man's image of a domestic sphere split between home-makers and bread-winners extended to his conception of the managerial sphere. Family images structured the relations of both home and work, blurring the neat lines which have traditionally been drawn between the two.[20] Sexual and family symbolism, Rosemary Pringle aptly remarks, 'is as central to work as it is to domestic relations'.[21]

In a material sense it was the labours of wives and secretaries that permitted organization men to pursue their 'family romances' with other men, or their quests for the perfect product. Women undertook the servicing work which made men comfortable in their environments, enabling them to channel their energies into the corporate life.[22] In this sense, the work of an office secretary in making coffee or tea, controlling access to managers, or organizing their timetables shared some similarities with the labours of wives in keeping house. These differences between the work of women and men were associated with equally profound psychic splits. The men depicted two kinds of women in their accounts: idealized 'good mothers' who supported their ambitions, and 'bad mothers' who wished to deprive them of power. The abilities of women in supportive functions such as personnel were frequently idealized, the men presenting their positive feelings towards such women as evidence of their commitment to equality. In fact, however, this fatherly concern threatened to limit the independence of women. In contrast, women in production jobs occasionally became objects of men's aggressive feelings, the woman's very competence seeming to indicate an ambition to rob men of their potency. Women managers of this generation also divided up the work world into nurturing and castrating mothers. They might deal with men's attempts at exclusion by demonstrating their skills at emotional labours, or by playing on men's insecurities about their masculinity. Men in particular were rarely conscious of the fantasy elements through which they transformed women managers into objects of love or persecution. At the same time, fantasies like these are significant because they motivated the discriminatory behaviour which researchers have shown operating at the points of recruitment, training, and promotion.

Family symbolism had an equally important place in relations between men, enabling them to transcend the cultural constraints of the work–home divide. We saw in Chapter 3 how relations between older and younger men might take on a variety of guises, ranging from father–son to sexually experienced older woman–boy virgin. The objects of production were endowed with a similarly polymorphous fantasy life in which masculine or feminine attributes might dominate. Men might celebrate a perfect product as a phallus, or, equally, as an object of heterosexual desire. The joy of production for this generation lay in the fact that it could be simultaneously 'begetting' and bread-winning, maternal and paternal. Relations like these brought men into intimate contact with each other. Yet the passions among men were repressed, to emerge in the heterosexual and familial imagery that men used to describe their work. Women's presence in management threatened the survival of close affections between men. A homosocial economy operated among men, was described in the language of heterosexual love, and was protected through the exclusion of real women.

So far I have emphasized how the organization man's identity as a man was confirmed by the gender regimes of work and home. The men I interviewed imagined themselves as bread-winners for family and company in their relations with partners and secretaries. In the case of women managers, the image of women as eternal dependants acted as a kind of 'exclusionary mechanism'. If in this way the organization man's fantasies directly reflected his social power, it is easy to overstate the case. Throughout we have observed the defensiveness of members of the post-war generation. They felt besieged on every side—from younger women and men competitors, from the tide of economic change, even from the wives and secretaries who facilitated their career success. Speaking with their 'corporate hat' on, as one man put it, they emphasized how important a skilled secretary was for the efficient running of a business. Yet a competent secretary might also cause men to feel that their own position was under threat. The men's attitude to women managers reflected a similar tension between utilizing the best talent available, and fearing women with independent career ambitions. Contradictions like these suggest that the organization man's hold over power was never entirely secure.

The course of business history also reveals how contingent the organization man's gender identity was. In terms of managerial authority, the post-war generation was betwixt and between. They were owner-managers, but they inherited the management culture of family capitalism. Lack of mobility between firms and relatively long career chains have prompted sociologists to label this cohort of managers as organization men *par excellence*.[23] Yet they embraced the professional ideal very reluctantly. Indeed, when talking about the business-school graduates, they defined themselves as anti-professionals. Moreover, the ideal of bureaucratic man itself seemed to disintegrate almost as soon as it was in place, undermined from within by industrial restructuring during the 1980s.[24] A changing economy and capital structure in manufacturing limited the organization man's ability to fashion a stable gender identity.

Reinard Bendix, writing about the passage of the United States from entrepreneurial to bureaucratic capitalism in the early twentieth century, has drawn attention to the difficulties which career managers faced in legitimating their new-found authority. Unlike entrepreneurs, these career managers had not proved their merits through the personal accumulation of capital. Their position rested instead on the market value of specialist skills.[25] In Bendix's view, the evolving 'spirit of managerialism'—symbolized in the work of F. W. Taylor and Scientific Management—functioned as an ideological tool which bolstered the status of non-owners by underlining their superior cognitive powers.[26] This work has argued that the legitimation of authority in business is also crucially a matter of gender. A gender perspective in the British case reveals just how incomplete the triumph of 'professionalism' was. British organization men faced similar dilemmas to their American counterparts in the post-war era of corporate capitalism. However, they did not opt completely for the mantle of rational man. Far from it, they struggled against an internalized view of management as a matter of pen-pushing. They might imagine themselves as entrepreneurs, placing their careers on the line with profitable but risky investments, or 'screwing' their suppliers down to the last penny, as if the company's capital was their own. Sometimes they sided with inheritors, emphasizing their loyalty to the founding families and upholding a conception of products as the bearers of company tradition. Alternatively, they might borrow the guise of 'hard' working-class masculinity, emphasizing the toughness they had developed through years of practical experience in manufacturing. Memories like these indicate that organization men felt a profound ambivalence about their place in the managerial and gender hierarchies. They could not rest easy with the image of themselves as thinkers; they had to be out there *doing* something. Historians of business describe the post-war years in terms of the triumph of the corporate economy. But the post-war gender hierarchy in manufacturing was down-side up. Organization men might have been the torch-bearers of a new, professional age, but they felt less manly than 'self-made' entrepreneurs, paternalistic inheritors, and (as one man expressed it) the 'horny-handed sons of toil' whom they managed.

Tensions like these between gender, class, and capital ownership were endemic in the stories of organization men. Their gender identities were also continually challenged by the changing fortunes of Britain's economy. We saw in Chapter 2 how the 1960s merger boom brought with it a renewed drive for profitability, as companies sought to protect themselves from take-over, or rationalize their acquisitions. This new orthodoxy clashed with the post-war emphasis on technical excellence as an end in itself. Increasingly it was the profitability rather than the function of products which counted. With the increasing emphasis upon efficiency, there was often a shift in the balance of power from the production functions to the newer disciplines of strategy, finance, and marketing. The recession of the early 1980s intensified the pace of change in manufacturing. Practices like subcontracting and the 'unbundling' of divisions from large corporations have played their part in eroding the bureaucratic ideal. The implications of these changes for managerial careers are profound. Rather than specialist skills in science or engineering forming the basis for a managerial appointment, what count today are the general-management techniques taught by business schools. Career chains are now shorter and jobs not so clearly delineated.[27] Mobility between firms is more common than in the post-war period. As Richard Scase and Robert Goffee comment, managers today are 'more likely to pursue "occupational" rather than "organizational" careers'.[28]

It was amidst the turmoil of industrial restructuring that I conducted my interviews. Some of the more senior managers had even taken a part in restructuring, selling off divisions of the business or contracting out for components they had once manufactured in-house. Thy tended to see such changes as symptoms of decline rather than renewal. Organization men clung to the cult of the producer but felt impotent to protect their love of products from the cost-cutting accountants and financiers. They responded to their marginalization by asserting the inherent superiority of their masculinity over that of the younger generation. Business-school graduates were thought to lack the discipline born of military service, with its enforced separation from women and family. Nor had they the experience of 'man management' which their seniors had built up over the course of an organizational career. The organization man's version of masculinity provided him with a means of asserting a kind of superiority in the face of economic threats. It made him more heroic than the younger managers in manufacturing, or the city whiz-kids and retailing managers who stole the public limelight in the 1980s. The battle between generations and industrial sectors for supremacy revolved partly around masculinity. Organization men cast aspersions on the masculinity of their formally trained successors by labelling them as mere professionals. Meanwhile, advocates of the enterprise culture trained their guns on organization men, who were accused of sheltering inside their organizations from the chill winds of competition.[29] Each side cast aspersions on the other's manhood, accusing it of having become the real bureaucrats.

While the lines of battle between organization men and their successors seemed clear during the 1980s, ironically there was growing confusion within more academic circles between 'hands-on' and rational–logical management styles. Once again, the conflicts within public discourses about management took a different form from the conflicts within particular business regimes. On the one hand, the art of management as an analytical process was elevated to new heights with the work of writers like Michael Porter. His extremely popular writings on competitive strategy adhered to impersonal, positivist methods of analysis. The arguments appealed by virtue of their clarity, and the supposition that economic prosperity would surely follow once a logical strategy had been formulated. On the other hand, there were sustained attempts to dismantle the masculine fantasy of management through deductive reasoning. This was especially true of Peters's and Waterman's *In Search of Excellence*, whose message quickly spread across the Atlantic to become part of 'new wave management' in Britain.[30] Peters's and Waterman's recommendation for flatter hierarchies, the blurring of functional divisions through project teams and total quality, became the catch-calls of the 1980s.[31]

In Search of Excellence claimed to liberate managers from the rational paradigm, but in so doing it reverted to the principles of post-war gender regimes. Paradoxically, while setting out an agenda for the restructuring which organization men resisted, Peters and Waterman echoed many of their sentiments. Both organization men and the 'new wave management' writers pointed their fingers at business schools for turning out passionless quantifiers. Top managers and staff were accused of having become isolated from realities outside company headquarters, particularly products and customers. In unison with organization men, Peters and Waterman called for 'love of product' to become once again the motive force for industrial endeavour.[32] As Peters and Waterman remarked, management is not about 'brain games in the sterile ivory tower, it's shaping values and reinforcing through coaching and evangelism in the field—with the worker and in support of the cherished product'.[33] There was one critical difference between this new managerialism and the views of organization men: where the latter regarded love of products as an end in itself, Peters and Waterman refashioned it in the context of a service-driven economy. Regardless of whether they sold hamburgers or cars, excellent companies were those which 'defined themselves as de facto service businesses'.[34] A perfect product was the result of a coming together of manufacturers and customers, and that could only occur once the financiers and strategy-makers were unthroned.

Gender was one of the subtexts in this battle within the ranks of professional business between product-orientated and 'rational' approaches to management. In their attempt to shift the balance of power, Peters and Waterman put gender images to good use. They emphasized the importance of 'irrational, intuitive' qualities for success, explicitly describing these as feminine.[35] National recovery, they argued, depended upon the debunking of analytical approaches, and greater respect for the emotional satisfactions afforded by work. Peters and Waterman sought to return managers to a polymorphous state in which masculine and feminine, 'hard' and 'soft' elements were combined. Where intuition had previously been dismissed as 'soft', Peters and Waterman counselled that 'soft is hard'.[36] The doctrine of scientific management claimed to be hard but was actually 'sterile'. Planning 'stamps all verve, life and initiative out of the company'.[37] The masculine image of the rational manager was thus challenged by demonstrating that seemingly feminine characteristics were actually potent managerial tools. Soft really could become hard.

The 1980s debates about the future of industry represented gender in diverse, often conflicting ways. At the level of national politics, the discourse of the enterprise culture resurrected images associated with the self-made entrepreneur, using them to cast aspersions on the manhood of organization men. Within management there were continued arguments about whether analytical or 'hands-on' styles should take precedence. These debates paralleled those which we observed in the literature on women in management, with its dilemma of whether individual women should seek success through 'masculine' or 'feminine' management styles. The one thing which all these discourses had in common was their engagement with gender images: unconsciously in the case of the national debates, semi-consciously in the case of business-school pundits, and overtly in the women-in-management literature. None of the streams mounted a direct challenge to the divide itself. Instead, business commentators invoked images of sexual difference as a means of arguing for the management style they favoured. The managerial world remained split in two, leaving even its most privileged actors, men like Sir John Harvey-Jones, struggling to heal the psychic and social rifts between masculinity and femininity, and become 'simultaneously strong and compassionate, stiff-lipped yet emotional'.[38]

Since the heyday of the 'organization society' in the 1960s there have been dramatic shifts in the locus of economic power, in the structure of manufacturing industries, and in the dominant dis-courses of management. The growing pre-eminence of service-sector industries during the 1980s raises the question of whether men's domination of management will disappear with the organization man himself. Existing research suggests a far-from-simple picture. Rosemary Crompton and Kay Sanderson, in their work on gender segregation in 1980s Britain, point out that it was the bastions of tra-ditional masculinity which suffered the heaviest job losses in the 1980s.[39] During this time women managers made their strongest gains in the financial sector, where Britain's future (at least at the time their book was published) looked brightest. These changes lead Crompton and Sanderson to be relatively optimistic. They claim that educated and qualified working women, in the restructured white-collar hierarchies particularly, are 'likely to be one of the most endur-ing phenomena carrying over into the twenty-first century'. Women will continue to be under-represented in comparison to men of the same level. Nevertheless, the 'impact of their presence upon the overall structure of material advantage and disadvantage . . . may be of greater significance than their numerical representation in the working population'.[40]

On the other side are those, also researching the service sector, who emphasize the ways in which masculinity and managerial cul-tures continue to be locked together. Cockburn's belief that the 'long agenda' of equality has scarcely been touched was based on work in a retailing firm which has achieved national recognition for its equal-opportunities programme.[41] Recent case-studies in banking suggest that, while women have moved into traditionally 'masculine' spheres like insurance sales, men still dominate the more senior, better-paid posts. Men continue to define which jobs are the 'bread-winning' ones.[42] Changes like these raise wider questions about gender and management which a study such as this, based as it is on one generation of men in one sector, cannot answer. What I have tried to show is that future research, as well as detailing the structural aspects of gender inequality, must also consider its symbolic and psychic dimensions.

NOTES

1. R. Crompton and K. Sanderson, *Gendered Jobs and Social Change* (London, 1990), 164, table 8.1.
2. Hansard Society, *Report of the Hansard Society Commission on Women at the Top* (London, 1990), 53. The first woman finance director to be appointed to a FTSE 100 Index company took up her post in mid-1991 (*Guardian*, 16 June 1991).
3. Hansard Society, *Women at the Top*, 8.
4. This is pointed out by Collinson, Knights, and Collinson in relation to the literature on sex discrimination (D.L. Collinson, D. Knights, and M. Collinson, *Managing to Discriminate* (London, 1990), 10–14).
5. D. L. Sheppard, 'Organizations, Power and Sexuality: The Image and Self-Image of Women Managers', in J. Hearn, D. L. Sheppard, P. Tancred-Sheriff, and G. Burrell (eds.), *The Sexuality of Organization* (London, 1989), 139–58.
6. Collinson, Knights, and Collinson, *Managing to Discriminate*, 85–93.
7. R. W. Connell makes a similar point about the tenuous masculinity of the office-worker in *Which Way Is Up? Essays on Class, Sex and Culture* (Sydney, 1983), 20–3.
8. Harvey-Jones, *Getting it Together: Memoirs of a Troubleshooter* (London, 1991), 373.
9. For excellent recent summaries of the women in management literature, see M. Alvesson, and Y. D. Billing, 'Gender and Organization: Towards a Differentiated Understanding', *Organization Studies*, 13/2 (1992), 73–102; C. Cockburn, *In the Way of Women: Men's Resistance to Sex Equality in Organizations* (London, 1991), ch. 2, 'Equal Opportunities: Rights and Wrongs'.
10. R. M. Kanter, *Men and Women of the Corporation* (New York, 1977), 22.
11. Ibid. 265–87.
12. See J. Acker, 'Hierarchies, Jobs, Bodies: A Theory of Gendered Organizations', *Gender and Society*, 4/2 (June 1990), 143.
13. Good critiques of this liberal stance are J. Webb, 'The Gender Relations of

Assessment', in J. Firth-Cozens and M. A. West (eds.), *Women at Work: Psychological and Organizational Perspectives* (Milton Keynes, 1991), 13–25; and J. Webb and S. Liff, 'Play the White Man: The Social Construction of Fairness and Competition in Equal Opportunity Policies', *Sociological Review*, 36/3 (1988), 532–51. The rich case-studies presented by Collinson, Knights, and Collinson amply show the limitations of formalization strategies. They reveal the ways in which gender inequality is 'produced and reproduced in routine practices'. Nevertheless the authors still end up advocating further professionalization of recruitment and promotion. The only additional requirements which they specify to this 'liberal' approach are the extension of career-break schemes, flexible working, and work crèches (*Managing to Discriminate*, 207–13).

14. Their most recent work is M. J. Davidson and C. L. Cooper, *Shattering the Glass Ceiling: The Woman Manager* (London, 1992).

15. C. L. Cooper and M. J. Davidson, *High Pressure: Working Lives of Women Managers* (Glasgow, 1982). Cooper and Davidson do point out the possibility of training programmes which would confront men with their 'myths', but they direct most of their consideration to the 'special needs' of women (p. 231).

16. J. Marshall, 'Issues of Identity for Women Mangers', in D. Clutterbuck and M. Devine (eds.), *Businesswoman: Past and Future* (London, 1987), 19. See also Marshall, *Women Managers: Travellers in a Male World* (Chichester, 1984), 19.

17. Marshall, 'Issues of Identity', 21; in a wry aside she comments that 'Equal opportunity to coronary heart disease is an "equality" we can do without' (p. 13).

18. J. B. Rosener, 'Ways Women Lead', *Harvard Business Review* (Nov.–Dec. 1990), 119–25; see also the debate in the Jan.–Feb. issue, 151–60.

19. C. Cockburn, 'Equal Opportunities: The Short and Long Agendas', *Industrial Relations Journal*, 20/3 (1989), 219–20.

20. For a commentary on sociology's foundation in the division between family and public domains, see L. Davidoff, '"Adam Spoke First and Named the Orders of the World": Masculine and Feminine Domains in History and Sociology', in H. Corr and L. Jamieson (eds.), *The Politics of Everday Life: Continuity and Change in Work, Labour and the Family* (London, 1990), 229–56.

21. R. Pringle, *Secretaries Talk: Sexuality, Power and Work* (Sydney, 1988), 216.

22. J. Finch, *Married to the Job: Wives' Incorporation in Men's Work* (London, 1983), 79, 108–9.

23. R. Scase and R. Goffee, *Reluctant Managers: Their Work and Lifestyles* (London, 1989), 3.

24. Indeed Scott Lash and John Urry claim that Britain never fully entered the 'modernist' era of scientific management (*The End of Organized Capitalism* (Cambridge, 1987), 9).

25. R. Bendix, *Work and Authority in Industry: Ideologies of Management in the Course of Industrialization* (Los Angeles, 1974), 287–9.

26. It also bolstered their authority as men, as Kanter points out (*Men and Women*, 20).

27. Scase and Goffee, *Reluctant Managers*, 10–11.

28. Ibid. 12.
29. See, e.g., Lord Young's speeches, where he criticizes 'corporate cultures' for suppressing enterprise (P. Morris, 'Freeing the Spirit of Enterprise: The Genesis and Development of the Concept of Enterprise Culture', in R. Keat and N. Abercrombie (eds.), *Enterprise Culture* (London, 1991), 32).
30. T. Peters and R. H. Waterman, *In Search of Excellence: Lessons from America's Best-Run Companies* (New York, 1982). For a good review of this literature, see S. J. Wood, 'New Wave Management?', *Work, Employment and Society*, 3/3 (Sept. 1989), 379–402.
31. Wood, 'New Wave Management?', 381.
32. Peters and Waterman, *In Search of Excellence*, 33.
33. Ibid., p. xxv.
34. Ibid., p. xxii.
35. e.g. their eight qualities of excellence are called 'motherhoods' (ibid. 11, 16).
36. Ibid. 11.
37. Ibid. 31.
38. Harvey-Jones, *Getting it Together*, 375–6.
39. Crompton and Sanderson, *Gendered Jobs and Social Change*, 165.
40. Ibid. 166.
41. Cockburn, 'Equal Opportunities', 212.
42. In their study of the 'Hamlet' banking group, Glenn Morgan and David Knights illustrate very well the threats which restructuring posed to male managers, and the intensity of their resistance. Generational tensions surfaced when an attempt was made to rationalize insurance sales, allowing the mainly female counter staff to take on selling. The older, paternalistic branch managers tried to support 'their' women staff, while younger salesmen fought to retain the high commission work. Despite this movement of women into insurance sales, a distinct division of labour remained, women handling the minor transactions inside the branch, whilst bigger policies such as life insurance were sold by largely male sales staff outside the branches (G. Morgan and D. Knights, 'Gendering Jobs: Corporate Strategy, Managerial Control and the Dynamics of Job Segregation', *Work, Employment and Society*, 5/2 (June 1991), 181–97).

APPENDIX I

The Social Backgrounds of Organization Men

While most studies of management centre on particular organizations or industrial sectors, this work has a generational focus. It is based on the life histories of senior managers who began their careers in the post-war years.[1] Of the twenty-five men and five women who make up the study, almost all were born in Britain in the inter-war period.[2] At the time of interview in 1987–8, they were in late career or recently retired. Similar cohorts have been portrayed in previous studies of management. Comparisons can be made, for example, with the middle-managers described by J. M. and R. E. Pahl in their 1971 study, and the senior managers interviewed by J. Fidler a decade later.[3]

In addition to age and seniority, a number of other features identify the interviewees as 'organization men'. Most had been career managers for the majority of their careers. All were career managers during the heyday of the 'organization society' in the late 1950s and 1960s. Thus, for the most part they did not have controlling financial interests in the firms they managed. Three began their careers as inheritors but sold their shareholding when the firm was publicly floated or taken over, so making the transition to career manager. A further seven had begun their careers as salaried employees but later started up their own businesses. In most management texts, these varieties of management are considered as quite distinct. By contrast, a life-history approach reveals just how frequently managers cross between the statuses of 'entrepreneur', 'inheritor', and 'career manager'. Despite this movement, all the managers in this survey had spent the bulk of their working lives as career managers.

Secondly, all had worked in manufacturing industries. While a diverse range of industries are represented in the book, three are mentioned in more detail: motor vehicles (Turner Motor Works, Hill Components, and Bridgend Motor Parts), petro-chemicals (Chemtex and Swan Oil), and electronics (Quantec, Fisher Electronics, and Winwood Appliances).[4] The motor-vehicles sector was of particular interest because of its tradition of promotion from engineering functions to management and its generally 'macho' reputation, while the latter two were key growth industries in the post-war period. At the same time, this work does not adopt a case-study approach. Rather it assesses the effect of changes in historical time—particularly shifts in capital structure and economic climate—on the organization man's identity as a man and manager. This required a sample with some more detailed studies of particular organizations, but which could also illuminate the range of businesses operating in the post-war period, from family-owned holding companies to multi-divisional public firms.

Thirdly, despite the movement which this study reveals between self-employed and salaried status, still most of the managers had pursued 'organizational' rather than 'occupational' careers.[5] They had gained promotion, as Mr Nash put it, by 'working their way up some company structure for twenty, thirty, forty years'. A comparison with the present generation of middle-managers illustrates just how strong the ethos of internal promotion was during the post-war years. Only a fifth of the managers in my study had moved two or three times, while a further fifth had moved four times or more. The remaining three-fifths had stayed with the one firm for the whole of their careers. The study carried out by Richard Scase and Robert Goffee in the mid-1980s conveys a quite different picture. Less than a third of their sample had stayed with the one firm, a particularly striking finding given that the majority of their cohort was in early and mid-career, and could be expected to move again in the future.[6] It is the post-war generation's lack of movement between firms which, more than anything else, leads me to call them 'organization men'.

Lack of mobility between firms is related to the fourth distinctive feature of this generation: training. They completed their education before the founding of business schools in Britain during the early 1960s. Thus, while over three-quarters had some form of tertiary education, they lacked the professional skills of their successors. Reflecting the post-war belief in modernization through the 'white heat of a new technological revolution',[7] over 40 per cent had qualifications in engineering and science.[8] Only 13 per cent had trained in general management, finance, or accountancy, disciplines which are today highly valued for senior management posts.[9] While interviewees lacked formal skills in management, the majority had military training. Almost half the men in this sample served in the war, while a further third—men who turned 18 after 1945—did two years' national service.[10] Most had been commissioned, and from this they had gained an interest in management, and 'hands-on' experience of it. For the post-war generation, national or war service took the place of formal management education. Lack of skills in the management professions, and the predominance of experience in technical functions, probably intensified the tendency to seek mobility within firms. The organization man's knowledge was largely firm-specific.

Class provides the fifth tie which bound this generation together. Ex-working- and lower-middle-class managers are probably over-represented here.[11] Even so, managers from middle-class families were still firmly in the majority. Almost half had fathers who were also managers, revealing a pronounced occupational ascendancy.[12] Two-thirds were grammar-school-educated. Most began their secondary education prior to 1944, in the period when grammar schools still charged fees. Twenty per cent attended a public school, while the rest (mainly ex-engineers) had been educated at secondary modern schools. By comparison, in his study of 1958, R. V. Clements found that, of the cohort aged between 20 and 35—the age group most similar to this one—almost half had attended a public school, while a little over a third had attended a grammar school.[13] Thus my sample is biased towards the ex-'scholarship boys' who, in the post-war culture, symbolized the passing-away of family capitalism, and the coming of age of the meritocracy.

The division of roles between male managers and full-time wives was a sixth factor which marks this generation out as distinctive. Over three-quarters of the wives of organization men in this study did not work after marriage.[14] A dramatically different picture emerges from Scase and Goffee's study of managerial life in the 1980s. Two-thirds of the men in their study had partners who worked, albeit typically in professional jobs at a lower grade than their husband.[15] While the jobs of wives still appear to be secondary to those of male managers, nevertheless the pattern of complete separation between bread-winners and home-makers is no longer the norm.

Finally, a comment on the research method. The interviews were open-ended in format. I tried to minimize my interventions so as to enable the interviewees to put as much structure on the narrative as possible. I simply asked managers to tell me their career history, making sure that they covered the broad areas of family background, education, and training, and job changes. My visits lasted from an hour and a half to a day. They often concluded with a trip through the works to explain the firm's products and manufacturing processes, and lunch or drinks, where I would be introduced to colleagues. I kept a journal of what happened during my visits, since these events were often as revealing as the recorded interview. The sample was built up through a combination of advertising in the BIM, IPM, and CBI newsletters, personal contacts, and suggestions from my interviewees. Given its relatively small size, I do not claim that the sample is 'representative' of post-war industrial managers in general. Instead my interest was in obtaining as full a picture as possible of the lives and views of individual managers.

NOTES

1. The sample is evenly divided between directors and middle to senior managers. I tried to interview as many directors as possible. The main reason for this was that, at the time of research, studies of gender segregation showed that, while women were beginning to enter middle-management positions, equivalent changes were not taking place in senior management. I wanted to understand more about the men who occupied boardroom posts, and how the culture of the boardroom might be linked to the exclusion of women.

2. In terms of nationality, the exception was an American-born head-hunter who had worked in the automobile industry. Two interviewees were born after 1939. One was

a woman born in 1945 (Mrs Finch), who worked in the insurance industry. I included her because of the difficulty in finding women middle and senior industrial managers of this generation. The other, a man born in 1942 (Mr Gidley), was interviewed because he had worked in the two key industries in the sample: petrochemicals and automobiles. The son of a managing director, he had gained a management post very early in his career, in 1961.

3. J. Fidler, *The British Business Élite: Its Attitudes to Class, Status and Power* (London, 1981); J. M. Pahl and R. E. Pahl, *Managers and their Wives: A Study of Career and Family Relationships in the Middle Class* (London, 1971).

4. Some of the historical details concerning these firms have been omitted for reasons of confidentiality.

5. These terms are used by R. Scase and R. Goffee, *Reluctant Managers: Their Work and Lifestyles* (London, 1989), 87.

6. Ibid. 197, table A5.

7. Harold Wilson's legendary election speech of 1964, quoted in M. J. Wiener, *English Culture and the Decline of the Industrial Spirit, 1850–1980* (Harmondsworth, 1985), 164.

8. 23% of the sample had qualifications in engineering and 17% in science; 23% had done arts, and a further 10% had qualified in law or law-related subjects.

9. This spread between science and engineering, arts and finance, broadly confirms R. V. Clements's 1950–5 sample (*Managers: A Study of their Careers in Industry* (London, 1958), 187, app. 2, table 34). Fidler's study of the mid-1970s shows up an interesting change; perhaps reflecting the overall shift towards financial management, 42% of the chief executives in his study had been trained in commerce or economics (*The British Business Élite*), table 4.5.

10. This echoes Fidler's finding that over two-thirds of chief executives had done national or war service (Ibid. 98–9).

11. Perhaps this stems from the particular desire of 'self-made' managers to tell their story. The narratives of such men took two main forms. In one genre interviewees depicted a victory of sheer ability over the privileges of class. Here the interview served a largely narcissistic function. In the other, acknowledgment was given to a series of people who had provided assistance, from the teachers at school and university, to older managers. In this case the interview enabled the respondents to give back something to the academic culture which had helped them, and also pass on their knowledge to a younger generation. See also J. Peneff, 'Myths in Life Stories', in R. Samuel and P. Thompson (eds.), *The Myths We Live By* (London, 1990), 36–40.

12. C. Erickson's study of the steel and hosiery industries in the late 1950s reveals a broadly similar pattern. 34% of managers in the steel industry had fathers who were also business men. In hosiery the connection was even more pronounced, 47% following their father into the same industry (*British Industrialists: Steel and Hosiery, 1850–1950* (Cambridge, 1959), 12, 93).

13. Clements, *Managers, 189*, app. 2, table 38.

14. Pahl and Pahl found that 15% of wives had employment outside the home; of these the majority worked part time (*Managers and their Wives*, 126).

15. Scase and Goffee, *Reluctant Managers*, 163, fig. 7.1.

APPENDIX II

Biographical Details

Aldridge, Sir Peter, Ex-Chairman, Chemtex
Aldridge was born in 1917. His father was a railway porter and his mother was a laundry worker. He left school at 16 in the middle of the 1930s depression, beginning his career as a clerk at a grocery store. Aldridge continued his schooling and subsequently his B.Comm. degree as an evening student, and just before the war he began working for Chemtex as an economist. After a period of six years in army intelligence, where he reached a senior rank, he married and returned to Chemtex, where he served in a number of overseas posts. Aldridge was instrumental in the 'palace revolution' at Chemtex in the early 1960s, where the post-war board of largely Establishment directors was pushed aside, and the legendary Lord Meadows took over as chairman. Aldridge became a finance director at this time, helping to implement the rapid expansion programme engineered by Meadows. He was appointed to the chair on Meadows's retirement in the mid-1970s, and retired himself in the late 1970s.

Baker, J., Contracts Director, Jennings Windows
Baker was born in 1928 in the small town where Jennings, a family firm until the mid-1960s, was based. His father worked for Jennings, as did many of his relatives. As he put it, 'This company was based on father, son, and grandfather, as the sort of construction of the business.' Baker went to the local grammar school, leaving at 16 and working for a short time as a junior clerk at Jennings before joining the army. He returned to the firm in 1948 with a commission, and took a job in Singapore as a trainee overseas sales representative. On his return in 1954 he married. In 1965 Jennings merged with another family firm, and two years later it was taken over by a large public company. Baker benefited in career terms from these changes. After a series of promotions from sales to research and development functions, he became a director of Jennings in 1983.

Bannerman, W. H., Bannerman and Associates, Management Consultants
Bannerman was born in 1932. His mother was a teacher and his father was an electrical engineer. After completing his matriculation at a grammar school,

Bannerman did an arts degree and then served in the RAF. He joined United Steel as a management trainee in 1955, and married two years later. Bannerman stayed at United until 1964, employed initially in the work study department, and later as a production manager. In his early thirties he moved to a consultancy firm which specialized in work-study methods. He was promoted to third in command there before founding his own consultancy business in the mid-1970s. Today he specializes in work with local authorities and public-utilities.

Baraclough, J. P., Personnel Director, VST Motor Parts
Baraclough's parents founded VST just after the war. The firm grew rapidly during the 1950s, and merged with another component manufacturer in 1960. Baraclough herself went to grammar school and did a B.Comm. degree before entering the firm as an office administrator in 1955, aged 23. She became personnel director in her late twenties, and shortly afterwards married VST's managing director. He was a career manager who had been brought in to VST from one of the major component suppliers. Baraclough's involvement in the firm began to wane after the merger, her marriage, and the birth of her children between 1960 and 1965. Her husband died during the 1960s, and Baraclough then returned full time to VST. During the recession of the 1980s the firm experienced severe job losses, which once again reduced her role in the firm. Although Baraclough still works at VST two days a week, and maintains a minority shareholding, she also holds non-executive directorships of a number of regional public utilities and banks, as well as the local chamber of commerce.

Briar, C., Ex-Director, Briar and Peacock
Briar's family owned and managed a food company. It was a large enterprise, with its own farms and plantations, warehouses, refineries, manufacturing and packaging plants, and world-wide subsidiaries. Born in 1926, Briar was educated at one of the Clarendon public schools. After matriculating in 1943 he joined the army, where he sought but failed to get a commission. Briar spent six months after the war at Briar and Peacock's West Indies operation ('a great adventure') before beginning work in one of the firm's London processing factories. He was married in the same year that he started as a trainee manager at the plant. With his uncle's guidance, Briar eventually became a director of the factory in 1959. In 1961 he took up a general management post at head office, where he stayed until 1972 as director of management services. He was appointed to the main board in 1972, and became managing director of its refining arm in 1975. Briar and Peacock was the target of a hostile takeover in the early 1980s, and at that point Briar decided to retire.

Dolan, F. C., Product Manager, Jennings Windows
Unlike his colleague Mr Baker, Dolan was not a local employee. Born in 1924 in a middle-class family (his father was a salesman), Dolan went to a minor public school, served in the RAF during the war, and then did arts at

Cambridge. He began with Jennings as a management trainee in 1950, marrying the following year. Like Baker, he has stayed with Jennings for the whole of his career, witnessing its transformation from a family-run enterprise to a public company, now three times the target of take-overs. He took a succession of overseas sales posts before becoming product manager in 1966, and has remained in this post for the past twenty years. As he explained, 'I haven't developed my personality strongly enough or imposed my personality on my colleagues enough. If I had done, I'd have probably been on the board . . .'

Dowell, P., Chairman, Hill Components

Dowell's father and uncles were automative engineers in the Midlands, while his mother worked as a nurse during the First World War. Dowell himself was born in 1925, attended grammar school until the age of 16, and trained as an accountant. He felt that the English preference for service work rather than 'proper work . . . like making things' had 'steered my father into suggesting that I didn't go into engineering'. Dowell's accountancy training was interrupted by the war, where he served in the navy and gained a commission. In 1949 he completed his articles in a family accountancy firm, married, and joined Hill Components. After moving through the ranks at Hill to become chief accountant, in 1964 Dowell took a general management post at the firm's spares division. His aim was, he explained, to get away from accountancy, which he 'didn't enjoy', and pursue instead the 'family background' of automotive engineering. In 1975 Dowell returned to head office as a general manager. In 1983 the company undertook a round of job cuts and restructuring, its financial problems compounded by the last remaining inheritor, who sold her shareholding at the depth of the recession. At this point Dowell was appointed chairman. He set about bringing together a new, younger board, and at the time of interview was considering the possibility of a 'friendly' take-over by a larger component manufacturer.

Duncan, W. D., Ex-Manager, Industrial Relations, Swan Oil

Duncan's father sold medical equipment, and his mother was the daughter of a Scottish Presbyterian minister. Duncan went to a public day school in Edinburgh, and gained a B.Sc. after serving in India during the Second World War. In 1951 he took a job at an oil refinery in Trinidad, and the following year he was married, his wife taking the post of company doctor at the same plant. Four years later Duncan moved to Swan Oil's R&D division as a research chemist. In 1958 he moved to the company's light-fuels division, where he was promoted through the ranks. Like his colleagues Greenwood, Jones, and Wright, Duncan gradually moved out of research in mid-career. He became head of personnel of a minor division in 1964, and in 1970 Duncan took up a post as personnel superintendent in one of Swan's refineries. He worked briefly at head office but did not enjoy this, and after a year there he took a sideways move to a further refinery, finishing his career in 1986 as an industrial relations negotiator.

Eagleton, M., Head-Hunter, Eagleton and Mills

Eagleton's parents ran a general store in Vermont, America. Eagleton was born in 1920, joined the US Army during the war, and then went to Yale university. He began working as a sales representative for an automobile manufacturer in the United States after the war, and was seconded to its British subsidiary in 1958. After five years here, running the British manufacturing plant, he was head-hunted by a US communications firm. Eagleton worked as a general manager in the British arm of the firm before setting out on his own as a head-hunter in 1968. Much of our interview was spent with him giving a potted biography of the senior British managers who were his clients. Reluctant to talk about his own career, he offered me instead the names of his clients in exchange for which 'we can develop it into a book. And I've got a couple of publishers who would just love it. Really, I'm serious. You'd better be working to a damn good outline, right now . . .'

Ellis, D., Managing Director, Hartley Electrical Contractors

Like his father, Ellis attended a grammar school and later trained as an electronic engineer at a London Polytechnic. He served in the navy in 1947–9, leaving at the age of 22 to take up a job as an engineer with one of Britain's largest electronic components firms. He stayed there for the next sixteen years, during which he married, and was promoted to product manager. In 1966 he took up a job as manager in another multinational components firm. During this time, however, 'at the back of my mind was the whole idea of starting my own business'. In 1969 he began working as a managing director of Hartley's, a small (forty employees), family-owned electrical contracting company. In 1972 he bought the owners out, and set up on his own.

Finch, J. S., Claims Manager, Neptune Insurance

Finch was born in 1945. After attending grammar school and secretarial college, her first job was in a small insurance broker's as a secretary. Two years later, in 1966, she was made assistant to the managing director. His intention was to train Finch as an insurance broker. However, during this time Finch married, and in 1968 she left work when she became pregnant. After two years she decided that 'it was obvious that I wasn't going to be the maternal type and stay at home, so I had to get back to work'. She took a job with General Insurance as an assistant to the training manager, and was sitting the qualifications to become a training manager herself when her husband moved his job. Then followed a succession of clerical jobs with insurance firms, Finch shadowing her husband's job moves each time. In the late 1970s she was divorced. She began at Neptune in 1980, having gained further qualifications in insurance. She has since been promoted from supervisor to claims manager.

Franks, H. G., Deputy-Director of Personnel, Quantec Computers

Franks's mother was a school teacher before her marriage, and his father was a mining engineer in the north of England. Born in 1933, Franks went from grammar school to a social studies course at university, and decided to become a personnel officer because 'I'm a person-oriented person. Clearly I liked inter-relating with people.' His first job was as a management trainee at an electronic components firm. He married a year after being appointed to his first management post, as personnel manager responsible for the recruitment of shop-floor staff. After short spells as a personnel manager at CA Steel, and as a lecturer in Business Studies at a polytechnic, in 1966 he took a job with Quantec, a multinational computer firm. He is now second in charge to Quantec's personnel director.

Gidley, C. R., General Manager, Marine Coatings
Gidley's father was sales director of a prominent European chemicals firm. Gidley himself was born in 1942, and attended one of the Clarendon public schools before starting in 1961 as a trainee manager with Deeks, a multinational chemicals and drinks firm. He married in 1967, four years after taking up his first management post. Gidley remained with Deeks as a sales manager until 1974, when the chemicals arm of the firm was taken over by an oil company. Gidley then decided to resign and join Plastex, a firm which manufactured plastic mouldings for the automobile industry. In 1979 he moved again, this time to become sales manager of a packaging firm. It went into receivership in 1980, and Gidley was unemployed for a year. Then in 1981 he joined a chemicals and paints firm as sales director of one of divisions. Dural sold off this division in 1984, leaving Gidley unsure of his future with the firm, since the parent company had decided to relocate the plant in the United States.

Gould, N., Ex-Company Secretary, Reed Shipping
Gould was born in East London in 1926. Her father worked as a journalist, but 'my mother was the ambitious one'. Gould went to the local grammar school, but, because of financial pressure, she did not do her matriculation, and instead trained as a secretary. She worked as a secretary in a number of firms in 1944–7, while studying in the evenings to become a draughtswoman. Having gained the necessary qualifications, in 1951 she married, but then decided not to pursue a career in architecture. Instead she took a job with Reed Shipping as a secretary, and quickly took over the responsibility for the day-to-day running of the Operations function. On the arrival of a new Operations manager in 1961, she was moved, against her wishes, to the Stores and Spares division. During the 1960s she qualified as a Chartered ship-broker, and became company secretary at Reed in 1974, aged 48. Gould retired in 1987, a month before our interview.

Grainger, D. T., Production Manager, Winwood Domestic Appliances
Grainger's father was a regular soldier, and Grainger grew up in English army communities in South Africa, India, Egypt, and Palestine. He returned to England with his mother in 1945 at the age of 15, and did an engineering apprenticeship. He worked in a small machine-tool factory after qualifying. In 1951 he married and began his national service with the army. On his return in 1953 Grainger took a job as a production engineer with the Turner Motor Works. In 1958 he started work with Winwood Appliances, initially as a

production engineer and later as works manager at the Winwood plant in Wales. Between 1967 and 1975 followed a string of production and manufacturing engineering jobs, each offered by his 'mentor', David Moss. In 1975 Grainger made the jump to general management, moving with Moss to Dealex Audio. Two years later Grainger was made redundant after his mentor left Dealex. Grainger secured a job with a British computer firm later that year, but was again made redundant in 1980, during the recession. A year later he returned again to Winwood, as a manufacturing engineering manager—a post similar to the one he had held at the time of his departure from the firm in 1967.

Greenwood, P. W., Ex-Personnel Manager, Swan Oil

Greenwood's father was a salesman but lost his job during the 1930s depression: 'You would say that the slump broke him.' Greenwood won a scholarship to a North London grammar school, leaving at 18 to enter the army. He spent from 1943 to 1947 in the services, where he was commissioned. Greenwood then did a B.Eng. at Cambridge, and won a scholarship to do a Masters in mechanical engineering. He began work with Oilco in 1952 as an instrumentation engineer, and was supported by his wife while he gained a further qualification in chemical engineering. Four years later he joined Swan Oil as a project engineer, at the age of 31. Like Duncan, Jones, and Wright, the other three Swan employees I interviewed, in mid-career Greenwood moved out of technical functions and into general management. He worked as refinery manager in Swan refineries in Britain, the Middle East, and Far East during the 1960s. In 1970 he moved across to the personnel function, and retired as director of recruitment at Swan head office.

Handley-James, J., Head of Government Relations, Chemtex

Handley-James grew up in India, her father a sea captain, her mother a nurse and 'a very radical liberal lady in the small "1" sense'. She completed her grammar-school education in Britain in 1937, and began working as an administrative assistant with the Board of Trade during the war. In 1939 she married a naval officer, but they separated in 1943. Shortly afterwards she began an arts degree at London University as an evening student, graduating with first-class honours in 1949. In 1950 she joined Chemtex as a researcher in the Government Relations department. She became deputy-head of this department in 1960, and department head in the late 1960s. These jobs involved working extensively with the three chairmen during this period: Sir John Bromley-Smith, Sir Ronald Meadows, and Sir Peter Aldridge (see above). Handley-James retired in 1980.

Johnson, D., Managing Director, Ablex Brazing

David Johnson's father was a clerk in the civil service. David went to a secondary modern school until he was 14, leaving to become a shop fitter in 1936. After a succession of semi-skilled jobs during the 1930s, he began working for a refrigerator manufacturer as a welder. As a result of this he became interested in welding, and started doing more skilled work at a sheet-metal firm. Johnson served in the RAF in 1940–6, during which he was commissioned and got married. At the end of the war he returned to his old firm as a foreman. In 1952 he obtained his first management job, as technical sales representative with a large iron foundry and agricultural machinery manufacturer. He became sales manager of the firm in the late 1950s, but left in 1970 to become general manager of Ablex, a small (fifty employees), family-run brazing firm. In 1980 Johnson bought the owners out, and he now runs the firm with his two sons.

Johnson, R., Managing Director, Bridgend Motor Parts

Reg Johnson is David's younger brother. He was born in 1935, thirteen years after David. His parents having separated, Reg lived with his mother until her death when he was 14, and then with his father. He left school at 15 and joined the civil service: 'I stuck that out for a few months and then that was it.' He lived on his own for three years before joining the navy in 1953. Reg quickly gained a reputation as a boxer, and became a full-time member of the navy boxing team. After leaving the navy he did an engineering diploma, going from there to an engineering job at an oil company. Two years later, in 1962, he moved to a large aeronautical engineering firm, where he held various production management jobs. In 1971 Reg joined Brigend, a family firm, as general manager. He subsequently bought out the previous owner, then sold the business to a multinational components firm, International Parts. In 1981 Johnson decided to buy back the business. Today it is a private company, employing around 100 staff.

Jones, H., Ex-Head of Recruitment, Swan Oil

Jones was born in 1920, the son of a solicitor. He attended a minor public school and started a B.Sc. at London University; however, his studies were interrupted by the war. Jones joined the army in 1940 as an officer, but, as his colleagues explained it, he had a 'bad war', being taken a prisoner of war in the Far East until 1946. In 1949 he completed his B.Sc., and joined Swan as a refinery technologist. Jones moved to an overseas post in operations in 1952, but suffered a nervous breakdown in 1955, and as a result was moved aside to a job in graduate recruitment. At the age of 40 he married, and soon afterwards was appointed to the post of staff manager at one of Swan's British refineries. Since then he has held a number of personnel jobs, both at head office and in the refineries, including refinery liaison, and staff development and services. He retired in 1980, with responsibility for head-office recruitment.

Lloyd, R. T., Managing Director, Sentinel Trucks

Lloyd's father was a successful entrepreneur. In the late 1940s he had opened a garage, selling petrol and repairing cars. The firm soon expanded into car and truck dealerships, and opened new outlets. Lloyd junior went to the local East London grammar school, but left in 1952 at the age of 15, keen to join the family business. He worked first as an 'apron boy', serving petrol, quickly moving up the hierarchy to become a 'parts man' and then an office manager. After serving as an engineer in the army and being commissioned, he returned in 1957 to manage one of the family's truck and car dealerships. After his father's death in the late 1950s the responsibility for petrol and vehicle sales was split between the two sons. R. T. Lloyd took over the vehicle sales in 1960—the year in which he also married. He decided to finance further expansion plans by floating his part of the company. As a result Sentinel grew rapidly through the 1960s into over twenty vehicle dealerships. In the late 1960s, however, the company was taken over by asset strippers. Lloyd bought back three of the family's original truck dealerships from the new owners, managing them as an entrepreneur until 1979, when he sold them off to a rival distribution network. Lloyd stayed on as managing director of one outlet, but bought it back once again in 1987.

Locke, C., Director, Locke International
Locke was born in 1933. She grew up on a large family estate where her father was head chauffeur: 'I can remember as a small girl, when he was . . . seeing [that] all the cars [were properly] cleaned and polished, lifting me in the back and sitting me on a pair of rugs and shutting the doors. And I would sit in this car . . .' Locke attended grammar school and won a scholarship to Lancaster University. She began a mathematics degree, but switched to engineering after hearing that the engineering professor wanted to 'make an experiment' by taking on a woman student. Upon graduating in 1955 Locke was unable to secure a post, but with the help of the professor, she eventually found employment in the United States as a trainee transport engineer. A succession of engineering and sales jobs followed, first in Britain and later in the Soviet Union. In 1963 Locke married, but her husband died six years later. After his death Locke took a job as a consultant with a major truck manufacturer, and a decade later, in the late 1970s, she founded her own transport consultancy firm, which at the time of interviewing did most of its business in the Soviet Union.

Nash, G. A., Director of Legal Affairs, Turner Motor Works
Born in 1938, Nash went to grammar school and then did law at university. He completed his two years' national service in the army, returning in 1961 to start in his uncle's legal practice as an articled clerk. After five years there, in 1966 Nash joined a large engineering firm in the north as a company solicitor, marrying in the same year. In 1969 he began with Turner, where he has moved up through the ranks from on-staff solicitor, to become director of his department: 'like it or not, I rank pretty high in the British company.'

North, N. S., Ex-Deputy Chairman, Chemtex
North's father was a post-office clerk in London. His parents wanted to give him a good education, so he was sent to a Catholic grammar school. North gained his O levels in 1942, but did not go on to matriculation because of family financial pressures. At the age of 16 he began as a clerk in an insurance firm, and two years later he started in a local department store in the accounts department. Inspired by one of the accountants there, he began

doing accountancy at night school, and in 1951 he qualified. North married in 1953, the same year that he started with Chemtex. He soon transferred to the Central Accounts department, where, after a number of promotions in the 1960s, he met the later chairman, Lord Meadows: 'Up until then my training had been pathetic, as a future manager of British industry. It had been awful.' North helped Meadows to fight off a take-over bid launched by a competitor in the early 1960s. After Meadows became chairman in the mid-1960s, North was appointed chief accountant of Chemtex in 1968; a director in 1970; and deputy-chairman in 1975.

Sorrell, R. S., Personnel Services Manager, Turner Motor Works
Born in 1926, Sorrell was a boarder at a minor public school before joining the RAF as an officer during the war. He was demobilized in 1946 and went on to Cambridge University, where he completed an arts degree. Turner took him on as a graduate management trainee in 1950, and he married in 1952, shortly after taking up his first management post. Seen as a 'high flyer', he was appointed to a series of jobs in personnel at head office—in recruitment and training, and later in industrial relations. In 1962 he was seconded to the overseas headquarters of Turner, coming back to a job as assistant personnel director in the British personnel division. In 1967, at the age of 40, he was 'pushed out' of head office to 'macho type industrial relations work' at the company's truck division: 'Here I was being sent back to a manufacturing activity at a top level personnel job, never having had, since when I started as a boy, any plant experience.' Sorrell failed to quell unrest at the plant, and as a result was 'demoted' two levels to a post in management training. Since then he has served in a number of training jobs in the personnel division.

Stewart, N. W., Ex-Deputy Chairman, Chemtex
Stewart's parents worked on an estate in the Midlands, his father as a gardener and his mother as a domestic. Born in 1927, Stewart won a scholarship to grammar school, but left in 1943 for financial reasons. He started work for Chemtex as a laboratory assistant, gaining his Higher National Certificate and then a B.Sc. in chemistry as an evening student. In 1952 Chemtex took him back as a research chemist in its Midlands laboratory, but he soon began to take on a more managerial role, being appointed section leader in 1953. He was married the following year. In 1957 Stewart moved down to the R&D division of the London head office, eventually being made head of the division in 1963. Like North, Stewart's career was taken in hand by Lord Meadows, who had recently been appointed to the chair at Chemtex: 'He got hold of me and said, "I want you to move."' Stewart gained commercial experience by taking a job as marketing manager in a cotton mill which Chemtex had recently acquired. Two years later he was appointed chairman of another textiles firm which Chemtex had taken over, which was on the point of bankruptcy. Stewart and Meadows 'got it all back and turned it around', and Stewart was rewarded with an appointment to the main board of Chemtex. He was made deputy-chairman in 1976, and retired shortly after our interview in 1988.

Summers, L. R., Owner-Director, CLB Electronics
Summers's father was a merchant in Liverpool. Summers went to grammar school in Liverpool, and, after matriculating, he left to join the navy, where he was commissioned. At university Summers completed a B.Sc. in electrical engineering, and in 1950 he began with a major electronic components manufacturer as an engineer. He was made an engineering development manager in the mid-1950s, during which time he also married. Summers left in 1957 to join a family firm, Bonflex, which sold specialist components. He stayed with Bonflex until 1962, when he founded his own components firm with another manager from the firm. Their business has grown considerably, and now employs 300 staff. Summers remains a co-director, but spends most of his time in London, working on new component designs, organizing finance, and pursuing his political and other interests.

Tinsley, C. W., Management Consultant, Regional University
Tinsley's father worked for the CEGB in a semi-skilled job. Tinsley himself went to grammar school, leaving in 1945 at the age of 16 to begin an engineering apprenticeship. He worked in a succession of steel manufacturing firms, first as a mechanical engineer and later—after completing an HNC and a graduate qualification in production engineering—as a production engineering manager. In the early 1960s he moved to a firm of management consultants, where he stayed for a decade, gradually moving out of engineering to financial and marketing consultancy. During the 1970s he worked in general management posts in a number of manufacturing and construction firms. He was made redundant in 1980, and went on to head a local chamber of commerce before being appointed director of management services at Regional University.

Van Hoffen, G., Ex-Commercial Director, Fisher Electronics
Van Hoffen's father was deputy managing director of Fisher Electronics, then a world leader in communications technologies. Van Hoffen junior attended a public school in South Africa before returning to London and joining Fisher (along with his three brothers) as a radio mechanic in 1943, when he was 17. He spent from 1946 to 1948 in the navy as a radar officer, and went from there to Cambridge to do a B.Sc. in electrical engineering. In 1952 Van Hoffen returned to Fisher, where he worked in the marine division in radar maintenance, and later as a contracts manager. In 1960—the year after his marriage—he was moved from the technical division to head office. There, in preparation for future promotion, he acted as assistant to a number of board members. Van Hoffen was managing director of the company's South Africa's operations from 1965 to 1969, and was called back to take up a post as operations manager in London. In 1971 he became commercial director. The company was taken over in 1981, and Van Hoffen was made redundant in the subsequent re-structuring; 'I felt a bit bitter . . . you're probably getting a sense of this.' He is now the general manager of a golf club.

Wright, F., Ex-Refinery Manager, Swan Oil
Wright's father was a painter and decorator. Wright won a scholarship to grammar school and got his matriculation before joining the RAF in 1939, aged 18. He served for the duration of the war, and was commissioned. In 1946 he married, his wife working as a teacher while he studied for his B.Sc. Wright's first job was with Swan as a trainee technologist. He subsequently worked in refineries in Australia, the Far East, and around Britain. In 1972 he was made general manager of Swan's South Refinery, where he remained until his retirement in 1981.

Bibliography

i. Books and Articles

ABERCROMBIE, N., 'The Privilege of the Producer', in R. Keat and N. Abercrombie (eds.), *Enterprise Culture* (London, 1991), 171–86.

ACTON SOCIETY TRUST, *Management Succession: The Recruitment, Selection, Training and Promotion of Managers* (London, 1956).

ACKER, J., 'The Problem with Patriarchy', *Sociology*, 23/2 (1989), 235–40.

——'Hierarchies, Jobs, Bodies: A Theory of Gendered Organizations', *Gender and Society*, 4/2 (June 1990), 139–58.

ALLEN, G. C., 'The Cult of the Amateur', in D. Coates and J. Hillard (eds.), *The Economic Decline of Modern Britain: The Debate between Left and Right* (Brighton, 1986), 153–9.

ALVESSON, M., and BILLING, Y. D., 'Gender and Organization: Towards a Differentiated Understanding', *Organization Studies*, 13/2 (1992), 73–102.

ANDERSON, P., 'The Figures of Descent', *New Left Review*, 161 (Jan.–Feb. 1987), 20–77.

ARNOLD, V., and DAVIDSON, M. J., 'Adopt a Mentor—The New Way Ahead for Women Managers?', *Women in Management Review and Abstracts*, 5/1 (1990), 10–19.

BADEN-FULLER, C., and HAMPDEN-TURNER, C., *Strategic Choice and the Management of Dilemma: Lessons from the Domestic Appliance Industry* (Centre for Business Strategy Working Papers, 51; May 1988).

BARNETT, C., *The Audit of War: The Illusion and Reality of Britain as a Great Nation* (London, 1987).

BARTOLOME, F., 'Executives as Human Beings', in J. H. Pleck and J. Sawyer (eds.), *Men and Masculinity* (Englewood Cliffs, NJ, 1974), 100–7.

BAXENDALE, J., 'Martin J. Wiener: English Culture and the Decline of the Industrial Spirit, 1850–1980', *History Workshop Journal*, 21 (spring 1986), 171–4.

BEECHEY, V., 'What's So Special about Womens' Employment? A Review of Some Recent Studies of Womens' Paid Work', *Feminist Review* (winter 1983), 23–45.

——'Women and Employment in Contemporary Britain', in V. Beechey and E. Whitelegg (eds.), *Women in Britain Today* (Milton Keynes, 1986), 77–131.

BENDIX, R., *Work and Authority in Industry: Ideologies of Management in the Course of Industrialization* (Los Angeles, 1974).

BENJAMIN, J., 'Master and Slave: The Fantasy of Erotic Domination', in A. Snitow, C. Stansell, and S. Thompson (eds.), *Powers of Desire: The Politics of Sexuality* (New York, 1983), 292–312.

BLY, R., *Iron John: A Book about Men* (Longmead, Shaftesbury, Dorset, 1991).

BOLOGH, R. W., *Love or Greatness: Max Weber and Masculine Thinking—A Feminist Inquiry* (London, 1990).

BRADLEY, H., *Men's Work, Women's Work: A Sociological History of the Sexual Division of Labour in Employment* (Oxford, 1989).

BURRELL, G., 'Sex and Organizational Analysis', *Organization Studies*, 5/2 (1984), 9–118.

——and HEARN, J., 'The Sexuality of Organization', in J. Hearn, D. L. Sheppard, P. Tancred-Sheriff, and G. Burrell (eds.), *The Sexuality of Organization* (London, 1989), 1–29.

CALAS, M. B., and SMIRICICH, L., 'Voicing Seduction to Silence Leadership', *Organization Studies*, 12/4 (1991), 567–602.

CALLAN, H., and ARDENER, S. (eds.), *The Incorporated Wife* (London, 1984).

CHANDLER, A. D., *The Visible Hand: The Managerial Revolution in American Business* (Cambridge, Mass., 1977).

——and DAEMS, H., *Managerial Hierarchies: Comparative Perspectives on the Rise of the Modern Industrial Enterprise* (Cambridge, Mass., 1980).

CHANNON, D. F., *The Strategy and Structure of British Enterprise* (London, 1973).

CHODOROW, N., *The Reproduction of Mothering: Psychoanalysis and the Sociology of Gender* (Berkeley, Calif., 1978).

CLARK, D. G., *The Industrial Manager: His Background and Career Pattern* (London, 1966).

CLEMENTS, R. V., *Managers: A Study of their Careers in Industry* (London, 1958).

CLUTTERBUCK, D., and Devine, M., *Businesswoman: Present and Future* (London, 1987).

COATES, D., and HILLARD, J. (eds.), *The Economic Decline of Modern Britain: The Debate Between Left and Right* (Brighton, 1986).

COCKBURN, C., *Brothers: Male Dominance and Technological Change* (London, 1983).

——*Machinery of Dominance: Women, Men, and Technical Know-how* (London, 1985).

——'Equal Opportunities: The Short and Long Agendas', *Industrial Relations Journal*, 20/3, (1989), 213–25.

——*In the Way of Women: Men's Resistance to Sex Equality in Organizations* (London, 1991).

COLEMAN, D. C., 'Gentlemen and Players', *Economic History Review*, 2nd ser., 36/1 (1973), 92–116.

——*Courtaulds: An Economic and Social History*, iii. *Crisis and Change* (Oxford, 1980).

——and McCLEOD, C., 'Attitudes to New Techniques: British Businessmen, 1800–1950', *Economic History Review*, 2nd ser., 39/4 (Nov. 1986), 588–612.

246

Collinson, D. L., 'Men Only: Theories and Practices of Job Segregation in Insurance', in D. Knights and H. Willmott (eds.), *Gender and the Labour Process* (London, 1986), 140–79.

——'Engineering Humour: Masculinity, Joking and Conflict in Shop-Floor Relations', *Organization Studies*, 9/2 (1988), 181–99.

——and Collinson, M., 'Sexuality in the Workplace: The Domination of Men's Sexuality', in J. Hearn, D. L. Sheppard, P. Tancred-Sheriff, and G. Burrell (eds.), *The Sexuality of Organization* (London, 1989), 91–110.

——Knights, D., and Collinson, M., *Managing to Discriminate* (London, 1990).

Connell, R. W., *Which Way is Up? Essays on Class, Sex and Culture* (Sydney, 1983).

——*Gender and Power: Society, the Person and Sexual Politics* (Cambridge, 1987).

Cooper, C. L., and Davidson, M. J., *High Pressure: Working Lives of Women Managers* (Glasgow, 1982).

Crompton, R., and Sanderson, K., *Gendered Jobs and Social Change* (London, 1990).

Dalton, M., *Men Who Manage: Fusions of Feeling and Theory in Administration* (New York, 1959).

Davidoff, L., '"Adam Spoke First and Named the Orders of the World": Masculine and Feminine Domains in History and Sociology', in H. Corr and L. Jamieson (eds.), *The Politics of Everday Life: Continuity and Change in Work, Labour and the Family* (London, 1990), 229–56.

——and Hall, C., *Family Fortunes: Men and Women of the English Middle Class, 1780–1850* (London, 1987).

Davidson, M. J., and Cooper, C. L., 'Women Managers: Their Problems and what can be Done to Help them', in C. L. Cooper and M. J. Davidson (eds.), *Women in Management: Career Development for Managerial Success* (London, 1984), 32–56.

——*Shattering the Glass Ceiling: The Woman Manager* (London, 1992).

Easlea, B., 'Patriarchy, Scientists, and Nuclear Warriors', in M. Kaufman (ed.), *Beyond Patriarchy: Essays by Men on Pleasure, Power, and Change* (Toronto, 1987), 195–216.

Edwardes, M., *Back from the Brink: An Apocalyptic Experience* (London, 1983).

Elbaum, B., and Lazonick, W., 'An Institutional Perspective on British Decline', in B. Elbaum and W. Lazonick, *The Decline of the British Economy* (Oxford, 1986), 1–18.

Erickson, C., *British Industrialists: Steel and Hosiery, 1850–1950* (Cambridge, 1959).

Fidler, J., *The British Business Élite: Its Attitudes to Class, Status and Power* (London, 1981).

Figlio, K., 'Oral History and the Unconscious', *History Workshop*, 26 (Aug. 1988), 120–30.

Finch, J., *Married to the Job: Wives' Incorporation in Men's Work* (London, 1983).

FLORENCE, P. S., *The Logic of British and American Industry: A Realistic Analysis of Economic Structure and Government* (London, 1972).

FREUD, S., *On Sexuality: 'Family Romances', in Three Essays on the Theory of Sexuality and other Works*, trans. J. Strachey (Harmondsworth, 1986).

——*Civilization, Society and Religion: Group Psychology, Civilization and its Discontents and other Works* (Harmondsworth, 1987).

FUSSELL, P., *The Great War and Modern Memory* (Oxford, 1978).

GAME, A., 'Secretaries and Bosses', *Journal of Pragmatics*, 13 (1989), 343–61.

GILLIS, J., *For Better, for Worse: British Marriages, 1600 to the Present* (New York, 1985).

GOFFEE, R., and SCASE, R., *Women in Charge: The Experience of Female Entrepreneurs* (London, 1985).

HACKER, S. L., 'The Eye of the Beholder: An Essay on Technology and Eroticism', in S. L. Hacker, *'Doing It the Hard Way': Investigations of Gender and Technology*, ed. D. E. Smith and S. M. Turner (London, 1990), 205–23.

HANNAH, L., 'Business Development and Economic Structure in Britain since 1880', in L. Hannah (ed.), *Management Strategy and Business Development: An Historical and Comparative Study* (London, 1976), 1–23.

——*The Rise of the Corporate Economy*, 2nd edn. (London, 1983).

HANSARD SOCIETY, *Report of the Hansard Society Commission on Women at the Top* (London, 1990).

HARVEY-JONES, J., *Getting it Together: Memoirs of a Troubleshooter* (London, 1991).

HAYES, R., and ABERNATHY, W., 'Managing our Way to Economic Decline', in E. Rhodes and D. Wield (eds.), *Implementing New Technologies: Choice, Decision and Change in Manufacturing* (Oxford, 1985), 169–75.

HEARN, J., and PARKIN, P. W., *'Sex' at 'Work': The Power and Paradox of Organisation Sexuality* (Brighton, 1987).

HENNIG, R., and JARDIM, A., *The Managerial Woman* (London, 1978).

HEWARD, C., *Making a Man of him: Parents and their Sons' Education at an English Public School, 1929–1950* (London, 1988).

HOCHSCHILD, A. R., *The Managed Heart: Commercialization of Human Feeling* (Berkeley, Calif., 1983).

HUDSON, L., and JACOT, B., *The Way Men Think: Intellect, Intimacy and the Erotic Imagination* (London, 1991).

HUNT, D. M., and MICHAEL, C., 'Mentorship: A Career Training and Development Tool', *Academy of Management Review*, 8/3 (1983), 65–78.

HUNT, J. C., *The Psychoanalysis of Fieldwork* (London, 1989).

IACOCCA, L., with W. Novak, *Iacocca: An Autobiography* (London, 1988).

IRIGARAY, L., *This Sex Which Is Not One*, trans. C. Porter with C. Burke (New York, 1985), ch. 8, 'Women on the Market', 170–92.

JEREMY, D. J., 'Anatomy of the British Business Élite, 1860–1980', *Business History*, 36/1 (March 1984), 3–21.

JEWSON, N., and MASON, D., 'The Theory and Practice of Equal Opportunities: Liberal and Radical Approaches', *Sociological Review*, 34 (1986), 307–34.

JOHNSON, B. S., *All Bull: The National Servicemen* (London, 1973).

JONES, R., and MARRIOTT, O., *Anatomy of a Merger: A History of GEC, AEI and English Electric* (London, 1970).

KANTER, R. M., *Men and Women of the Corporation* (New York, 1977).

KNIGHTS, D., and MORGAN, G., 'Corporate Strategy, Organizations, and Subjectivity: A Critique', *Organization Studies*, 12/2 (1991), 251–73.

LANNING, G., PEAKER, C., WEBB, C., and WHITE, R., *Making Cars: A History of Car Making in Cowley . . . by the People who Make the Cars* (London, 1985).

LASH, S., and Urry, J., *The End of Organized Capitalism* (Cambridge, 1987).

LEGGE, K., 'Women in Personnel Management: Uphill Climb or Downhill Slide?', in A. Spencer and D. Podmore (eds.), *In a Man's World: Essays on Women in Male Dominated Professions* (London, 1987), 33–61.

LEVINSON, D. J., *The Seasons of a Man's Life* (New York, 1978).

LEWIS, J., *Women in Britain since 1945: Women, Family, Work and the State in the Post-War Years* (Oxford, 1992).

LEWIS, P., 'Mummy, Matron and the Maids: Feminine Presence and Absence in Male Institutions, 1934–63', in M. Roper and J. Tosh (eds.), *Manful Assertions: Masculinities in Britain since 1800* (London, 1991), 168–90.

LEWIS, R., and STEWART, R., *The Boss: The Life and Times of the British Business Man* (Phoenix, 1961).

LOCKE, R., *The End of the Practical Man: Entrepreneurship and Higher Education in Germany, France and Great Britain, 1880–1940* (London, 1984).

——*Management and Higher Education since 1940: The Influence of America and Japan on West Germany, Great Britain and France* (Cambridge, 1989).

LODGE, D., *Ginger, You're Barmy* (Harmondsworth, 1982).

McDOUGALL, J., *Theatres of the Mind: Illusion and Truth on the Psychoanalytic Stage* (London, 1986).

McKENDRICK, N., 'The Enemies of Technology and the Self-Made Man', general introduction to R. Church, *Herbert Austin: The British Motor Car Industry to 1941* (London, 1979), pp. ix–li.

——'Gentlemen and Players Revisited: The Gentlemanly Ideal, the Business Ideal, and the Professional Ideal in English Literary Culture', in N. McKendrick and R. B. Outhwaite (eds.), *Business Life and Public Policy: Essays in Honour of D. C. Coleman* (Cambridge, 1986), 98–137.

McNALLY, F., *Women for Hire: A Study of the Female Office Worker* (Surrey, 1979).

MARSHALL, J., *Women Managers: Travellers in a Male World* (Chichester, 1984).

——'Issues of Identity for Women Managers', in D. Clutterbuck and M. Devine (eds.), *Businesswoman: Past and Future* (London, 1987), 11–30.

MARX, K., and ENGELS, F., *Collected Works, iii. Marx and Engels: 1843–1844* (London, 1975).

MERTON, R. K., *Social Theory and Social Structure* (New York, 1968).

METCALF, A., and HUMPHRIES, M. (eds.), *The Sexuality of Men* (London, 1985).

MILLS, A. J. 'Organizations, Gender and Culture', *Organization Studies*, 9/3 (1988), 351–69.

——'Gender, Sexuality and Organization Theory', in J. Hearn, D. L. Sheppard, P. Tancred-Sheriff, and G. Burrell (eds.), *The Sexuality of Organization* (London, 1989), 29–45.

——and MURGATROYD, S. J., *Organizational Rules. A Framework for Understanding Organizational Action* (Buckingham, 1991).

MILLS, C. W., *White Collar: The American Middle Classes* (New York, 1951).

MITCHELL, J. (ed.), *The Selected Melanie Klein* (London, 1986).

MORGAN, D. H. J., *'It Will Make a Man of You': Notes on National Service, Masculinity and Autobiography* (Studies in Sexual Politics, 17; University of Manchester, Department of Sociology, 1987).

——*Discovering Men* (London, 1992).

MORGAN, G., *Images of Organization* (London, 1986).

——and KNIGHTS, D., 'Gendering Jobs: Corporate Strategy, Managerial Control and the Dynamics of Job Segregation', *Work, Employment and Society*, 5/2 (June 1991), 181–97.

MORRIS, P., 'Freeing the Spirit of Enterprise: The Genesis and Development of the Concept of Enterprise Culture', in R. Keat and N. Abercrombie (eds.), *Enterprise Culture* (London, 1991), 21–38.

MORT, F. 'Boys Own? Masculinity, Style and Popular Culture', in R. Chapman and J. Rutherford (eds.), *Male Order: Unwrapping Masculinity* (London, 1988), 193–225.

NEWTON, P., 'Who Becomes an Engineer? Social Psychological Antecedents of a Non-traditional Career Choice', in A. Spencer and D. Podmore (eds.), *In a Man's World: Essays on Women in Male Dominated Professions* (London, 1987), 182–203.

NICHOLSON, N., and WEST, M., *Managerial Job Change: Men and Women in Transition* (Cambridge, 1988).

NOE, R. A., 'Women and Mentoring: A Review and Research Agenda', *Academy of Management Review*, 13/1 (1988), 65–78.

OCHBERG, R. L., 'The Male Career Code and the Ideology of Role', in H. Brod (ed.), *The Making of Masculinities: The New Mens' Studies* (Boston, 1987), 173–95.

PAHL, J. M., and PAHL, R. E., *Managers and their Wives: A Study of Career and Family Relationships in the Middle Class* (London, 1971).

PASSERINI, L., 'Work Ideology and Consensus under Italian Fascism', *History Workshop*, 8 (autumn 1979), 82–108.

PENEFF, J., 'Myths in Life Stories', in R. Samuel and P. Thompson (eds.), *The Myths We Live By* (London, 1990), 36–49.

PENROSE, E., *The Theory of the Growth of the Firm* (Oxford, 1959).

PERKIN, H., *The Rise of Professional Society: England since 1880* (London, 1989).

PETERS, T., and WATERMAN, R. H., *In Search of Excellence: Lessons from America's Best-Run Companies* (New York, 1982).

PETTIGREW, A., *The Awakening Giant: Continuity and Change in Imperial Chemical Industries* (Oxford, 1985).

PLUMMER, K., *Documents of Life: An Introduction to the Problems and Literature of a Humanistic Method* (London, 1983).

POLLARD, S., *The Genesis of Modern Management: A Study of the Industrial Revolution in Great Britain* (London, 1965).

——*The Development of the British Economy, 1914–1980*, 3rd edn. (London, 1983).

PORTELLI, A., *The Death of Luigi Trastulli and other Stories: Form and Meaning in Oral History* (New York, 1991).

PORTER, M., *The Competitive Advantage of Nations* (London, 1990).

PRINGLE, R., *Secretaries Talk: Sexuality, Power and Work* (Sydney, 1988).

——'Bureaucracy, Rationality and Sexuality: The Case of Secretaries', in J. Hearn, D. L. Sheppard, P. Tancred-Sheriff, and G. Burrell (eds.), *The Sexuality of Organization* (London, 1989), 158–78.

PURCELL, K., 'Gender and the Experience of Employment', in D. Gallie (ed.), *Employment in Britain* (Oxford, 1988), 157–86.

RAVEN, J., 'British History and the Enterprise Culture', *Past and Present*, 123 (May 1989), 178–204.

RAW, C., *Slater Walker: An Investigation of a Financial Phenomenon* (London, 1977).

READER, W. J., *Imperial Chemical Industries: A History*, ii (Oxford, 1975).

REICH, H. M., 'The Mentor Connection', *Personnel* (Feb. 1986), 50–5.

RILEY, D., *War in the Nursery: Theories of the Child and Mother* (London, 1983).

ROPER, M., 'Fathers and Lovers: Images of the "Older Man" in British Managers' Career Narratives', *Life Stories/Récits de vie*, 4 (1988), 49–58.

——'Yesterday's Model': Product Fetishism and the British Company Man, 1945–85', in M. Roper and J. Tosh (eds.), *Manful Assertions: Masculinities in Britain since 1800* (London, 1991), 190–212.

——and TOSH, J., 'Historians and the Politics of Masculinity', in M. Roper and J. Tosh (eds.), *Manful Assertions: Masculinities in Britain since 1800* (London, 1991), 1–25.

ROSENER, J. B., 'Ways Women Lead', *Harvard Business Review* (Nov.–Dec. 1990), 119–125.

ROTHWELL, S., 'Positive Action on Women's Career Development: An Overview of the Issues for Individuals and Organizations', in C. L. Cooper and M. J. Davidson, *Women in Management: Career Development for Managerial Success* (London, 1984).

ROYLE, T., *The Best Years of their Lives: The National Service Experience, 1945–63* (London, 1988).

SAMPSON, A., *The Anatomy of Britain Today* (London, 1965).

——*The New Anatomy of Britain* (London, 1971).

——*The Changing Anatomy of Britain* (London, 1982).

SAMUEL, R., and THOMPSON, P. (eds.), *The Myths We Live By* (London, 1990).

SANDERSON, M., *The Universities and British Industry, 1850–1970* (London, 1972).

SCASE, R., and GOFFEE, R., *The Real World of the Small Business Owner* (London, 1980).

————*The Entrepreneurial Middle Class* (London, 1982).

————*Reluctant Managers: Their Work and Lifestyles* (London, 1989).

SCHEIN, E., *Organizational Culture and Leadership* (London, 1985).

SCOTT, J., 'Gender: A Useful Category of Historical Analysis', *American Historical Review*, 91/5, (1986), 1053–75.

SEGAL, L., 'Look Back in Anger: Men in the 50s', in R. Chapman and J. Rutherford (eds.), *Male Order: Unwrapping Masculinity* (London, 1988), 68–97.

————*Slow Motion: Changing Men, Changing Masculinities* (London, 1990).

SHEPPARD, D. L., 'Organizations, Power and Sexuality: The Image and Self-Image of Women Managers', in J. Hearn, D. L. Sheppard, P. Tancred-Sheriff, and G. Burrell (eds.), *The Sexuality of Organization* (London, 1989), 139–58.

SMITH, D. E., *The Everyday World as Problematic: A Feminist Sociology* (Milton Keynes, 1988).

SNOW, C. P., *The New Men* (London, 1954).

SOFER, C., *Men in Mid-Career: A Study of British Managers and Technical Specialists* (Cambridge, 1970).

SOMMERVILLE, J., 'The Sexuality of Men and the Sociology of Gender', *Sociological Review*, 37/2 (May 1989), 277–308.

STANWORTH, P., and GIDDENS, A., 'An Economic Élite: A Demographic Profile of Company Chairmen', in P. Stanworth and A. Giddens (eds.), *Élites and Power in British Society* (Cambridge, 1974), 80–101.

SUMMERFIELD, P., *Women Workers in the Second World War: Production and Patriarchy in Conflict* (London, 1984).

THEWELEIT, K., *Male Fantasies: Women, Floods, Bodies, History* (Cambridge, 1987).

THOMPSON, P., *The Voice of the Past: Oral History*, 2nd edn. (Oxford, 1988).

THOMPSON, P., and McHUGH, D., *Work Organisations: A Critical Introduction* (London, 1990).

TOLSON, A., *The Limits of Masculinity* (London, 1977).

TREMAYNE, S., 'Shell Wives in Limbo', in H. Callan and S. Ardener (eds.), *The Incorporated Wife* (London, 1984), 120–35.

TURNER, G., *Business in Britain* (London, 1969).

WAINWRIGHT, H., 'Women and the Division of Labour', in P. Abrams and R. Brown (eds.), *UK Society: Work, Urbanism and Inequality* (London, 1984), 198–246.

WAJCMAN, J., *Feminism Confronts Technology* (Cambridge, 1991).

WALBY, S., *Patriarchy at Work: Patriarchal and Capitalist Relations in Employment* (Cambridge, 1986).

WEBB, J., 'The Gender Relations of Assessment', in J. Firth-Cozens and M. A.

West (eds.), *Women at Work: Psychological and Organizational Perspectives* (Milton Keynes, 1991), 13–25.

——and Liff, S., 'Play the White Man: The Social Construction of Fairness and Competition in Equal Opportunity Policies', *Sociological Review*, 36/3 (1988), 532–51.

Weber, M., 'Bureaucracy', in H. Gerth and C. W. Mills (eds.), *From Max Weber: Essays in Sociology* (London, 1948), 196–267.

Wheatcroft, M., *The Revolution in British Management Education* (London, 1970).

Whitley, R., Thomas, A. and Marceau, J., *Masters of Business: The Making of a New Élite?* (London, 1984).

Whyte, W. H., *The Organization Man* (Middlesex, 1963).

Wiener, M. J., *English Culture and the Decline of the Industrial Spirit, 1850–1980* (Cambridge, 1981; repr. Harmondsworth, 1985).

Williams, C. L., *Gender Differences at Work: Women and Men in Nontraditional Occupations* (Berkeley, Calif., 1989).

Willis, P., 'Shop-Floor Culture, Masculinity and the Wage Form', in J. Clarke, C. Critcher, and R. Johnson (eds.), *Working-Class Culture: Studies in History and Theory* (London, 1979), 185–201.

Wilson, E., *Only Halfway to Paradise: Women in Postwar Britain, 1945–1968* (London, 1980).

Winnicott, D. W., *Playing and Reality* (London, 1988).

Witz, A., *Professions and Patriarchy* (London, 1992).

Wood, S. J., 'New Wave Management?', *Work, Employment and Society*, 3/3 (Sept. 1989), 379–402.

Woodward, J., *Industrial Organization: Theory and Practice*, 2nd edn. (Oxford, 1980).

Young, M., and Willmott, P., *The Symmetrical Family: A Study of Work and Leisure in the London Region* (London, 1973).

ii. Reference

Dictionary of Business Biography: A Biographical Dictionary of Business Leaders Active in Britain in the Period 1860–1980, 3 vols. (London, 1985).

Director, Institute of Directors (London), 1970–89.

Financial Times, 1985–91.

Guardian, 1985–91.

Manager, subsequently *Management Today*, 1955–89.

Proceedings of the London School of Economics Seminar on Problems in Industrial Administration, 1950–70.

Who's Who, 13th Annual Edition (1985).

Index